Sorcerer's Stone

For Chloe~
Discover Alchemy!
Dennis W. Hauck

Sorcerer's Stone

A Beginner's Guide to Alchemy

DENNIS WILLIAM HAUCK

CITADEL PRESS
Kensington Publishing Corp.
www.kensingtonbooks.com

CITADEL PRESS BOOKS are published by

Kensington Publishing Corp.
850 Third Avenue
New York, NY 10022

All Kensington titles, imprints, and distributed lines are available at
special quantity discounts for bulk purchases for sales promotions,
premiums, fund-raising, educational, or institutional use. Special book
excerpts or customized printings can also be created to fit specific needs.
For details, write or phone the office of the Kensington special sales
manager: Kensington Publishing Corp., 850 Third Avenue, New York,
NY 10022, attn: Special Sales Department; phone 1-800-221-2647.

First printing: June 2004

10 9 8 7 6 5 4 3 2

Printed in the United States of America

Library of Congress Control Number: 2004103784

ISBN 0-8065-2545-2

❧ Contents ❧

ᴐ Introduction ᴐᴄ

MY INITIATION INTO ALCHEMY took place while I was still a graduate student in mathematics in the mid-1970s. I enrolled at the University of Vienna to study the work of one of its professors, the logician Kurt Gödel. In 1931, Gödel proved that all axiomatic systems (such as math and logic) were inconsistent. His incontestable proof sent shock waves through the academic community. Mathematicians had been trying for decades to prove that mathematics was a perfect system of knowledge that could lead us to a perfect understanding of the universe. But Gödel exposed the "Queen of the Sciences" as nothing more than a common harlot. The meticulous proofs of mathematics had no more to do with higher truths than the steps in popular parlor games. There were reports of mathematicians committing suicide after reading his proof.

The quiet and reserved Viennese professor unveiled the fundamental chaos in the roots of mathematics. He showed that *any* logical system was inherently flawed by inconsistency, indecision, and incompleteness. Like an earthquake, his proof destroyed confidence in purely logical processes, and the aftershocks are reverberating through the sciences to this day.

Philosophers argued over whether Gödel's work proved the existence of God, and scientists scrambled to apply his discoveries to their work. Fractals and chaos theory, fuzzy logic, and artificial intelligence are the direct result of his work. From such everyday devices as cell phones, computer games, and digital thermometers to the Star Wars defense system, the ascetic professor from Vienna reshaped our world.

Gödel's Proof is both elegant and complex, and it took me many months to work through it. His ingenious proof caused a funda-

mental shift in the way I looked at the world. I realized that finding truth requires both rational and irrational methods in an intuitive merging of thought with feeling. Our thoughts alone are no
match for the mysteries of the universe.

As I began searching for tools in this new way of knowing, the
first thing I discovered was that the ancients were fully aware of this
special state of consciousness. The merging of thought and feeling
was called the "Sacred Marriage," a union of soul and spirit that
gave birth to higher consciousness. Egyptians described the child of
this union as the "Inheritor" and the new consciousness as "Intelligence of the Heart." Medieval alchemists named the offspring of
the sacred marriage the "Philosopher's Child." This innocent child
carried the magical "Philosopher's Stone," an indestructible state of
mind that gave its possessor perfect understanding. Because of its
power to change both personal and objective reality, the stone of
the alchemists was also known as the "Sorcerer's Stone."

When I finished my research, I tried to pull all the diverse philosophical ideas into something solid (like a stone) that I could use in
the everyday world. Then, one day, at the end of my rope and
despairing of ever finding a way to apply these principles, I headed
for the university library just to be near books. Often when I am
empty and confused, the answer just presents itself through some
chance occurrence in a library: a book lies on a desk opened to a
page containing just what I need, or a book falls off a shelf that I was
meant to read. Psychologist Carl Jung experienced similar synchronistic revelations and attributed them to his "library ghost." Well, my
library ghost led me to the basement archives, although it was not
just one book that jumped out at me. It was a whole roomful.

The cold, musty room was filled with old alchemy texts. The
university was founded in 1385, when Vienna and nearby Prague
were at the center of European alchemy, and the room was an
uncirculated storage area for the old Latin and German books.
What grabbed my attention as I paged through the books was not
the elaborate typestyles of the words but the strange and deeply
meaningful illustrations, which seemed to communicate their
wisdom not through my brain but through my guts.

Grotesque creatures fought each other inside huge glass retorts. Lizards frolicked in the flames of a bonfire; two lonely fish swam toward each other under the sea; a lion sat on its hind legs devouring the sun. An eagle flying high in the air was incongruously chained to a toad crawling on the ground. A wolf and dog battled in the middle of a deserted town. A slithering winged serpent entwined itself around a female corpse lying in an open grave. Another serpent lay nailed to a cross. Snakes and dragons chased their own tails in neverending circles. A naked king and queen embraced in a rocky grotto as the sun and moon eclipsed in the sky above. A two-headed hermaphrodite stood in triumph on top of a fire-breathing dragon. A warrior clad in armor wielded his gleaming sword high in the air before slicing open a giant egg. Everywhere, ravens sat observing scenes of death and transformation, while gods and goddesses from mythology pointed earnestly at bubbling cauldrons and blazing furnaces.

When I started reading the books, I found no explanations for the mysterious pictures and the texts were full of riddles and allusions to unknown substances. Yet between the lines and within the silent images, I felt great truths were being revealed. My friends started calling me "Monk" because I sat all day in the library transcribing books and all night meditating on Xerox copies of the drawings.

It soon became obvious that the alchemists were talking about universal spiritual principles that could be demonstrated in their laboratories. Alchemy was a lot more than just a precursor to chemistry. It was a union of science and religion based on an ancient method of finding truth that combined all ways of knowing.

One thing lacking in my studies, however, were the "oral teachings" that could only be transmitted one-on-one from an alchemist. I was surprised to discover that there were still alchemists practicing in Europe, and I set out to find one. After months of searching, I finally received a referral from an elderly gentleman I met in a coffeehouse in Bolzano in northern Italy. The old man was a member of the Solificati, a secretive group of magicians and alchemists that formed in the early fifteenth century. He gave me the phone number of an alchemist living in Prague.

I set up a meeting with the alchemist at his house in the Josefov section of Prague. The referral from the Solificati greatly impressed the alchemist for he immediately agreed to instruct me in alchemy. All I had to do was agree to a yearlong commitment and bring a carton of Camel cigarettes for him and a box of Mozart Kugeln (chocolates) for his wife every time I visited.

So, every "Day of Mercury" (Wednesday) for a year, I rode the train the short distance from Vienna to Prague. Back then, the city was behind the Iron Curtain, and the thirty-minute journey took hours. As an American, I was usually detained and searched for cash, maps, and other contraband. At the same time, the United States government was keeping tabs on my movements. My brother was in the Air Force and had a high security clearance working in missile silos in Minot, North Dakota. He was suddenly reassigned to a base in the Texas desert as a barracks painter. He lost his security clearance because I was spending so much time behind the Iron Curtain.

I stuck out my apprenticeship and learned a lot about the practical, psychological, and spiritual practices of alchemy. The first thing I learned was that these three aspects of the Great Work always went together. No transformation was complete and lasting until it simultaneously occurred on the physical, the mental, and the spiritual levels. The goal was to surrender your personal identity and turn your consciousness into Mercury, the mirror-like liquid metal of the alchemists that, on the mental level, takes on the shape and character of whatever the light of consciousness focuses on. In other words, to know something alchemically, you have to *become* it.

Another idea my teacher kept stressing was that the Sorcerer's Stone is worthless unless it is a "living stone." You cannot change anything with dead words from a dead part of you. Alchemy spreads like any other life form, though the process of seeding and multiplication. "It takes a seed of gold to make gold," say the alchemists.

Now with this book, I pass on a seed of gold to you, the reader. Even if you know nothing of the ancient art, it will slowly grow in you, provided you give it your attention and keep it alive.

Sorcerer's Stone

1

What Is Alchemy?

THE FIRE BURNED STEADILY within the athanor, the cylindrical brick furnace at the center of the alchemist's laboratory. Midway up the athanor, two holes glowed like eyes gazing out into the darkened room, while occasional puffs of falling ash issued from a wider opening below. On top sat a huge glass retort, its single opening stopped with clay; inside the glass, a heavy mass of dark green mud folded about itself in slow, swirling currents.

The writhing blob of matter was known as the First Matter and it represented months of hard work roasting, pulverizing, dissolving, and breaking down materials said to contain the mysterious essence. This primordial, chaotic mass was the goal of all alchemists and they believed that once they had isolated enough First Matter, they could purify it and produce the magical Sorcerer's Stone that would in turn perfect anything. Of course, just how to accumulate and purify the First Matter was the greatest secret in alchemy.

Along the wall to the right of the athanor, two shelves stretched the length of the room. The upper shelf held the dried carcasses of assorted frogs, birds, and rats, while less identifiable creatures peered out from preservative-filled jars. The alchemists believed the life force was a subtle substance that could be separated from living things and used to impart health to others or even give life to inanimate objects. Many famous alchemists claimed to have created little beings (called *homunculi*) by infusing the life force into flasks of chemical compounds.

On the lower shelf along the same wall were assorted vials, vessels, crocks, and burlap bags holding various powders and liquids, each one carefully marked with a unique symbol. Linger too long in this section of the lab, however, and your senses were overcome by a biting odor, like a mixture of rotten eggs and vinegar. Many alchemists became gravely ill by experimenting with unknown compounds and caustic metals. One ill-fated British alchemist used to demonstrate the affinity of mercury for gold by sticking his big toe in a saucer of mercury while holding a gold coin in his mouth. Within a half-hour, the coin was coated with a silvery layer of mercury that had traveled through his blood. Unfortunately, he was only able to perform the feat a few times before he died of mercury poisoning.

Beneath the two long shelves in the laboratory sat a narrow workbench piled with odd-looking utensils and glass beakers that contained assorted colored powders. At the center of the bench, next to a small herb press, a balancing scale seesawed aimlessly, caught in a passing draft of air. Meanwhile, in the dark space underneath the table, an iron cauldron full of decomposing organic matter gurgled suspiciously. This tub was known as the "digester," in which materials were allowed to rot and break down by an alchemical operation called putrefaction.

Against the opposite wall, there stood two sturdy bookcases stuffed with stained papers, old manuscripts, and leather-bound books. Between the bookcases, an empty chair sat in front of a broad wooden desk. On the cluttered desktop, next to an open notebook, a quill pen waited patiently in its inkwell. This is where the alchemist recorded the results of his experiments, using not only measurements and the written word but bizarre diagrams and drawings of eerie creatures and mythological figures intended to capture the experience on as many levels of interpretation as possible.

On the back wall of our medieval laboratory, a bewildering array of glass vessels hung supported on wooden pegs. Flasks, beakers, cylinders, and retorts of all sizes spread across the entire wall. Nearby, a cluttered array of copper tubing zigzagged upward from a thick, pear-shaped clay vessel on the floor. Known as a "serpent condenser," the giant air-cooled apparatus was used for distilling the foul-smelling solution poured off from the digester. Distillation purified even the foulest liquid and also concentrated the strength of whatever essences were present. Not only could one make alcoholic spirits and essential oils using distillation but also produce specific herbal tinctures and elixirs as well.

Next to the serpent condenser, a large dark curtain hung suspended from the ceiling and was carefully draped completely around a small altar on the floor. This tent or tabernacle formed a private meditation space for the alchemist, and as much work was done within this sacred tabernacle as was carried on in the laboratory. Alchemists spent many hours in solitary contemplation, attempting to purify and focus their minds.

Hidden somewhere in the meditation area of the laboratory could usually be found the alchemist's incubator. This insulated, copper-clad wooden box was perhaps the most sacred spot in the lab. The sealed container, kept warm by the fermenting matter within, was where the alchemist directed his thoughts and visualizations. It was during the process of fermentation that the magical First Matter was most exposed and most open to the influence of the alchemist. However, if anyone other than the alchemist touched or even looked upon this box, all was lost. In the beginning, the subject of the alchemist's work was easily corrupted by another's impure thoughts, which is why the alchemist always kept his work secret—even from other alchemists.

To alchemists, consciousness is a force of nature that can be harnessed and purified through prayer and meditation and then added to the experiment just like a chemical ingredient. This esoteric part of the experiment is absolutely necessary and explains why many alchemical experiments cannot be duplicated in a chemical laboratory. Chemistry operates by rearranging atoms like so many billiard balls—a methodology much too crude for the alchemist. From the alchemist's viewpoint, chemistry is an artificial science that deals only with the external forms in which the elements manifest.

Modern chemists, who believe their experiments take place only on the physical level, see no need to purify themselves or meditate prior to beginning an experiment.

To an alchemist, on the other hand, entering a laboratory emotionally upset or focused on one's ego and not the greater universal pattern to be revealed in the experiment destroys the delicate connection with the subtle level of reality on which the alchemist hopes to work. In other words, the alchemist's attitude has a lot to do with the outcome of the experiment. This idea is very similar to the Observer Effect, a proven tenet of quantum physics, in which the expectations of the experimenter have been shown to influence the outcome of experiments in nuclear physics. The atomic level of reality can be considered more subtle or "spiritual" than the gross physical level at which we all live. Yet somehow, the alchemists knew that consciousness was the tool through which man could access that invisible level underneath our everyday reality. Like a modern quantum physicist, the alchemist is always looking for the most subtle level of reality, the deepest underlying pattern that explains physical reality.

From our modern materialistic viewpoint, it is hard for us to imagine how much a part of their experiments were the alchemists. All matter was alive, and they sympathized with the subject of their work every time they exposed it to fire, submerged it in acid, or bathed it in cooling waters. When working at the athanor, they breathed in unison with their bellows, taking in deep breaths and exhaling evenly as the air rushed out of the narrow spout of the bellows to fan the fire. When the fire needed to be hotter and the pace of squeezing quickened, so did the alchemist's breathing, until the sound of the bellows and the alchemist's lungs merged into a single cadence. As the temperature of the fire increased, so did the glowing warmth in the alchemist's body. This uncanny identification with the processes in the laboratory was absolutely essential. The alchemist and his work fed on each other. The alchemist suffered with his work, felt its same temperament, and changed with it. For if the experiment was truly a success, the alchemist too was transformed. The key to this whole magical process was the conscious connection or "correspondence" the alchemist was able to forge between his own mind and the "mind of nature," as expressed in the experiment.

The alchemist's idea of the "mind of nature" was very similar to our modern notion of evolution. Over time, nature seems to be perfecting itself. It may take millions of years but eventually a species transforms itself in response to some great need and a new species, more able to survive in the world, comes into existence. The Great Work of alchemy has always been to find ways to speed up this natural process of perfection. In the words of the modern French alchemist, Jean Dubuis: "Alchemy is the art of manipulating life and consciousness in matter, to help it evolve, or to solve problems of inner disharmonies."

The alchemists believe that everything carries the energetic seed or pattern of its own perfection and it is the job of the alchemist to resurrect these essences of perfection that are trapped in matter— to bring them to light and allow their full expression in time and space. They see this guiding pattern of perfection as an inner spirit that exists in all matter, from a dull gray lump of lead to a living human being.

In the alchemical view, matter is alive and the metals grow naturally in the earth's interior furnace by alchemical processes that act on the First Matter. Since all things in nature are charged with the divine spirit or life force and therefore aspire to a higher, more perfect state, metals, too, gradually evolved over time.

The alchemists believed that the metals actually grew inside the earth. The first form of the metals is the base metal lead, which evolves into tin, which evolves into iron, which becomes copper, then mercury, then silver, and finally culminating in gold, the most matured metal. Gold was the final perfection of all the metals, as indicated by its beauty and superior properties. In other words, by natural processes the metals transmuted from baser or "lower" metals, such as lead and tin, into more noble or "higher" metals such as silver and gold.

The alchemist's task, therefore, is to speed up nature's work by transforming the metals in the laboratory into higher forms. Such artificial transmutations by the alchemists were believed to encourage the overall pattern of transformation on our planet and contribute to the evolution of everything, including human beings. To alchemists, the whole universe is slowly evolving toward perfection.

What makes humans different from ordinary matter is that we can consciously participate in our own process of transformation. Since we are all part of nature, we all participate in alchemy whether we know it or not. We can proceed as alchemists and try to intentionally manifest our perfected nature, or we can spend our lives (or lifetimes) unconsciously cycling through worldly experiences that finally bring inner spiritual resources to the surface. In this sense, alchemy is really a science of soul, a truly unique discipline in the history of the world that combines the tools of both science and religion and uses both intellect and intuition. According to this deeper tradition, the gold of alchemy is hastened perfection in the highest sense—the divinization of matter and of human beings.

In the most basic sense of the word, alchemy is simply the art of transformation. It is an art in the sense that it seeks change not by mechanically forcing nature to do its will but rather by encouraging certain latent patterns to come alive and grow. The alchemists viewed the growth of minerals, plants, animals, or the evolution of whole species as alchemical processes going on in the laboratory of nature. Indeed, for the alchemist *all* matter is alive and has the potential for growth and change.

Anyone who works creatively with matter comes to the realization that it is alive to some extent. Craftspeople and artists know the materials they use have an inner life of their own—unique histories, properties and possibilities. They realize they must feel and understand this life so that a creative relationship exists between them.

So, in the final analysis, alchemy is an art that can only be practiced by those who possess artist's tools—the inspired presence and purified imagination necessary for creative transformation. While the laboratory procedures necessary for alchemical preparations may be taught to just about anybody, in much the same way as a chemist learns formulas from textbooks, the results that such a person could accomplish would be without life, and no alchemical transformation into something new and fundamentally different could take place.

In the next chapter, we will learn where the principles of alchemy originated and how the alchemists applied them to their work through the ages. Then we will learn some basic alchemical techniques and use them to begin the Great Work in earnest. Like every initiate on the path of alchemy, our goal is to become awakened to the energy of creation and use it in our transformations. The way to do that was first expressed in a mysterious document known as the Emerald Tablet.

The Magical Message of the Emerald Tablet

The Emerald Tablet is at the center of Western alchemy and contains concepts crucial to understanding alchemy as it is practiced around the world. According to legend, the Emerald Tablet was an artifact brought to Egypt by godlike visitors over twelve thousand years ago. The tablet contains the essence of alchemical philosophy and is said to contain a formula for the perfection of anything, whether it be a metal or the human soul. Nearly every medieval alchemist had a copy of it hanging on his laboratory wall and constantly referred to the secret formula it contained.

It is not just the ancients who appreciated the tablet. "The Emerald Tablet," said noted Jungian author Dr. Edward Edinger, "is the cryptic epitome of the alchemical opus, a recipe for the second creation of the world." Esoteric scholar John Matthews wrote: "There is no getting away from the fact that the Emerald Tablet is one of the most profound and important documents to have come down to us. It has been said more than once that it contains the sum of all knowledge—for those able to understand it."

The secret formula contained in the Emerald Tablet became known as the Emerald Formula. It consists of seven consecutive steps that lead to a new level of creation no matter what the "substance" of transformation may be. The alchemists interpreted these steps in terms of seven chemical operations that they performed on the "matter" of their work to perfect it. We will examine this formula in detail in the ensuing chapters. For now, however, we are going to devote some time to gaining a deeper understanding of the Emerald Tablet.

What the Emerald Tablet Tells Us

The Emerald Tablet is organized in seven rubrics or paragraphs. They are called rubrics (from the Latin *rubeo*, meaning "red") because, in the Latin translations, the first letter of each paragraph was highlighted in red ink. It should be noted that when the tablet refers to the "Universe," it is talking about the material universe in which we live. When it speaks of the "Whole Universe," it is referencing not only the material universe (Below) but also the spiritual universe (Above). See if you can sense the secret formula hidden in the words of the Emerald Tablet as you read the following version.

THE EMERALD TABLET

In truth, without deceit, certain, and most veritable.

That which is Below corresponds to that which is Above, and that which is Above corresponds to that which is Below, to accomplish the miracles of the One Thing. And just as all things have come from this One Thing, through the meditation of One Mind, so do all created things originate from this One Thing, through Transformation.

Its father is the Sun; its mother the Moon. The Wind carries it in its belly; its nurse is the Earth. It is the origin of All, the consecration of the Universe; its inherent Strength is perfected, if it is turned into Earth.

Separate the Earth from Fire, the Subtle from the Gross, gently and with great Ingenuity. It rises from Earth to Heaven and descends again to Earth, thereby combining within Itself the powers of both the Above and the Below.

Thus will you obtain the Glory of the Whole Universe. All Obscurity will be clear to you. This is the greatest Force of all powers, because it overcomes every Subtle thing and penetrates every Solid thing.

In this way was the Universe created. From this comes many wondrous Applications, because this is the Pattern.

Therefore am I called Thrice Greatest Hermes, having all three parts of the wisdom of the Whole Universe. Herein have I completely explained the Operation of the Sun.

The first rubric asks us to come to a higher awareness and open up to deeper truths. The second rubric presents the Doctrine of Correspondences, which describes a vertical relationship between the realm of spirit Above and the realm of matter Below. This is the so-called Vertical Axis of reality, which the alchemists felt they could enter in their meditations. The Horizontal Axis is our normal material world. A wonderful example of experiencing the vertical axis is a work in the *Corpus Hermeticum* called the "Divine Pymander" (or "Divine Mind"). It is allegedly written by Hermes Trismegistus and describes his meeting with the Divine Mind and what it revealed to him about the nature of reality.

The third rubric elaborates on the nature of the One Thing, which is the subject of the tablet. The alchemists have usually interpreted the One Thing to mean the First Matter or Universal Life Force, and this rubric describes its characteristics. The first two sentences of this rubric present the Four Elements in the order of Fire, Water, Air, and Earth. Associated with each of these elements are the first four operations of alchemy: calcination, dissolution, separation, and conjunction. These will be explained in Chapter 13 (Operations of Alchemy).

The fourth rubric is the most mystical part of the Emerald Tablet and seems to be telling us how to enter the spiritual realm Above. It also describes the last three alchemical operations of fermentation, distillation, and coagulation (explained in Chapter 13:

Operations of Alchemy). The fifth rubric describes the result of the previous conditions, which is the purified Quintessence.

The sixth rubric suggests that the previous rubrics have described a specific universal pattern that leads to transformation on all levels of reality. It is not only the formula that the alchemist follows in his work, but also the overall pattern of nature in the evolution of matter.

The seventh and last rubric identifies the author of the tablet as "Thrice Greatest Hermes." Hermes is the Greek name of the Egyptian God of Wisdom, Thoth, who was said to have introduced writing, mathematics, and music to the world. In the Roman tradition he was known as Mercury. His Latin name is Hermes Trismegistus, which means "Thrice Greatest Hermes." Hermes (or Thoth) is thrice greatest because he has gained knowledge on all three levels of reality: the physical plane, the mental plane, and the spiritual plane. The Operation of the Sun is the complete explanation of the workings of the universe, which he has revealed in the Emerald Tablet.

It is best not to overanalyze the Emerald Tablet but rather seek a deeper connection with its truths by reading it many times until it begins resonating with you in some way. Carry a copy of the tablet with you and read it at various times of the day to see how the meanings change. You may want to rewrite it in a way that makes more sense to you. It seems that just about every alchemist from Albertus Magnus to Isaac Newton had their own personal translation of the tablet.

Experiment 1: The Emerald Tablet Engraving

In this experiment in the Inner Laboratory, we will try to gain a deeper appreciation of the Emerald Tablet by studying a wonderful engraving that is said to have captured the meaning of the tablet and contains all the symbols of alchemy. It is called the *Tabula Smaragdina*, which is Latin for "Emerald Tablet." Created by artist Matthieu Merian, it was first published in 1618 in Daniel Mylius's *Opus Medico-Chymicum* ("The Medical-Chemical Work").

Figure 1. The *Tabula Smaragdina* engraving illustrates the principles of the Emerald Tablet and is said to contain all the symbols of alchemy. (Daniel Mylius, *Opus Medico Chymicum*, 1618)

The engraving (see figure 1) depicts the birth of the Stone as it leaves heaven (the spiritual realm above) and enters earth (the material realm below). The engraving is in the style of a mandala, in which one focuses on the center of the drawing (the Stone) and tries to incorporate all the surrounding images and symbols in one vision of truth. Many medieval alchemists sat staring at it for hours trying to absorb its power.

Immediately one notices the sharp division into the Above and the Below. Above, the larger Sun of the One Mind, whose rays encompass the whole universe, rises behind the Sun of Heaven or what is known by Hermeticists as "Mind the Maker." This intermediate stage is dominated by twenty-nine cherubs or archetypal forces, which can be seen as the crystallized thoughts or Word of God.

The three smaller Suns floating among the angels represent the three heavenly substances or principles expressed as the Holy Trinity. The center sun is the *Tetragrammaton* or Ineffable Name of God written in Hebrew; to the left is the Son of the Sun or the sacrificial Lamb of God; and to the right is the Dove or Holy Ghost hidden in matter. The alchemists were very careful not to appear blasphemous and often concealed their symbols in Christian terms. Any alchemist of the time would immediately recognize these as the alchemical principles of Sulfur, Mercury, and Salt respectively. Known as the Three Essentials, they were spiritual forces at work on every level of reality and are explained in more detail in the next chapter.

The Below is divided into two areas: the daytime (solar or masculine) left side and the nighttime (lunar or feminine) right side. In Chinese alchemy, these two opposing forces in the created world are known as yang (masculine) and yin (feminine).

On the solar side at the bottom left corner is a lion standing upright like a man. Known as the Red Lion, he represents the fiery, masculine, intellectual energy of the Work. Behind him is a fence, and a village can be seen in the distance. The lion is wearing a collar of stars that represents the archetypal forces emanating from the constellation of Leo, which figured so prominently in Egyptian alchemy. Leo is offering a naked man a thirteen-rayed Sun, symbol of Hermetic wisdom.

On the lower right (or lunar) side of the drawing is a stag standing upright like a man. He is the mythological Acteon, the "Fugitive Stag," who represents the watery, feminine, emotional energy of the Work. Acteon was a hunter who fell in love with the Greek fertility goddess Artemis (or Diana to the Romans) when he saw her bathing naked in a pond. Acteon could not control his passion and was turned into a stag. Each of his twelve antlers has a star above it representing the inexorable forces of the zodiac in our lives. The three-leafed clover in his left hand symbolizes the primal Three Essentials of creation. In his right hand is the Moon in all its changeable faces, which he is handing to a naked woman.

The man and woman in the lower part of the drawing are called Sol and Luna. Sol, whose genitals are covered by the sun, represents the masculine or aggressive archetype. Luna, whose genitals are covered by the crescent moon, represents the feminine or passive archetype. The stream of stars flowing from her right breast is the Milky Way. She holds a bunch of grapes in her left hand, which symbolizes the sacrificial life force she gives to the world. Both Sol and Luna are chained to the Clouds of Unknowing and do not see the larger pattern of the universe.

On the chests of the man and woman are the symbols for both the sun and moon. In other words, Sol contains the seed of the feminine within him, and Luna contains the seed of the masculine within her. The meaning is much the same as the Tai Chi symbol in which the yang (masculine) energy is constantly changing into yin (feminine) energy because each carries the seed of the other. This is the basic rhythm of the material universe in which the interplay of positive and negative forces drives creation.

In the bottom corners of the drawing are two large birds. The one on the right is the Phoenix, the mythological bird of spirit who rose from its own ashes to be reborn. The bird on the left is an eagle (Aquilla), the worldly bird of soul. On the masculine side under the wings of the Phoenix are the elements of Fire and Air; on the feminine side under the wings of Aquilla are the elements of Water and Earth. The meaning and relationships of the Four Elements are described in Chapter 3 (Principles of Alchemy).

At the center of the lower part of the drawing is a figure representing the alchemist. He stands at the center of the Mountain of the Philosophers holding two starry hatchets representing the higher faculty of discernment. The alchemist has cut through the Chains of Unknowing and has seen the greater pattern of the universe. The alchemist represents a balancing and integration of the masculine and feminine powers to his left and right. Half his frock is black with white stars and the other half is white with black stars. This represents the alchemist's living embodiment of opposites in which each half of his frock contains the seed of its opposite. The fire shooting out from the mountain to his right and the water streaming forth to his left are the primal forces of spirit and soul. Their union is depicted by the two lions with a single head upon which the alchemist stands. Pouring out of the lion's mouth is the magical elixir created by the union of opposites, which the alchemists also referred to as the Mother of the Stone.

The three rows of plants growing up the Mountain of the Philosophers contain ciphers for the operations of alchemy expressed in the work with minerals, plants, and the metals. All the rows culminate in the symbol for gold at the summit. It is here the Clouds of Unknowing part to reveal the hidden processes of evolution.

At this point in the Work, the alchemist can access the powers Above by aligning himself with the Cosmic (or Vertical) Axis of reality. This hidden entryway to the spiritual realm can by seen by drawing a line from the elixir pouring out of the lion's mouth at the bottom of the drawing, through the body of the alchemist and the symbol for gold, to bisect the name of God at the top of the drawing. As the alchemist travels in this vertical orientation, he first encounters the Ring of Heavenly Bodies in which the seven larger stars represent the five visible planets with the sun and moon. These are the seven alchemical operations of transformation, which are explained in detail beginning in Chapter 5 (Climbing the Ladder of the Planets).

After penetrating this ring, a semicircle of five scenes that lead to the Stone is encountered. The birds of spirit shown in each scene correspond to the five visible planets. From left to right: the Black Crow of Saturn, the White Goose of Jupiter, the Rooster of Mars, the Pelican of Venus and, finally, the Phoenix of Mercury.

At the center of the drawing is a large sphere made up of seven concentric rings, which are layers that must be peeled away to reach the Stone. The outer ring contains the twelve signs of the zodiac, the karmic and astrological forces in the individual that must be overcome. The second ring is inscribed with three Latin phrases meaning "Year of the Winds," "Year of the Sun," and "Year of the Stars." These are the archetypes of time and space that must be transcended during the Work. The third ring describes the three kinds of Mercury (Common Mercury, Bodily Mercury, and Philosophical Mercury) that must be used to reach the Stone. The fourth ring names the three kinds of Sulfur (Combustible Sulfur, Fixed Sulfur, and Volatile or Ethereal Sulfur) that must be utilized in the Work. The fifth ring names the three types of Salt or essences (Elementary Salt, Salt of the Earth, and Central Salt) that are revealed during the Work. Thus, the Fifth ring represents the Fifth Element or Quintessence, which carries the purified central essences of the substance being work on.

The sixth ring has a message written in Latin that warns: "You must find the four grades of Fire of the Work." This refers to the four kinds of fire the alchemist uses to purify matter. They are explained in Chapter 3 (Principles of Alchemy).

The seventh innermost ring depicts the Sorcerer's Stone. It shows a large upward-pointing triangle of Fire, which is the purified consciousness that is at the heart of the Stone. Within that triangle is the symbol for Mercury or the exalted light of mind. To the upper left of the large triangle is a smaller downward-pointing triangle representing celestial Water, which is divine grace. To the upper right is a small upward-pointing triangle representing Fire, which is the universal spirit of perfection and evolution. At the bottom is the Star of David, which combines the symbols for Water and Fire and is another symbol for the Stone. At the very center of the inner circle, inside the cipher for Mercury, is a single dot. This is the Monad or One Point, the center of the entire drawing and around which both heaven and earth revolve.

2

The Golden Thread That Runs Through Time

THE TEACHINGS OF THE EMERALD TABLET are one of the earliest known expressions of the "Perennial Philosophy," so called because it keeps turning up in so many different cultures and ages despite efforts by those in authority to suppress or destroy it. Medieval alchemists referred to these teachings as the Underground River, which flowed through time carrying the ancient wisdom. The Perennial Philosophy is based on the notion that the physical world is a manifestation of a greater spiritual reality. "The nature of this reality," notes author Aldous Huxley, "is such that it cannot be directly or immediately apprehended except by those who have chosen to fulfill certain conditions, making themselves loving, pure in heart and poor in spirit." Getting beyond one's personal ego and becoming an "empty cup" seems to be the fundamental condition for experiencing this higher reality.

The Emerald Tablet implies that if we can connect with this higher reality through the purification of consciousness, we can alter physical reality by changing the higher spiritual ideal or archetype on which it is based. This concept of mind over matter is described in the dictum "As Above, so Below." That is the basic idea behind all alchemy and magic, and it had its origin in ancient Egypt.

According to legend, the first alchemist was Thoth, who lived in Egypt during a time known in the ancient texts as *Zep Tepi*, when godlike beings roamed the earth and shared their knowledge with mankind. Thoth (or Tehuti, which is his most ancient name) was part of a "Group of Nine" who arrived in Egypt with an advanced spiritual technology that enabled them to manipulate matter. Thoth was an intermediary between the godlike beings and the humans of the time. He was known as a scribe, the inventor of the sacred language of hieroglyphics (literally, "Holy Writing").

Thoth was often portrayed as an ibis (a tall bird with a long curved bill) and was also associated with baboons. His symbol was a pair of serpents twisted around a central staff (the caduceus). Since snakes represent the life force in most ancient cultures, the caduceus become the symbol of healing and medicine. There is a remarkable similarity between Thoth's caduceus and the structure of the DNA molecule, the double helix of proteins that is the blueprint of all life. Perhaps this further explains his odd association with baboons. Could Thoth have manipulated the genetic material of baboons or apes to speed up the evolution of mankind? Such an act would certainly be in line with his role as the first alchemist.

The legend continues to about 10,000 B.C., when Thoth, knowing a great flood was about to envelope the planet, sealed his scrolls inside a great stone pillar as a kind of time capsule of wisdom for later generations. He also inscribed a succinct summary of his teachings on a gemstone tablet and sealed it in another great pillar. These two pillars survived the Great Flood and were later discovered by Egyptians. They are mentioned in texts dating to the New Dynasty (1550–1050 B.C.), a period when alchemy flourished in Egypt. They were also described by travelers to Egypt, including the Greek historian Herodotus who visited Egypt in 400 B.C. He called them the "Pillars of Hermes."

According to some accounts, the scrolls and tablet of Thoth were removed from the pillars and moved for safekeeping to the Temple of Amen, which is the oldest temple in Egypt. The ancient temple is located in Siwa, hundreds of miles from Cairo in the middle of the Libyan desert. Only priests and pharaohs were allowed to view the sacred texts at Siwa. It was not until Alexander the Great conquered Egypt and became its Pharaoh in 332 B.C. that knowledge of the ancient documents spread. Alexander traveled to Siwa, retrieved the sacred writings of Thoth, and put them on public display in Heliopolis in 330 B.C. The tablet Thoth inscribed has become an object of veneration and amazement to this day. One traveler, who had seen it in Heliopolis, wrote: "It is a precious stone, like an emerald, whereon these characters are represented in bas-relief, not engraved into the stone. It is esteemed above two thousand years old. Plainly, the matter of this emerald had once been in a fluid state like melted glass, and had been cast in a mold, and to this flux the artist had given the hardness of a natural and genuine emerald, by his art." This ancient gift of Thoth to the people of earth became known simply as the Emerald Tablet. According to Hermetic historians, Alexander built the great library at Alexandria primarily to house and study the Thothian scrolls.

How the Arabians Saved Alchemy

The demise of Egyptian alchemy began when the Romans took control in the first century B.C. The Romans considered the alchemists a dangerous group of freethinkers and tried to suppress their activities. Finally, worried that alchemists were planning to fund a rebellion, Diocletian (emperor of Rome 284–305 A.D.) ordered the destruction of all alchemical writings in Egypt. In 313, after Emperor Constantine declared Christianity the official religion of the Roman Empire, alchemists and other philosophers of nature were severely persecuted. Fortunately, a mystical group of Christians, known as the Nestorians, smuggled many of the alchemical manuscripts into Persia and shared them with the Arabs.

By 400 A.D., all that survived of Egyptian alchemy were a few key texts that were translated into Arabic by Alexandrian scholars and the cache of Nestorian texts. Alchemy took root in the Arabian lands and Arab alchemists played a key role in preserving the Egyptian source documents. In fact, our word "alchemy" comes from the Arabian phrase "al-khemia," which literally means "from the black soil of the Nile Delta." Significantly, Egyptian alchemists had used the term "khem" to refer to the First Matter or life force, which they believed was carried by the fertile, black dirt in the delta. Thus, esoterically, the word "alchemy" really means "from the First Matter."

Knowledge of "al-khemia" spread through Babylon to the Orient around 500 A.D. and finally reached Europe with the Moorish invasion of Spain in 711. The earliest surviving copy of Thoth's Emerald Tablet is in an Arabic book from 650 A.D., which was later translated into Latin in Spain. The Emerald Tablet quickly became the bedrock on which European alchemy was based. The universal alchemical principles concealed in the tablet were considered so powerful that they were kept secret from the common people and expressed openly only in private oral teachings. In books, they were concealed in arcane drawings, secret ciphers, and contradictory terminology, so that only initiates could understand them.

During this period, the influence of Arabian alchemists was especially strong. The writings of Geber (721–815), Rhazes (860–932), and Avicenna (980–1036) were capturing the imaginations of scholars around the world, and a new era of alchemy ensued that lasted nearly a thousand years. Geber (Jabir ibn Hayyan) was so careful to conceal the true principles of alchemy that his works rarely made sense, and the term "gibberish" originally referred to his writings. Nonetheless, to the initiated, Geber was deeply revered. He introduced new operations in alchemy and explained the transformation of metals in terms of idealized substances he called Sulfur and Mercury.

These were not the common elements of the same name but universal or archetypal qualities common to all things. Common sulfur and mercury only carried the "signatures" or physical characteristics of these archetypes. Since common sulfur (also known as brimstone or "burning stone") was bright yellow, formed colorful compounds, was easily detected by its biting odor, and could be easily ignited, it represented the fiery or energetic properties expressed in the properties of plants and metals. Because of its yellow color and inner fire, sulfur was also associated with the sun and its metal, which is gold.

Common mercury, on the other hand, had no color of its own and reflected whatever light or image was cast on it. The odorless liquid metal quickly extinguished flames and actually absorbed other metals placed into it, including gold. Thus, mercury represented the watery, hidden, or occult properties expressed in the properties of plants and metals. To distinguish these philosophical ideals from their common counterparts, the alchemists referred to them as Philosophical or "Sophic" Sulfur and Mercury and usually capitalized them.

Female alchemists from the Middle East also became widely known in Europe. Cleopatra (not the famous seducer of Roman generals but an Alexandrian alchemist of the third century) invented the modern still. Maria Prophetissa (also known as Mary the Jewess), who lived around 300 A.D., invented several important alchemical devices, including the "bain marie" or Mary's bath, which is a double-boiler system that evenly distributes heat to substances undergoing transformation. She emphasized the importance of joining opposites. "Invert nature," she explained, "and you will find that which you seek." "Join the male and the female, and you will find what is sought." She is also famous for this mystical cry: "One becomes two, two becomes three, and by means of the third and fourth, it achieves unity; thus the two are but one."

With the Crusades, the Arabian texts on alchemy were further dispersed throughout Europe by the Templars and others who had fought in the Holy Lands. The alchemical explanation of nature spread throughout Europe in the writings of three gifted alchemists: Albertus Magnus (1205–1280), Roger Bacon (1214–1294), and Arnold of Villanova (1235–1311). As with most alchemical writings, their treatises contained not only mystical theories but also practical recipes; for example, Arnold of Villanova gave the distillation of wine as an illustration of the process of spiritization, while Roger Bacon gave a formula for gunpowder to demonstrate the hidden fire of sulfur. He also gave directions for constructing a telescope to keep track of celestial events for planning experiments. But Geber's Sulfur-Mercury model continued to dominate medieval alchemy.

"Alchemy is a science teaching how to transform any kind of metal into another through the use of the proper medicine," noted Roger Bacon in his *Mirror of Alchemy*. "Alchemy therefore is a science teaching how to make and compound a certain medicine, which is called the Elixir, which when cast upon metals or imperfect bodies of any kind, it fully perfects them in the very projection. The natural principles of this Elixir can be found in the mines and are Sulfur and Mercury. All metals and minerals, whereof there be sundry and diverse kinds, are begotten of these two. But I must tell you that nature always intends and strives to the perfection of Gold, yet the many accidents coming between change the metals. For according to the purity and impurity of the two aforesaid principles (Sulfur and Mercury), pure and impure metals are engendered."

Medieval alchemists believed that if you changed the signatures (physical characteristics) of substances, you also changed their "sophic" or archetypal properties. In the Emerald Tablet, this principle is described as "As Above, so Below." For instance, if ordinary shiny liquid mercury is transformed into a dull, solid amalgam by adding lead, sophic mercury has been created. By a similar process of working with the most basic signatures of the metals, the medieval alchemists believed it was possible to change one metal into another. Thus, if you were able to change the gray color of lead into a yellowish hue, you were on your way to making gold. Of course, this seems very simplistic to us, but it shows how important the concept of signatures was to the alchemist.

By working with the metals so closely and paying such attention to their physical properties, the early alchemists were aware of the regularity of properties reflected in the modern Periodic Table, in which the characteristics of the elements repeat in an eightfold cycle. "The metals are similar in their essence, and differ only in their form," summarized Albertus Magnus. "One may pass easily from one to another, following a circle [or cycle]." The alchemists' attempts to transform base metals into gold also resulted in the discovery of acids, alcohols, and hundreds of new compounds. Alchemy became the leading intellectual movement in Europe, even to the point where some universities started replacing the works of Aristotle with texts attributed to Thoth and Hermes. Even clerics of the Church became practicing alchemists. It was the heyday of alchemy.

The Mystery of Nicolas Flamel

During this momentous period in the history of alchemy, reports of alchemical transmutations circulated widely and samples of alchemical gold were to be found in most of the courts of Europe. One of the best documented cases of an alchemist succeeding in changing lead into gold during this time was that of Nicolas Flamel. The strange facts of Flamel's life are available for anyone to consider and all the public records relating to his life are still intact: his birth certificate (born 1330; died 1418), his marriage contract to his wife Pernelle, his last will and testament, deeds of his generous gifts of properties to charity, and commissions of monuments to his memory. In viewing these records, it becomes obvious that this poor bookseller, who worked out of his home in Paris, suddenly became very rich and started giving away large sums of money and valuable property to those in need. His explanation was that he had discovered the ancient alchemical secret of making gold.

Flamel was an educated man with a passion for the Hermetic arts and a driving desire to discover the Philosopher's Stone, the perfected essence of matter that embodied the deepest secrets of transformation. Whatever profits he made, he quickly invested in alchemy books, and he firmly believed that one day he would find a book that held the answers he was seeking. He even dreamed of an angel coming to him and promising him that he would one day find the book. "Look well at this book," she told him. "At first you will understand nothing in it—neither you nor any other man—but one day you will see in it that which no other man will be able to see."

One day, a young Jewish man came to him with a rare alchemy book to sell, and Flamel gladly paid him the requested price of two florins without further bargaining. It was a period in which Jewish people were being expelled from France and many of them were

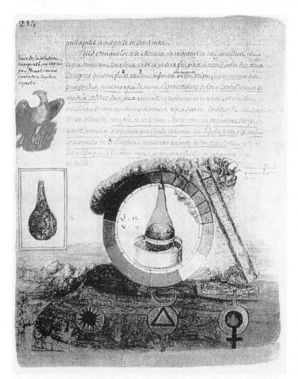

Figure 2. A page from the notebooks of Nicolas Flamel shows the vessel of transformation and various symbols for the operations of alchemy. (Nicolas Flamel, *Livre des Figures Hierogliphiques*, 1410)

selling treasured possessions before fleeing into Spain. According to Flamel, the book had an ancient binding of worked copper, on which were engraved curious diagrams and certain characters, some of which were Greek and Hebrew and others in an unknown language. The pages of the book were not parchment but were made of the bark of young trees that were covered with script written with an iron point. The pages were divided into groups of seven and consisted of three parts separated by a page showing a strange and unintelligible diagram. The edges of the book were covered in gold leaf, and the title page listed the author as "Abraham the

Jew—Prince, Priest, Levite, Astrologer, and Philosopher." There
were curses against anyone who read the book who was unworthy
of its contents, and every page carried an unknown word
(*Maranatha!*) that seemed to be a warning of some sort. In his
Book of the Hieroglyphic Figures, Flamel wrote:

> Once I had this beautiful book in my possession, I did nothing
> but study it night and day, learning very well all the operations it
> described, but not knowing with what material it should be
> started. This caused me great sorrow, kept me in solitude, and
> made me sigh incessantly. My wife Pernelle, whom I loved like
> myself, was greatly astonished at this, so I showed her this beau-
> tiful book, with which, the moment she saw it, she fell as much
> in love as I, taking extreme pleasure in contemplating the beau-
> tiful covers, engravings, images, and portraits, of which figures
> she understood as little as I did. Nevertheless, it was for me a
> great consolation to talk about it with her, and to consider what
> could be done in order to find out their meaning.

Although Flamel was initiated into alchemy and was familiar
with the ciphers and symbols of the alchemists, nothing in the book
made any sense to him. He even copied pages from the book and
displayed them in his store hoping someone might understand
them. After twenty-one years, Flamel had still not understood the
book and he made the desperate decision to travel to Spain to seek
the help of Jewish scholars who had fled there to escape persecution
in France. In Leon, he met a Jewish scholar who was familiar with
the book of Abraham the Jew and wanted very much to see it for
himself, but the man died on their return journey. Flamel had
copied a few pages from the book and the man had recognized
some of the script as ancient Chaldean; he translated several pages.
That was enough for Flamel to begin translating the remaining
pages, and in another three years he and his wife had finished the
complete translation.

According to his diaries, he strictly followed the instructions of
Abraham the Jew and changed a half-pound of mercury first into

silver and then into pure gold. Simultaneously, wrote Flamel, he accomplished the same transmutation in his soul. After only three transmutations of mercury into gold, Flamel was rich beyond his dreams, yet he kept none for himself. Instead, he established houses for the poor, founded free hospitals and schools for the blind, rebuilt statues and monuments, renewed abandoned cemeteries, and endowed churches throughout France. At nearly all his charities, Flamel commissioned strange stones or plaques containing alchemical symbols.

Alchemists still make the pilgrimages to his former charities, such as the former site of Saint-Jacques-la-Boucherie Church at Tour de Saint-Jacquesnear Chatêlet and the Cemetery of the Innocents. In 1786, all the bodies in the cemetery were exhumed and moved to the Paris catacombs under Denfert Rochereau. However, Flamel's house is still standing at 51 rue Montmorency, which is near rue Montorgueil in Paris.

Flamel continued his lifelong labor of copying manuscripts and studying alchemy but soon lost interest in making gold. He realized that love of gold metal could destroy him, and he closed Abraham's book and never shared its contents with anyone. He felt that the transmutations had started a greater spiritual gold growing within him and his wife Pernelle that was worth more than any material possession. He continued to live the quiet life of a scribe and scholar and wrote many important books on alchemy but never divulged the secrets of the book of Abraham. He and his wife lived long lives into their eighties. It was as if he knew when he wanted to die, and he carefully settled his affairs and planned how he was to be buried. He had his tombstone prepared beforehand. His stone shows a bright sun above a key and a closed book in the middle of various figures. Many have taken it to mean that Flamel chose not to share the key to alchemy with an immature and impure world. It can still be seen at his gravesite in Paris at the Musée de Cluny at the end of the nave of Saint-Jacques-la-Boucherie Church.

After his death, word quickly spread of his accomplishments in alchemy and his house, monuments, and even his grave were nearly destroyed by people searching for gold or the alchemical powder of projection that would enable them to create gold. Perhaps Flamel was right in his assessment of the human soul not being ready for the truths of alchemy. Flamel bequeathed his library to a nephew named Perrier, whom he had initiated into alchemy. Perrier kept the family secrets and Flamel's library was passed down from generation to generation. One of his descendants named Dubois demonstrated what he called his ancestor's power of projection in the presence of Louis XIII and successfully transmuted leaden balls into gold.

Cardinal de Richelieu heard of the demonstrations and imprisoned the man for questioning. The cardinal eventually condemned the man to death and seized all his property, including the book of Abraham the Jew. The cardinal also ordered the original home searched, and at the same time, someone moved the huge tombstone on Flamel's grave and pried open the coffin. According to reports of the time, no body was found, which only compounded the mystery. Undaunted, the cardinal built an alchemical laboratory at the Chateau of Rueil, which he often visited to study the manuscript and to try to understand the sacred hieroglyphs and rediscover the secret of creating gold. Fortunately, the ambitious politician never succeeded in cracking the key of Abraham the Jew. After Cardinal de Richelieu died, the book itself was never found, although copies of the drawings had been made and were widely circulated.

The Paracelsian Revolution

In the hundred years after Flamel's death, his intuition about the evils of man's fixation on gold came true and alchemy suffered as greed and avarice dominated alchemical experiments. As a result, the deeper philosophical foundations of alchemy were in disarray. About this time, the iconoclastic alchemist Paracelsus (1493–1541) appeared on the scene and cleaned up the philosophical underpinnings of alchemy. He expanded Geber's Sulfur-Mercury theory by the addition of Salt as the third member of what he called the Tria Prima

(Three Essentials). Salt represented matter and the materialization of spiritual principles. Its characteristics were non-flammability and fixity, and mystically it was associated with the body of man. The definite association of Mercury, Sulfur, and Salt with spirit, soul, and body (respectively) was made by Paracelsus. He stated:

> Know, then, that all the seven metals are born from a threefold matter, namely, Mercury, Sulfur, and Salt, but with distinct and peculiar colorings. Mercury is the spirit, Sulfur is the soul, and Salt is the body. The soul, which indeed is Sulfur, unites those two contraries, the body and the spirit, and changes them into one essence.

Another of Paracelsus' key concepts was that of the mysterious First Matter as it exists in the body and how it could be used in healing. According to Paracelsus, during a person's life, there is present a finely diffused form of matter, like a vapor filling not merely every part of his physical body but actually stored in some parts. It is a subtle matter constantly renewed by the vital chemistry; a matter as easily disposed of as the breath, once the breath has served its purpose. Paracelsus named this First Matter of life the *Archaeus*, meaning the "oldest principle" present in the body. The *Archaeus* has a magnetic nature and radiates within and around living bodies. The *Archaeus* is the spark of life within us that originated with the Universal Spirit. He wrote:

> The *Archaeus* is an essence that is equally distributed in all parts of the human body. The *Spiritus Vitae* (Spirit of Life) takes its origin from the *Spiritus Mundi* (Spirit of the Universe). Being an emanation of the latter, the *Archaeus* contains the elements of all cosmic influences and is therefore the cause by which the action of the cosmic forces act upon the body."

The revolutionary ideas of Paracelsus would substantially change and invigorate alchemy. By introducing Salt, he refocused the attention of alchemists to the problems of the real world of matter and human suffering. He began a new era of alchemy that emphasized the use of the metals and minerals as part of medicine, and alchemists became more like pharmacists than philosophers. Almost single-handedly, Paracelsus rescued alchemy from the puffers (materialistic alchemists who sought to make gold for their own personal gain) and gave it a new orientation in the service of mankind. As the founder of iatrochemistry (from the Greek words for "medicinal chemistry"), Paracelsus added minerals, metals, and chemical compounds to the physician's arsenal of herbs and plants. He also discovered the basic principle of homeopathy—the idea that substances that make us sick can also, in much smaller quantities, make us well by eliciting a healing response from the body. Despite his contributions to scientific method, however, Paracelsus always believed that alchemy was a form of magic and too much reliance on intellect instead of intuition would spell disaster for the world. "Magic," he explained, "has the power to experience and fathom things which are inaccessible to human reason; for Magic is a great secret wisdom, just as reason is a great public folly."

Unfortunately, Paracelsus was not a very appealing person and had few friends. With his squat, pear-shaped body, large misshapen head, and protruding lips, he was not a handsome man. But what really repulsed people was his antagonistic, in-your-face demeanor and his relentless air of self-importance. His real name was Philippus Aureolus Theophrastus Bombastus von Hohenheim, but he took the Latin name "Paracelsus" (meaning "Beyond Celsus") to show that he surpassed the great Aulus Celsus, a revered Roman physician who wrote the first European medical text in 1478. Paracelsus was so confrontational in discussing his ideas that his middle name (Bombastus) became synonymous with the loud and self-reverent speaking style of "bombastic" people.

Yet this rude little man was a formidable debater who argued with great vigor and seasoned his words with biting sarcasm and dramatic demonstrations. To attract more people to his lectures, Paracelsus spoke in the common language (German) instead of scholarly Latin. His vitriolic tirades made his lectures extremely popular and attractive to inquisitive young minds who carried his ideas throughout Europe. In 1523, he caused a great scandal by publicly burning the works of the Arabian alchemist Avicenna and the Roman physician Galen to show it was time to move beyond their orthodox ideas. He even attacked the venerated Greek philosopher Pythagoras for "polluting" the sciences with "mere speculation" devoid of any observation of nature. In 1527, while teaching at the University of Basil, he presented a lecture to the medical faculty in which he accused them of killing their patients with their "dangerous cures" and challenged them to burn their outdated textbooks, to "get off the couch and get to work" experimenting for new and better methods of healing. He was run out of town by the incensed doctors, who nearly tarred and feathered him. After that episode, Paracelsus was rarely invited to speak at universities, although he traveled extensively throughout Europe and continued spreading his inflammatory ideas. Finally, the formidable powers of the Church warned him to tone down his rhetoric or be burnt at the stake for blasphemy.

There was simply no denying that Paracelsus was a heretic. He began his popular treatise, *Aurora of the Philosophers*, with the unequivocal statement that the Egyptian god Thoth was in fact Adam, and the Pillars of Hermes were not pillars but stone tablets that contained the secrets of nature written in the sacred language of hieroglyphics. In the same treatise, he claimed that after the Great Flood, Noah discovered Thoth's tablets on Mount Ararat and the teachings of Thoth were passed down to Abraham and became the common foundation of Judaism, Christianity, and Islam. According to Paracelsus, the Three Magi (Magicians) who brought gifts to the infant Jesus were really alchemists following the ancient Egyptian path of wisdom.

Although chastised for his presumptive arrogance, Paracelsus was truly an egoless man furiously focused on higher truths who dedicated his life to finding the "chief and supreme essence of things." To him, this divine Quintessence could only be glimpsed through extreme honesty, mental purgation, and spiritual purification. His search for this "perfect substance"—a supreme life force that contained the "essence of all celestial and terrestrial creatures"—continuously humbled him. An alchemist might discover the "wonderful and strange effects" of this substance but such effects were not to be mistaken for the Thing Itself. According to Paracelsus, its exact nature was "impenetrable even to the wisest of the Magi [magicians]."

The Church eventually lost its patience with this stubborn little man and banished him to a hotel room in Salzburg, Austria. Not surprisingly, Paracelsus continued writing his inflammatory texts. Finally, at the age of forty-three, he died under mysterious circumstances in his hotel room. His body was quickly buried before anyone could examine it and it was rumored that physicians from the faculty of the University of Vienna had hired an assassin to silence him. Yet even death could not silence the great Paracelsus. His books inspired many revolutionary advances in the healing arts and even to this day, the sick and infirm travel to his grave in Salzburg seeking a miraculous cure from the father of modern medicine.

Isaac Newton and the Black Dragon

One of the most important alchemists of the seventeenth century is hardly recognized for his work in this field, yet Sir Isaac Newton, the famous mathematician and scientist, spent most of his life pursuing alchemy. He wrote over a million words on the subject that have never been published because, after his death in 1727, the Royal Society deemed them "not fit to be printed." The papers were rediscovered in the middle of the twentieth century and most scholars now concede that Newton considered himself first and foremost an alchemist. It is now thought that Newton's laws of light and gravity were inspired by his alchemical work. Alchemical theory equates light with Mercury and the force of gravity with Salt. These concepts are explained in the next chapter.

When Newton worked in his lab, he demanded complete privacy, although his servants still kept a close eye on their eccentric master. One of his servants wrote:

Figure 3. The alchemist's work in the laboratory required prayer and meditation, as well as practical experimentation. (Heinrich Khunrath, *Amphitheatrum Sapentiae*, 1602)

He very rarely went to bed until two or three of the clock, sometimes not till five or six, lying about four or five hours, especially at springtime or autumn, at which time he used to employ about six weeks in his laboratory, the fire scarce going out night or day. What his aim might be I was unable to penetrate into.

As a practicing alchemist, Newton spent days locked up in his laboratory, and not a few researchers have suggested that he finally succeeded in transmuting lead into gold. Perhaps that explains one of the oddest things about his life. At the height of his career, instead of accepting a professorship at Cambridge, he accepted a position as director of the Mint with the responsibility of securing and accounting for England's repository of gold.

Newton was a traditional alchemist in the sense that he accepted the idea that alchemy originated with Thoth in ancient Egypt. He prepared his own translation of the Emerald Tablet and kept it hidden safely in his laboratory. "Like all European alchemists from the Dark Ages to the beginning of the scientific era and beyond," noted Michael White in *Isaac Newton: The Last Sorcerer* (Addison-Wesley 1997), "Newton was motivated by a deep-rooted commitment to the notion that alchemical wisdom extended back to ancient times. The Hermetic tradition—the body of alchemical knowledge—was believed to have originated in the mists of time and to have been given to humanity through supernatural agents."

By 1669, Isaac Newton's lifelong work in alchemy had focused almost entirely on antimony, a metal that was to remain near the center of his thoughts for the rest of his life. Antimony is steel gray in color, but it can tarnish to much darker grays. Its metallic luster is often hidden by the tarnish. It is an extremely brittle, crystalline metal that is in the arsenic group of elements and is considered poisonous. Antimony was recognized in compounds by the ancients and was known as a metal at the beginning of the seventeenth century. The word "antimony" is from the Greek words *anti* and *monos* meaning "not alone." There is a legend that antimony was first named by Basil Valentine, who secretly added the poisonous metal to the food of Dominican monks in order to determine its effects on humans. A natural emetic, the antimony made the monks vomit and suffer from severe nausea. He therefore named the metal "anti-mony" meaning "anti-monks." The alchemists called this potent metal the "Black Dragon."

Antimony regulus is a star-shaped form produced by purifying antimony ore and heating it to a high temperature. The alchemists named this peculiar signature of antimony after the Regulus, the bright double star near the heart of the constellation Leo. The name is derived from the Latin *regulus*, meaning "lesser king." Because the regulus of antimony combines readily with gold (which is the true king), it became important to the process of extracting the precious metal from minerals and an object of considerable experimental interest to seventeenth-century adepts. About the process of making the regulus, Newton wrote:

> These rules in general should be observed. First, if the fire be quick. Second, if the crucible be thoroughly heated before anything be put in; third, if metals be put in successively according to their degree of fusibility from [iron], copper, antimony, tin, to [lead]. Fourthly, that they stand some time after fusion before they be poured off accordingly to the quantity of regulus they yield to keep it from hardening. Fifthly, that if you would have the saltpeter flow without too great a heat, you may quicken it by throwing in a little more saltpeter mixed with $\frac{1}{8}$ or $\frac{1}{16}$ of charcoal finely powdered. Thus with a good quick and smart fire, the ore gave a most black & filthy scoria, and the regulus after a purgation or two, starred very well. On a clear, uncloudy, and windless day, the regulus will become starred quite easily when you're ready, and sufficiently skilled in the process. The clear weather helps considerably, but then so does the bond between the matters and the operator.

The term "starred" was used by Newton in its most literal sense. For if the antimony has been properly purified, it forms long and slender crystals. During cooling the crystals in turn form triangular branches around a central point, taking on the aspect of a silver star. Newton found in the star signature of antimony the possibility of gaining cosmic knowledge in connection with the heavens.

In 1704, Newton used the Regulus of Mars (iron) as a reflecting mirror in a telescope to peer into space. His reflecting mirror was a curved mirror that gathered in light and reflected it back to a point of focus. His telescope opened the door to magnifiying objects millions of times—far beyond the power of any single lens.

To obtain a very shining mirrorlike surface, Newton then used silver to obtain the lunar regulus. Using methods developed by Nicolas Flamel, Newton amalgamated this regulus with thrice distilled mercury, which once washed, is a perfect reflecting mirror.

It was thus his alchemical work with antimony that guided Newton's interest in light and the gravity of heavenly bodies. By 1675, he began publishing his breakthrough papers on light and gravity. Newton had observed that the lines of crystals appeared to radiate out from the center of the star regulus and noted that they "might just as well be considered as radiating into the center, which gives them the character of attraction rather than the character of emission." It is likely at this point that the concept of gravitation "in which the lines of attraction run in to and converge in a center point" may have occurred to him.

Like Nicolas Flamel, Newton recognized that through the numerous "eagles" (distillations), the crystalline structure of the regulus was progressively adjusting and rising in a set pattern toward a cubic fundamental matrix. The cubic structure is the most perfect of the crystals having perfect right angles and equilateral triangles in its arrangement. This matter is the seed risen to its highest purity. Beyond this limiting point, the pattern breaks down. In fact, distilling the regulus amalgam more than nine times generally leads to an explosion. By repeated distillations, the material continued to change, after which it met a limit or final state. In this behavior of the regulus, one can see the seeds of Newton's mathematics of progression and limits, his theory of "fluxions" (calculus).

Despite his fascination with antimony, the regulus was not the goal of Newton's work. He looked upon the star as a most promising step in the creation of the Philosophical Mercury, the *Materia Prima* or First Matter from which all substances are formed. In the mid-1670s, Newton composed a long and polished paper entitled *Clovis* ("The Key"). This amazing document was the culmination of years already spent in the meticulous study of the star regulus in the hope of extracting Philosophical Mercury from common metals. Newton believed he had succeeded in doing just that.

According to his notes, he had found the Philosophic Mercury so sought after by the alchemists. Applying this new form of Mercury to the metals caused little trees of tiny crystalline branches to grow within them. In his view, he had given life to the metals. When he applied his new Mercury to gold, it also came alive but in the purest and most perfect life of all the metals. He believed the Philosophic Gold produced by this method was living gold that possessed magical powers. He even hinted that he had multiplied common gold ("caused it to grow") by mixing it with his Philosophic Gold. If true, it helps explain why this famous scientist was appointed Warden and then Master of the British Royal Mint.

As confirmation of his work, the *Cauda Pavonis* (Peacock's Tail), the multicolored tail of the peacock prophesied by ancient alchemists as the work came to a close, unfolded before Newton's very eyes. Nicolas Flamel had experienced the same thing while manipulating the regulus amalgam with gold and silver. Newton wrote:

> I know whereof I write, for I have in the fire manifold glasses with gold and this mercury. They grow in these glasses in the form of a tree, and by a continued circulation the trees are dissolved again with the work into a new mercury. I have such a vessel in the fire with gold thus dissolved, but extrinsically and intrinsically into a mercury as living and mobile as any mercury found in the world. For it makes gold begin to swell, to be swollen, and to putrefy, and to spring forth into sprouts and branches, changing colors daily, the appearances of which fascinate me every day. I reckon this is a great secret in Alchemy.

However, Newton was fearful that the secret would leak out into the world and cause dangerous political and social consequences, since mankind was not yet ready for such power to transform matter.

Like Albert Einstein trying to stop his theories from being used as atomic weapons, Newton was fearful his work would be exploited by evil men.

In 1676, after fellow member of the Royal Society Robert Boyle disclosed he had discovered a special mercury that grows hot (incalescent) when mixed with gold, Newton was afraid Boyle had made the same discovery. He wrote him a letter cautioning him to keep everything secret:

> It may possibly be an inlet to something more noble, not to be communicated without immense damage to the world if there should be any verity in the Hermetic writers, therefore I question not but that the great wisdom of the noble Author will sway him to high silence till he shall be resolved of what consequence the thing may be either by his own experience, or the judgment of some other—that is of a true Hermetic Philosopher—there being other things besides the transmutation of metals, if those great pretenders brag not which none but they understand.

In this respectful but pleading letter, we see that Newton was no common puffer but a spiritual alchemist of the first caliber. He truly believed that if the gates of wisdom were breached, the spoils of alchemy would go to vulgar materialists. Flamel and Newton, like all true adepts of alchemy, revered the Divine Plan. Boyle was one of a new breed of materialistic alchemists (who came to be known as "chemists") who subscribed to the spreading philosophy of Descartes that separated body and physicality from spirit and soul and denied the existence of such occult (hidden) forces as alchemical correspondences, chemical synchronicities, and invisible influences.

Rise of the Puffers

The fascination with gold during the Middle Ages produced a new class of mercenary alchemists known as "puffers," who sat at their furnaces constantly fanning their bellows, hoping to produce gold by working with external fires and never calling forth the inner, magical "secret fire" of the initiated alchemist. Using only physical methods and trickery, the puffers convinced princes and kings to finance their endeavors, although not a few went to the gallows when they were unable to produce more gold than they consumed. A few heads of state, such as Frederick of Wurzburg, actually maintained special gilded gallows for hanging alchemists.

At the height of the puffer craze in the sixteenth century, Paris, Vienna, Prague, and dozens of other European cities were home to alchemical workshops in which greed was the ruling passion. The puffers' laboratories can still be seen in Prague in the *Zlata Ulicka* ("Golden Alley"), which dates back to the time of emperors Maximilian II (1564–1576) and Rudolph II (1576–1612). Mercenary-minded alchemists, seduced by the allure of multiplying gold, degenerated into quacks and charlatans, and eventually brought alchemy into disrepute. England and several other countries banned alchemy and prohibited the circulation of gold and silver created by alchemists.

Modern chemistry, with its materialistic approach, actually arose from the erratic work of the puffers in the Middle Ages. The laboratory work of the puffers was geared toward manipulation of substances for personal or commercial gain. Puffers saw no value in spiritual techniques.

Nonetheless, spiritual alchemists suffered along with the puffers and were forced to practice their art in secrecy. By the late sixteenth century, alchemy was in philosophic disarray and was regarded as the most confused and difficult philosophical system in the world. French historian Albert Poisson noted in his *History of Alchemy* (1891):

> Scholasticism with its infinitely subtle argumentation, theology with its ambiguous phraseology, astrology so vast and so complicated, are only child's play in comparison with alchemy.

The demise of alchemy in Europe began in the late eighteenth century with the complete rationalization of science and the commercialization of chemistry. By the time Antoine-Laurent Lavoisier's chemical textbook (*Basic Characteristics of Chemicals*) was published in 1789, alchemy had degenerated from a practical path of spiritual perfection into a competitive race for commercial products to put up for sale on the economic merry-go-round. It was far from Egypt's ancient Science of Soul, which presented alchemy as a spiritual discipline designed to accelerate human evolution.

True alchemy could simply not survive in the new atmosphere of materialism and industrialization because the key to success in the ancient art lay in being able to work simultaneously on all levels of reality—not only on the physical level but on the psychological and spiritual as well. The alchemist's laboratory was a sacred place "between worlds" that could not be entered without becoming psychologically purified and spiritually energized, and things took place in the alchemist's laboratory that could never be reproduced in a chemist's lab. The central work in alchemy—the operation of the Stone—simply was not within reach of the chemist, for the methods involved the workings of an eagerness or inspiration, a fertilizing or generative element, suggesting that the alchemists had discovered some secret of life which, carried into metallurgy, produced effects unknown today.

What exactly were those unknown effects and how were they produced? What mysterious processes went on in the alchemists' laboratories? What was the secret formula contained in the ancient Emerald Tablet? Why did alchemists give up any prospect of a normal life to spend day and night tending their fires and performing incomprehensible experiments with dangerous chemicals? Why all the secrecy? Did any alchemist ever succeed? These are just a few of the questions that will be answered in the coming chapters. Before a true understanding is possible, however, each of us must become initiated into the mysteries of alchemy. That initiation begins in earnest in the next chapter.

3

The Principles of Alchemy

HERE IS A TANTALIZING ALCHEMICAL RIDDLE from the seventeenth century. In fact, if you really understand the answer, there is no need for you to read the rest of this book, for you are already an alchemist who has drunk from the Holy Grail of alchemy. Go out into the world now and accumulate as much of this substance as you can find for it is the key to all transformations. However, if you are like most of us and the riddle remains a riddle, then embark on the greatest journey of your lifetime and seek the answer to the riddle wherever it leads you.

> The key to life and death is everywhere to be found, but if you do not find it in your own house, you will find it nowhere. Yet, it is before everyone's eyes; no one can live without it; everyone has used it. The poor usually possess more of it than the rich; children play with it in the streets. The meek and uneducated esteem it highly, but the privileged and learned often throw it away. It is the only thing from which the Philosopher's Stone can be prepared, and without it, no noble metal can ever be created.

From the riddle, certain characteristics of the answer can be discerned. First, the answer to this riddle is the key that unlocks the door to wealth, health, enlightenment, and even immortality. Yet this great treasure is "everywhere to be found." The Renaissance alchemist George Beatus describes its power and also warns about its misuse:

I am a poisonous dragon, present everywhere and to be had for nothing. My water and fire dissolve and compound. Out of my body you shall draw the Green and Red Lion, but if you do not exactly know me, you will destroy your five senses with my fire. I give you faculties both male and female and the powers of both heaven and earth. I am the Egg of Nature. I am dark and bright; I spring from the earth and come out of heaven. I am the Carbuncle of the Sun. I am a most noble, clarified earth by which you may turn copper, iron, tin, and lead into most pure gold.

Another characteristic of the answer to the riddle is that it is something that can only be discovered and understood by first going within our own "house," which could also be our own body or mind. This thing is so mysterious and ineffable that it really cannot be spoken of directly at all. The only way to truly understand it is indirectly, through its corresponding signatures within our own bodies and souls. Sometimes these intimations are only obvious at quiet times, or when we focus our undivided attention on the present moment, or enter deep meditation seeking to learn the true nature of reality.

The riddle also suggests that people who blindly follow socially accepted values, beliefs, and behavior, are no longer connected to the mystery of this thing and therefore "throw it away." It is something often rejected as irrelevant or easily taken for granted. It seems the more civilized or "adulterated" we become, the less we appreciate this fundamental aspect of reality. But the alchemists knew the crucial importance of this thing, which exists both within us and in the natural world. German alchemist Heinrich Khunrath said:

This is the true Light of Nature, which illuminates all the God-loving philosophers. It is in the world, and the whole edifice of the world is beautifully adorned and will be naturally preserved by it. But the world knows it not. Above all, it is the subject of the great Stone of the philosophers which the world has before its eyes and yet knows it not.

Medieval alchemists frequently referred to this thing as "the cornerstone the builders forgot." In other words, it is something important that is not an integrated part of our current civilization.

Perhaps the biggest clue to the answer to the riddle is that it is "the only thing from which the Philosopher's Stone can be prepared." The ancient Greek alchemist Zosimos realized that the answer to this riddle, once known and purified, becomes the much-sought-after Philosopher's Stone. You can see the similarities in his description of the final goal of all alchemists: "In speaking of the Philosopher's Stone, receive this stone which is not a stone, a precious thing that has no value, a thing of many shapes that has no shape, this unknown which is known by all."

What is your answer? When the AlchemyLab.com Web site first appeared on the Internet, it required visitors to enter the answer to this riddle before gaining entry to the site. The problem was that no one was getting into the Web site, so the creators had to open the site to everyone. Most modern people have no idea what the riddle is about. Among the thousands of wrong answers were a few that came very close, such as imagination, love, light, consciousness, thought, sun, moon, time, energy, ether, god, joy, spirit, soul, heart, blood, chaos, fire, water, air, earth, sulfur, mercury, salt, quintessence, and the stone. Even such answers as urine, menses, manure, and dirt would be considered by alchemists to be fitting responses.

The First Matter

As far as the alchemists were concerned, there was only one correct answer to the riddle and it was the "First Matter." However, that is like answering a riddle with another riddle. The First Matter is the most nebulous concept in alchemy and very difficult to define in everyday terms. The *Lexicon of Alchemy* (Martin Ruland, 1612) lists over eighty definitions for the First Matter (*Materia Prima*). The alchemists themselves never fully agreed on what it was, and there are at least two hundred different descriptions in the literature. In

Figure 4. The First Matter of the alchemists is everywhere, but no one notices it. (Michael Maier, *Atalanta Fugiens*, 1617)

fact, many of the answers to the riddle given above are acceptable synonyms for the First Matter.

The reason the First Matter is so hard to describe is that it is everything and it is nothing. It is the primordial chaos, the infinite cornucopia from which the myriad of all created things emerges. With this primordial chaos is contained the germ or seed of potencies of all things that ever existed and of all that ever will exist in the future. It is the *Anima Mundi* (Universal Soul) and the very body of nature. The primordial matter focuses the archetypal powers that form minerals and metals, vegetables and animals, and everything that exists. All forms are hidden within its depths, and it is therefore what philosophers call the true *principium* or beginning of all things.

Even such things as urine and manure also have a ring of truth in talking about the First Matter, since they are things associated with the life force that humans tend to reject or not want to touch. Similarly, the whole concept of the First Matter has been rejected by modern civilization. The reason our culture has rejected the idea of the First Matter is that its first characteristic is that it exists in a state between matter and energy, between manifested and unmanifested. Our materialistic world has no room for such a gray area of reality. For us, things are either real or unreal. However in ancient times, that concept was extremely important to understanding the workings of the universe.

In ancient Egypt, the First Matter was the subject of the Emerald Tablet, which referred to it as simply the "One Thing." It is the primordial chaos of the universe fashioned into material reality by the thoughts (or Word) of the One Mind. The idea of One Mind (or Spirit) seeking expression in the material universe dates back at least as far as the ancient Egyptians. Priestly alchemists denoted the First Matter with the hieroglyph known as "kh," which looks like a circle with two wide horizontal black bands running through it. This symbol of the First Matter is the first hieroglyph that makes up the Egyptian word "khem," which is the root of our word "alchemy." It is also the only hieroglyph that continues to baffle Egyptologists. Other hieroglyphs are associated with common items such as a basket, stool, owl, vulture, etc. However, this particular one has both tangible and intangible nuances. The easiest definition is "black matter that is alive" but what exactly is that? Most language experts have translated it as "placenta," while others feel it might mean "fertile dirt" or "living black soil." In fact, it is the holy script for the First Matter, the basic stuff of the universe from which all things have sprung.

In ancient China, philosophers referred to the First Matter as the "Tao," which is an equally difficult term to describe. The Tao is the unborn origin of the universe, the chaotic source of all that exists neither in heaven nor on earth but in between. It is described in the *Tao te Ching*: "There is a thing confusedly formed, born between heaven and earth. Silent and void, it stands alone and does not change, goes round and does not weary. It is capable of being the mother of the world."

Alchemists of both East and West understood the cyclic nature of the First Matter, as it was created and destroyed, born and reborn throughout time. The Eastern symbol, the Tai Chi (or Yin-Yang diagram) shows black and white semicircles in an endless spiral of changing into one another, each containing the seed of the other. In the West, the symbol of the First Matter was the Uroboros (or Ouroboros), the snake or dragon eating its own tail. Sometimes two serpents (or dragons) were shown, with a lighter, winged serpent above and a darker, walking serpent below. Such symbols carry profound meaning and show how important was the First Matter to the process of life on all levels of body, mind, and spirit. Psychologist Carl Jung commented on this symbology in his *Mysterium Conjunctionis*:

> In the age-old image of the uroboros lies the thought of devouring oneself and turning oneself into a circulatory process, for it was clear to the more astute alchemists the *Materia Prima* of the art was man himself. The uroboros is a dramatic symbol for the integration and assimilation of the opposite, i.e., the shadow. This feedback process is at the same time a symbol of immortality, since it is said of the uroboros that he slays himself and brings himself to life, fertilizes himself and gives birth to himself.

Not surprisingly, finding the First Matter was a major problem for the alchemists. The ancient texts never described directly, only teased the initiate into accepting it without actually ever naming it. The adepts said that it was the alpha and omega, the beginning and end of all things, everywhere to be found, always available, easily directed by thoughts, yet overlooked by the masses as useless.

Because the First Matter was said to be present in every human being but rejected by most, literal-minded alchemists searched for it in cisterns and manure heaps, or in the night sweat of the elderly, even in the urine of young boys and the menses of pubescent girls, where it was thought to be purer than in adults.

Knowing that the First Matter could be corrupted by thoughts, the savvy alchemist most often searched in the bosom of nature herself, in the distant forests and mountains, for quiet sacred sites where he suspected it had accumulated. The alchemist traipsed deep into the forest searching for the blackest, purest dirt, far off the beaten path of both man and animal. Often, he spent weeks wandering until he found just the right spot. Then, by the light of the moon, he dug a deep hole to expose the virgin soil, which he hoped still contained traces of the First Matter. He carefully shoveled the sacred earth into a gunny sack and lugged it back to his laboratory. Sometimes, on cool spring nights, the alchemist drove wooden pegs into the ground and spread flax cloths over them to collect the morning dew, believing that in the process of condensing from the air, the pure moisture would trap traces of hidden matter that coagulated in the darkness of the night. Early the following day, he wrung the precious moisture from the cloths into clay crocks and immediately sealed them for later experimentation.

The Four Elements

According to the ancients, the First Matter has a fourfold structure, which they attributed to the existence of four archetypal forces or elements of creation and named Earth, Water, Air, and Fire. Obviously, the Four Elements of the alchemists are not our everyday ideas of earth, water, air, and fire, which are only the physical expressions of their respective archetypes. "There are four common elements," wrote Polish alchemist Michael Sendivogius (1566–1636), "and each has at its center another deeper element [the archetype] which makes it what it is. These are the four pillars of the world. They were in the beginning evolved and molded out of chaos [First Matter] by the hand of the Creator; and it is their contrary action which keeps up the harmony and equilibrium of the mundane machinery of the universe; it is they, which through the virtue of celestial influences, produce all things above and beneath the earth."

Thus, the Four Elements are named for those fundamental archetypes within matter and are symbolic of their metaphysical qualities. As archetypes, the elements are beyond any rational explanation and must be experienced to be understood. French philosopher Gaston Bachelard (1884–1962) concluded that the Four Elements resulted from "material image-making" or "the materialization of imagery" within the One Mind of the universe. He looked at the interaction of the elements from the point of view of what each sought. "Earthly joy is riches and impediment," he said. "Aquatic joy is softness and repose; fiery pleasure is desire and love; airy delight is liberty and movement."

In *Answers from the Elements*, Sufi alchemist Rumi describes the elements as expressions of the love of the universal soul for the divine spirit:

> Last night I asked the moon about the Moon, my one question for the visible world, Where is God? The moon says, I am dust stirred up when he passed by. The sun: My face is pale yellow from just now seeing him. Water: I slide on my head and face, like a snake, from a spell he cast. Fire: His lightning—I want to be that restless. Wind: Why so light? I would burn too if I had a choice. Earth, quiet, impregnated: Inside me I have a garden and an underground spring.

The ancient Greeks did a lot of philosophizing about the nature of the First Matter (which they called *hyle*), and from that it is thought the doctrine of the Four Elements emerged. The first philosopher to formalize these principles was Empedocles, a Greek philosopher and healer who lived around 450 B.C. In his *Tetrasomia* ("Doctrine of the Four Elements"), he stated that all matter is comprised of four roots (or elements): Earth, Water, Air, and Fire.

Figure 5. Through the circulation and transformation of the Four Elements and the corresponding humors, a human being is balanced and integrated. (Leonhard Thurneysser, *Quinta Essentia*, 1574)

According to Empedocles, Fire and Air are "outwardly reaching" elements, reaching up and out, whereas Earth and Water turn inward and downward. In his view, and that of later alchemists, the elements are not only material substances but also spiritual essences. To show their archetypal power, Empedocles associated each element with a god. "Hera rules the fruitful earth," he wrote. "Hades the central fire, Zeus the luminescent air, and Persephone the mollifying water."

The elements were animated through the interaction of two great living energies Empedocles called Love and Strife (*Eros* and *Eris*). Love he associated with the goddess Aphrodite, and Strife with the god of war, Ares. This simple view explained nearly every aspect of the world of the Greeks. Love and Strife were primordial gods who predated the gods of Olympus. This idea is very much like the Eastern tradition of Yin and Yang, with Yin being the passive feminine energy of Love and Yang being the aggressive masculine energy of Strife. Egyptian alchemists associated the feminine (Love) energy with the Moon and masculine (Strife) energy with the Sun, while European alchemists associated the feminine energy with the Queen and the masculine energy with the King.

Aristotle (350 B.C.) further developed the theories of Empedocles by explaining them in terms of their qualities. In his view, the elements arose from the interplay of the ideal (or archetypal) properties of hotness and coldness, and dryness and wetness. Fire (dry and hot) and Water (wet and cold) are polar opposites, as are Earth (dry and cold) and Air (wet and hot). Wet and dry are the primary qualities. Wet (moistness) is the quality of fluidity or flexibility, which allows a thing to adapt to its external conditions, whereas Dry (dryness) is the quality of rigidity, which allows a thing to define its own shape and bounds. As a consequence Wet things tend to be volatile and expansive, since they can fill spaces in their surroundings, whereas Dry things are fixed and structured, since they define their own form. Aristotle predicted that one material could be transformed into another by altering the mix of its archetypal elements and their qualities.

The symbols used by the alchemists for the elements have a lot to say about their archetypal origins. The symbol for Fire is an upward-pointing triangle – △ – since Fire with its hot and dry qualities is the most volatile element and seeks to ascend. The symbol for Water is a downward-pointing triangle – ▽ – since

Water with its cold and moist qualities seeks to descend or condense. Fire and Water are the two purest elements, and the other
two elements of Air and Earth are considered to be more material
versions of them. Thus, the symbol for Air – **△** – is the upward-
pointing triangle of Fire with a horizontal line through it. Air is hot
and moist and seeks to ascend, but its moist component blocks the
full ascent of the Fire principle, as indicated by the horizontal line
in the triangle. Thus Air is suspended in time and space, caught
between the extremes of the Above and the Below. The symbol for
Earth – **▽** – is the downward-pointing triangle of Water with a
horizontal line through it. Earth is cold and dry and seeks to
descend, but its dry component blocks the full descent of the Water
principle, as indicated by the horizontal line in the triangle. Thus
Earth is suspended in time and space and is what the alchemists
would call the least volatile or most fixed of the elements.

Another Greek philosopher, considered to be the father of medicine, Hippocrates (400 B.C.), added his own spin to the theory of
the elements by applying them to human psychology. He viewed
the elements as bodily fluids he called "humors" (see figure 5). In
Hippocrates' system, Fire is associated with the choleric humor of
yellow bile, which is carried in cholesterol as a by-product of digestion and energy transformation in the body. Aristotle would say
the choleric force is hot and dry. Choleric people therefore tend to
be energetic, active, moving, "on-fire," and enthusiastic.

Water is associated with the phlegmatic humor of phlegm, which
represents the clear fluids of the body carried by the lymphatic
system and secreted by the mucous membranes. Phlegmatic people
are cold and wet in Aristotle's terms and tend to be in touch with
their feelings and can be moody and brooding. The Water element
is associated with dissolution, diffusion, union, and transformation,
and people in whom the Phlegmatic humor is predominant tend to
be flowing and flexible, letting their feelings guide them, and ori-
ented toward emotional harmony.

Air is associated with the sanguine humor of the blood, which
distributes oxygen throughout the tissues of the body. The word
"sanguine" refers to a ruddy complexion in which the blood flows

close to the skin. Oddly, Hippocrates had no idea that the blood distributes "air" through the body, yet he made the connection using ancient esoteric doctrines and his own intuition. Sanguine people tend to be very changeable and even flighty, perhaps a little irritable yet basically optimistic, and full of personal integrity. According to Aristotle, such people are hot and wet in their elemental qualities.

Earth is associated with the melancholic humor of black bile, which probably refers to waste products associated with digestion such as the stools, from which useful energy has been removed leaving only the dregs of matter behind. Melancholic people tend to be apathetic, passive, stubborn, sluggish, and rigid yet practical. Since Earth is the principle of structure and materialization, the melancholic humor is dominant in the person who focuses on physical reality and tends to exhibit the qualities of perseverance, inflexibility, realism, and pragmatism. In Aristotle's terms, such people are cool and dry.

Carl Jung's theory of personality types is clearly derived from the humors of Hippocrates. The four basic Jungian types are each associated with a humor: feeling (Fire, choleric), thinking (Water, phlegmatic), intuition (Air, sanguine), and sensation (Earth, melancholic). By combining the polarities of introversion (a person focused on inner feelings and thoughts) and extroversion (a person focused on outer relationships and external objects), Jung developed eight personality types. In psychology, we also find the four humors expressed as the personality variables in the popular Myers-Briggs test. In the Luscher Color personality profile, the Fire color red has the qualities of excitement, activity, and self-confidence. The Water color blue is associated with relaxation, satisfaction, and self-moderation. The Air color yellow has qualities of free-thinking, change, and self-development. The Earth color green is associated with solidity, persistence, and self-respect.

Jung saw the Four Elements as archetypes existing in the collective unconscious and thus present in everyone. Jung considered Fire and Air the active, masculine elements and Water and Earth the passive, feminine elements. In Jungian psychology, it is the degree of development of each of the Four Elements in our conscious mind balanced with the unconscious retention of the remaining elements that determine our personality and attitude. In other words, this indwelling fourfold structure of our personality originates from the creation of ego out of the chaos of the unconscious, just as the fourfold structure of the universe was created by the action of the One Mind on the First Matter.

In alchemy, as in psychology, the goal is to develop a balance of the elements within the individual. Even Empedocles noted that those who have nearly equal proportions of the Four Elements are more intelligent and have the truest perceptions of reality. Personal transformation and individual integration are dependent upon balancing the elements within the psyche, and the deeper relationships of the elements (whether they oppose or complement one another) determine whether we are basically happy and balanced or develop neuroses, phobias, and other psychological disturbances. According to Jung, when two opposing elements encounter each other in the personality or are brought to the surface in a situation, there are three possibilities: 1) they may generate psychic energy; 2) they may neutralize each other; or 3) they may combine or unite. In alchemy and psychology, the third case is the most profound, for the union of opposite elements is the Conjunction of Opposites (*Coniunctio Oppositorum*), the creation of a higher unity and transcendence of conflicting polarities.

Experiment 2: Balancing the Elements

As we have noted, Aristotle considered the Four Elements as composed of the qualities of hot and cold, dry and moist. All the elements originated by impressing these qualities on the First Matter, and one element could be changed into another by altering these qualities. For instance, when the qualities of moist and cold are imposed on the First Matter, the element Water results, but if we boil Water, it is changed into Air (steam) by substituting the quality of hot for that of cold. In the following experiment in the inner laboratory of our mind, we will work to transform the humors using a procedure the alchemists called the Rotation of the Elements.

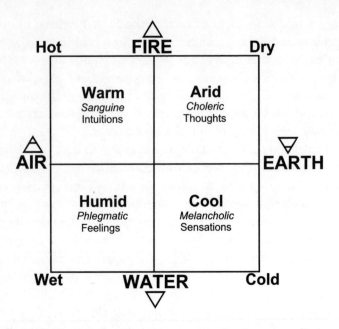

Figure 6. The Square of Opposition shows the relationships between the Four Elements and the qualities that transform them. (D. W. Hauck)

In this experiment, first try to determine which element (or humor) is predominant within you using the descriptions in the preceding section. Try to be objective and pick only one primary humor that seems to fit you. For help, you might want to take the Myers-Briggs test or quizzes contained in such popular books as *The Four Temperaments* by Randy Rolfe (Marlowe & Co. 2002). You may also want to consult a close friend or family member to find out how they would classify you.

Once you have determined your dominant humor, use the ancient Rotation of the Elements procedure to create the perfect balancing humor within you. This procedure is based on Aristotle's Square of Opposition (see figure 6), which depicts all the relationships between the qualities and the elements. The elements form a cross within the square, and each element is composed of two qualities shown in the corners of the square. Thus, Earth is dry and cold, Water is cold and moist, Air is moist and hot, Fire is hot and dry. The qualities form a diagonal cross (or "X") of opposition within the square. Changes in the qualities of the elements cause movement through the square. You could also say that the "strife between opposites" is the motor of rotation. Cold becomes hot, hot becomes cold, moist becomes dry, dry becomes moist.

Hot (or heat) in the upper-left-hand corner is the primary quality, and Fire at the top of the square is the most active element and the agent of transformation. Water at the bottom of the square is the most passive element and represents the agent of coagulation or the current situation. The "natural" circulation of the elements in the square begins with the process of adaptation (Water), and continues through expansion (Air), production (Fire), and retraction (Earth). The same pattern of movement through the elements can be seen in many elemental rotations, including the seasons (winter, spring, summer, fall), the ages of man (childhood, youth, maturity, old age), and the cyclic rise and fall of nations and ideas.

There are four rules that determine movement within the Square of Opposition. First, movement is in a clockwise rotation starting at Fire. This is where the work of alchemical transformation begins. You will notice that as you move through the square, each element follows its dominant quality. Therefore Fire is predominantly hot, Earth is predominantly dry, Water predominantly cold, Air predominantly moist. The turning square is an elemental rotation driven by the qualities: hot on the top, dry on the descending side, cold on the bottom, and moist on the rising side. "It is clear that generation of the elements will be circular," explained Aristotle, "and this mode of change is very easy because corresponding qualities are present in adjacent elements."

Second, direct transformation of opposite elements into one another is not impossible. We can move around the square, but not across it. Thus Water cannot be transformed directly into Fire, since they have no common quality; however, Water can be transformed by first changing into Air or Earth. Then, the Air or Earth is transformed into Fire.

Third, the qualities are inversely proportional to each other. That means that the higher the intensity of an *earlier* quality in the rotation, the greater the rate of increase in the following quality. Or alternatively, the higher the intensity of a *later* quality in the rotation, the more the preceding quality decreases. For instance, increasing hot increases dry but decreases moist. Or looking at the elements, heat causes Earth to lose its rigidity or dryness and melt (become more flexible or moist), which makes it Water. Further heating decreases the cold of the Water and increases its hot quality, which makes it boil and turn into Air (steam). When Air is heated, its moisture is reduced, and it rises higher into Fire. When Fire becomes cold, it loses its heat and becomes Earth (ashes) again.

Fourth, whenever there are two elements with a common quality, the element in which it is not dominant is "overcome" or "conquered" by the one in which it is dominant. This property is known as the Cycle of Triumphs and was first noticed by alchemist Raymond Lully (1229–1315); for example, when Water combines with Earth, the Earth is overcome, because they are both cold, but cold dominates in Water. Therefore, Water overcomes Earth and the result will be predominantly cold. According to this scheme, Fire overcomes Air, Air overcomes Water, Water overcomes Earth, and Earth overcomes Fire. Generally, the more subtle (or spiritual) element overcomes the grosser (or more material) element.

To balance your dominant element (or humor) find its opposite element on the cross within the square. You want to increase the presence of this neglected element to balance your temperament. However, since they are opposite, you must work through one of the adjacent elements; for example, if your dominant element is Water and you want to balance it with more Fire in your personality, begin by working with the adjacent element (Air or Earth) for which you feel you have the greatest affinity or with which you are the most comfortable. If you choose the path of Air, you need to work to increase the quality of moist, which means becoming more flowing and allowing emotional energy to surface. If you choose the path of Earth, you need to do the opposite and try to become less flowing and more controlling of emotional energy.

The process is really simple when you work with it awhile. Meditate on the different expressions of the qualities as the alchemists did. The archetypal relationships between the elements are so plainly depicted in the Square of Opposition that it is an amazingly versatile tool for all kinds of transformation. The alchemists used these same relationships and progressed through the Square of Opposition whether they were doing laboratory experiments, producing medicines, or working on their own personal transformations.

It is even possible to work in reverse (counterclockwise) rotation, which is known as the Death Rotation. The ancient Greek philosopher Heraclitus (500 B.C.) described the process thus: "Fire lives the death of Earth, and Air lives the death of Fire; Water lives the death of Air, and Earth lives the death of Water." In his book *Purifications*, Empedocles uses the reverse rotation to cleanse the soul of broken promises, crimes against humanity, and other bad karma. The process must be repeated in numerous rebirths and lasts for "thrice ten thousand years."

The Quintessence

The Quintessence of the alchemists is often described as the Fifth Element, not because it was considered one of the elements but because it was beyond the elements in both form and function. It was seen as something new and wonderful in creation that transcended the limitations imposed by the Four Elements. "The Quintessence is a thing," wrote Isaac Newton, "that is spiritual, penetrating, tingeing, and incorruptible, which emerges anew from the Four Elements when they are bound together."

The Quintessence has been described as luminous but invisible to ordinary sight. In medieval alchemy, the term Quintessence was synonymous with the elixir and was thought to contain the same magical ingredient. Like Pythagoras before him, Paracelsus believed the Quintessence is what the stars are made of and that within every living thing there exists a hidden star that was that thing's Quintessence. Indeed, one of the symbols for the Quintessence is the star. Another symbol is a pentagram inscribed in a circle, dividing it into five equal sections. The pentagram symbol is thought to represent the body of man. Alchemist Benedictus Figulus describes the Quintessence further in his book *The Golden Casket*:

> For the elements and their compounds, in addition to crass matter, are composed of a subtle substance or intrinsic radical humidity, diffused through their elemental parts, simple and wholly incorruptible, long preserving the things themselves in vigor. Called the Spirit of the World, it proceeds from the Soul of the World [First Matter]. This is the one certain Life filling and fathoming all things, so that from the emanations of sentient beings, there is formed the One Living Machine of the Whole World. This spirit by its virtue fecundates [fertilizes or brings to life] all subjects natural and artificial, pouring into them those hidden properties that we call the Fifth Essence or Quintessence. But this Fifth Essence is created by the Almighty for the preservation of the Four Elements of the human body, even as Heaven is for the preservation of the Universe. Therefore is this Fifth Essence a Spiritual Medicine, which is of Nature and the Heart of Heaven and never of a mortal and corrupt quality that makes all life possible. It is the Fount of Medicine, the preservation of life, the restoration of health, and in this may be the cherished renewal of lost youth and serene health be found.

Perhaps a picture of the true nature of the Quintessence is beginning to emerge. Often, when one is stymied by the indirect terminology of Western alchemists, it is fruitful to turn to the writings of their Eastern colleagues. In Chinese alchemy, the Fifth Element is Wood, which is a product of the plant kingdom and things that grow. In Taoist alchemy, the Quintessence is known as *chi*, an unseen energy that flows through the body and can be accumulated and directed in moving meditations such as performed in Tai Chi and Chi Kung. In Tantric alchemy, the Quintessence is the *kundalini* sexual energy coiled like a sleeping serpent at the base of the spine. In Hindu alchemy, the Quintessence is the spirit of breath known in Sanskrit as *prana*. This is very similar to the Western concepts of *pneuma* (Greek) and *rauch* (Hebrew).

In all these traditions, both East and West, there is only one thing that the Quintessence can be. It is the *life force* itself. That explains why the alchemists did not consider the Quintessence to be a product of the Four Elements, but a separate principle altogether through which all the elements could be tamed or controlled. Most alchemists believed the Quintessence had nothing at all to do with the Four Elements, but rather emerged from an even more primordial state known as the sacred Trinity or the Three Essentials.

The Three Essentials

It was Paracelsus who first organized the Three Essentials of Sulfur, Mercury, and Salt into powerful universal tools that gave alchemists great insight into the nature of reality. Sometimes called the Three Universals, the Three Supernals, the *Tria Prima*, or simply the Trinity, they are three fundamental forces that are present on all levels of reality. These three principles emerge from a common source, the First Matter, and are indistinguishable from their source in their powers of transformation. They also appear at the end of the Great Work as principles integrally bound up in the Philosopher's Stone, which was often symbolized by a three-headed serpent. The serpent represents the Three Essentials, for "the Stone is single in essence, but triple in form."

The Three Essentials are further defined by how they behave in fire. Sulfur is seen as what fuels the fire or what is changed in the fire. Thus, oil, fat, wood, and coal are all forms of Sulfur. Mercury is what goes unchanged or what is released or evaporated in the fire, and it is associated with the smoke, moisture, and light issuing from a fire. The new principle of Salt exhibits a fixed nature that resists the fire and is found in the ashes. As Paracelsus put it: "The fire is Mercury; what flames and is burnt is Sulfur; and all ash is Salt." In the burning of wood, for instance, Sulfur is that which is consumed in the fire; Mercury is the hot vapors that rise from the fire; and Salt is the ashes.

Figure 7. The Bird of Hermes shows the father of alchemy as a mythical creature whose tail entwines the Three Essentials of Salt, Sulfur, and Mercury. (Giovanni Nazari, *Metamor Fosi Metallico*, 1564)

Just as a plant yields the Three Essentials when it is decomposed, so do all things break down into their essential components. Even human beings consist of Salt (body), Mercury (spirit), and Sulfur (soul). In the most general terms, Sulfur is the fiery, solar, active, yang, masculine principle that gives us our individual identity or soul. It mediates between body and spirit and blends them into a unitary presence that liberates the soul bound up in matter and eventually perfects its inner nature.

Mercury is the watery, lunar, passive, yin, feminine principle that represents the universal spirit or life force in all things. It should be noted that Mercury is feminine only in relation to Sulfur. When Mercury mediates between Sulfur and Salt, it acts as the mother of the Stone, the carrier of the new life. In all other instances Mercury is considered androgynous or hermaphroditic (literally, Hermes + Aphrodite). Mercury is always considered a living and changeable force, having all the characteristics of the First Matter. This Original Mercury is for many alchemists, in the East and the West, the First Matter that all alchemists seek.

Salt is actually the key to alchemy, the beginning and end of the Great Work. It is the imperfect matter at the beginning of the experiment that has to be destroyed and dissolved to release its essences, which are reconstituted into the more perfect form at the end of the experiment. Salt is the mediator between Sulfur and Mercury and their balancer and gives reason and purpose to the dance of the opposites. Salt is seen as the child of the marriage of the King (Sulfur) and Queen (Mercury), the son of the Sun and Moon. Salt represents matter and the materialization of spiritual principles, and it is associated with the human body. Its physical characteristics are non-flammability and fixity, and it often appears as a precipitate or powder at the end of alchemical experiments.

For modern alchemists, too, the Three Essentials are the guiding principles of their work. Salt still represents matter, but Sulfur is seen as energy or emotions, and Mercury is the connecting principle of light or consciousness. Today, alchemy and science (especially quantum physics) are converging on a single view of the universe. Einstein's equation of the universe ($E=mc^2$) is as valid in alchemy as it is in modern physics. Energy (E) is Sulfur; mass (m) is Salt; and light (c) is Mercury. For both alchemist and physicist, energy and matter are really the same thing whose expression and form is determined by the intermediary of light. In fact, if that little "c" in Einstein's equation stood for "consciousness" instead of "light," there would be no difference between alchemy and modern science.

The Secret Fire

"Learn to know what is alchemy," Paracelsus tells us, "that it is only that which makes the impure pure by means of fire. Though not all fires do burn, it is however only fire and continues to be fire." Fire was the most important element to the alchemists for it was the agent of change, the revolutionary first step in any transformation. As Paracelsus implies, there were different kinds of fire that ranged from the grossest (most material) to the subtlest (most spiritual). The alchemists recognized four grades of Fire with which they could work. The lowest grade of fire was known as the Elementary Fire, which was the common fire we are all familiar with. Alchemist Antoine-Joseph Pernety wrote in 1758:

> The Elementary Fire, which is the fire of our stoves, is impure, thick and burning. This fire is sharp and corrosive, ill-smelling, and is known through the senses. It has for its abode the surface of the earth and our atmosphere and is destructive; it wounds the senses, it burns, it digests, concocts, and produces nothing. It is external [to the alchemist] and separating.

The highest grade of fire was the Celestial Fire, a white fire that the alchemists considered the burning brilliance of the Mind of God itself. According to Pernety, the purest grade of fire is the fiery power of God's will. He described it thus: "The Celestial Fire is very pure, simple and not burning in itself. It has for its sphere the ethereal region, whence it makes itself known even to us. Celestial

Fire shines without burning and is without color and odor, though it is sensibly exhaled. It is gentle and known only by its operations."

Between these two extremes of Elementary Fire and Celestial Fire, the alchemists postulated two other gradients. One was the Central Fire hidden within matter at its very center. Central Fire is the fire of creation, the embedded Word of God, in all manifested objects. According to Pernety:

The Celestial Fire passes into the nature of the Central Fire; it becomes internal, engendering in matter. Though the Central Fire [within matter] is pure in itself, it is mixed and tempered. It engenders and enlightens sometimes without burning, and burns sometimes without giving any light. It is invisible and therefore known only by its qualities. The Central Fire is lodged in the center of matter; it is tenacious and innate in matter; it is digesting, maturing, neither warm nor burning to the touch.

There is yet a fourth grade of fire, and it was the primary fire with which the true alchemist worked. They called it their "Secret Fire" because of its invisibility, and they went to great lengths to disguise its true nature. Pernety notes:

The fire of the sun could not be this Secret Fire. It is interrupted, unequal, and does not penetrate. The fire of our stoves, which hinders the union of the miscibles and consumes the bond of the constituent parts, could not be the one. The Central Fire, which is innate in matter, cannot be that Secret Fire so much praised, which causes the corruption of metallic germs, because the heat which engenders is internal and innate in matter, and that which corrupts is external and foreign to matter.

So, the Secret Fire is "external" to matter yet is somehow able to change it or cause its "corruption." Actually, the Secret Fire is part of the life force of the alchemist himself. Says Pernety: "This heat is very different within the generation of the individuals of the three kingdoms; the animal possesses it in a much higher degree than the plant." From these clues, we can discern that the Secret Fire is actually the life force itself, the Quintessence of matter.

In his book *Alchemy*, Franz Hartmann states that we all carry the Secret Fire within us:

> The Secret Fire of the alchemists is sometimes described as *kundalini*, the serpentine working power in the body of the acetic. It is an electric, fiery, occult power, the great pristine form which underlies all organic and inorganic matter. It is an electro-spiritual force, a creative power which, when aroused into action, can as easily destroy as it can create. This is the reason why the secrets of alchemy can not be divulged to the idle-minded or curious, and why only those who have gained the power to control their own self may be told how that power can be aroused in man.

The true nature of the Secret Fire was known and concealed ever since the invention of writing by Thoth, the father of alchemy. It is the true subject of his Emerald Tablet. "In allegories and fables," remarks Pernety, "the philosophers have given to this Secret Fire the names sword, lance, arrows, javelin, etc. It is the Fire which Prometheus stole from heaven, which Vulcan employed to form the thunderbolts of Jupiter, and the golden throne of Zeus." The Secret Fire is the breath of God, the Fifth Element, the Quintessence, the Original Mercury, and the First Matter. They all carry its great secret, a subtle force the alchemists tried to accumulate, control, and direct. Their goal was the same as that of Nature: the spiritization and perfection of matter through the workings of the invisible fire of the life force.

4

The Kitchen Alchemist: Making Tinctures and Elixirs

NOW THAT YOU HAVE BECOME FAMILIAR with the basic principles of alchemy, you can begin applying them immediately in the real world—right in your own kitchen. You do not need a fancy laboratory to make tinctures, elixirs, and essential oils, and you do not have to be an adept in the secret art to learn how to "charge" your formulations with healing energy or tailor them for specific transformations. Most of us already know how to do this. As one Sufi alchemist put it: "All the qualities of a good spiritual alchemist can be found in the person who can cook an egg perfectly."

The Alchemy of Cooking

Most people do not think of cooking as a kind of alchemy, but a little reflection on the actual processes involved makes the alchemical connection clear. Instead of beakers and flasks, the cook works with pots and pans, but the transformative elements—Fire, Water, Air, and Earth—are the same. The cook, like the alchemist, transforms matter through the application of fire. The cook dissolves, emulsifies, aerates, separates, macerates, blends, coagulates, and works through the same operations. And like alchemists, cooks add a deeper part of themselves to their "Opus." For every key idea in alchemy, there is a corresponding representation in the kitchen. As Above, so Below!

In the kitchen, the Four Elements find their most general expression in the four natural food groups. Nurturer foods (milk, nectars, soups, sauces, teas, eggs, beverages, and some vegetables like watermelons) are liquid foods that carry the signature of the Water element. Hunter foods (meat, fish, fowl, and spices used to cure meat) are of the masculine Fire element. Cultivator foods (harvested fruits and vegetables and cheese) are created from skills given by the Air element. Gatherer foods (grains, nuts, roots, berries, mushrooms and some wild vegetables) are gifts from the Earth element. Furthermore, each of these food groups is related to one of the Four Humors in people. The melancholic Earth humor's brooding connection with nature and stubborn attention to the land is seen in the Gatherers. The phlegmatic Water humor's tranquil and deliberate care is evidenced by the Nurturers. The sanguine Air humor's lively and optimistic approach can be found among the Cultivators, and the choleric Fire humor's active and excitable lifestyle is characteristic of the Hunters.

By working with all the "elements" expressed in foods and the corresponding temperaments in people, cooking can actually become a path to personal transformation. In planning a meal, the higher cook must consider not only the hidden properties of the physical foodstuffs but also the bodily, mental, and spiritual makeup of the persons who are going to eat the food. In the simplest case, for instance, angry or hyper individuals might be fed a diet high in Water element foods to calm them down, but lethargic or depressed people should eat Fire element foods to energize them. Worldly people should eat mostly Air element foods to spiritize them, while an intellectual or overly religious person should eat a diet of Earth element foods to ground him. The goal is not to neutralize the powers of the personality but to balance those forces into a resilient and whole individual. There are many guides available to the esoteric properties of herbs and foods. *Herbs in Magic and Alchemy* (C. L. Zalewski, Prism Press 1999) is an excellent source, and the Alchemical Properties of Foods Index (www.AlchemyLab.com/guideto.htm) lists planetary and elemental associations for hundreds of common foods.

As in alchemy, there is an invisible Fifth Element to consider in cooking aside from the basic Four Elements. The Fifth Element in food is that part that carries the etheric or spiritual essences of the material food, its vital force or Quintessence. The Quintessence of a meal is the sum of the ineffable spiritual and psychic essences that are introduced into a meal by the cook. If a meal is prepared and served in the right way (with the correct attitude or ritual), then the hidden Quintessence can be assimilated by all those present.

The savvy cook, who understands the basic principles of transcendental gastronomy, realizes that mundane meal times are opportunities for spiritual transformation. In other words, you can make use of the kitchen cauldron to get what you want through cookery by creating esoterically charged menus. One of the primary rules of alchemical cooking is that the preparer's attitude is a hidden component of the meal. As the alchemists would say: "Everything carries the signature of its creator."

No matter how hard the fast-food chains try to capture the image of wholesomeness in their advertising, they will never succeed in replacing a mother's cooking because industrial food preparation simply has no intrinsic or transcendental value. Cooking for the soul means cooking with care and imbuing food with positive psychic energy. It means knowing the esoteric properties of foods and learning to balance the elements in our bodies and minds. Alchemical cooks are able to turn their kitchens into sacred spaces, where the wonders of creation are played out.

Experiment 3: Preparing Clairvoyant Ruby Jelly

The importance of proper attitude in preparing alchemically active substances was emphasized by the French alchemist Michel de Notredame (1503–1566). He is better known simply as Nostradamus, whose amazingly accurate predictions have astounded the world. Michel actually gave part of the credit for his abilities to the following recipe, which is taken directly from his personal notebooks. He believed his "Clarified Ruby Jelly" made him clairvoyant and increased his psychic powers. He suggested that it was of such a refined nature that it should be eaten regularly only by the nobility. The primary ingredient is cherries, whose esoteric properties include increasing one's ability to foresee the future. Cherries are still used in divinatory rituals in many cultures throughout the world. However, Nostradamus's instructions make it clear that the most vital ingredient in his jelly is the way it is prepared. Without the proper attitude and rituals to create a sacred cooking space, the jelly "would alter considerably and be of no use."

Start by de-stemming and cleaning seven pounds of ripe Bing cherries. Discard any green or yellow cherries. Add two pounds of sugar to a large bowl and mash the cherries roughly in your hands, allowing the juice, seeds, and skins to fall directly into the bowl of sugar. Nostradamus warns that the crushed cherries and juice must fall into the sugar directly from your hands or else the esoteric energy will be lost. His method is designed to allow the sugar to absorb the fruit's essence immediately and acquire its purest signature. Heat the concoction for ten minutes over a moderate flame until the sugar is completely dissolved, *then* strain the mixture to remove the seeds, skins, and solids. Do not remove these "dregs" beforehand! Continue heating the juice until it begins to boil, and then turn down the heat to a gentle simmer, being very careful not to burn any material at the bottom of the pan. In another ten minutes, after the juice has thickened considerably, pour into canning jars. "My jelly may be given to a prince or noble lord," wrote Nostradamus, "or also to someone with a severe fever or who does not feel well, and such a person will find that it is invigorating and exceptionally pleasant. And if you make it as I have described here, without doubt it will turn out excellent."

Practical Alchemy: The Art of Spagyrics

Spagyrics (pronounced "spa-*jir*-ics") is applied alchemy, especially when the methods are used to isolate the essences of herbs and plants. Paracelsus invented the word by combining the two Greek words *spao* (tear apart) and *ageiro* (gather together). So the term spagyrics really means to tear apart and bring back together again. That is, tear apart to reveal the essences and then bring back together in a higher or more purified form. The object of spagyrics is to isolate the living essences and underlying signatures of something. "Spagyria," said Paracelsus, "teaches you to separate the false from the true."

In the laboratory, the opposing principles of "tearing apart" and "bringing together" are the main processes of working with herbs, flowers, and other plants to make medicinal elixirs, tinctures, balsams, and powders. First the plant is reduced to its most basic signatory essences and then the essences are further purified and recombined to make an entirely new compound. According to alchemical philosophy, this is simply provoking the natural evolution of matter, exalting substances to their most perfect or truest and most universal expressions.

These inner essences or "strengths" carry the archetypal signatures of the plant—what Paracelsus called its "star." By the Doctrine of Correspondences ("As Above, so Below"), a plant's inner star or essence is closely related to the stars above in the heavens. Plants are "ruled" by heavenly bodies, because their inner, microcosmic stars correspond to universal, macrocosmic stars. This is as true in people as it is in plants. In general terms, then, the "star" is the truest part of anything, the divine thought that gives things their form and being. By opening up something and revealing its star, you can use its incorruptible power to affect other things in predictable ways. "One must understand," elaborated Paracelsus, "that the medicine must be prepared in the stars and that the stars become the medicine."

Obviously, spagyrics is very different from modern pharmacology, in which the esoteric characteristics of substances are completely ignored. Most modern physicians rely entirely on the gross or chemical properties of drugs to treat disease and forget that they are really dealing with the life force of an individual being. Modern medicine has taken a stubbornly linear and physically aggressive approach to "fighting" disease as if it were somehow a foreign army invading the patient. As a result, physicians are caught in a never-ending spiral of developing new drugs as the life force adapts to the gross effects of the previous "wonder" drug. The key is to learn to redirect the life force itself.

Spagyrics is also different from homeopathy, although both systems make use of the essences of herbs and plants. In general, spagyric preparations are not diluted or "potentized" in the homeopathic sense. In homeopathic work, minuscule doses of a compound are used to treat a disease in which large doses of the same compound would produce symptoms *similar* to those of the disease in the hopes of eliciting a healing response from the body. On the other hand, modern medicine is allopathic; that is, it uses compounds that elicit symptoms directly *opposite* to those produced by the disease.

Although allopathic in approach, spagyrics is more holistic than either allopathy or homeopathy. It seeks to balance forces in the body by working on all levels, invoking the signatures of plants in the Below and the corresponding planetary forces in the Above, as well as requiring the conscious participation of both the patient and the practitioner, who represent the forces "In Between." Spagyric compounds work on very subtle levels and trying to use them either allopathically or homeopathically can have unpredictable results. Unlike nearly every other type of medicine, true spagyrics are considered living essences that grow stronger with age and maintain the characteristic ability to "adapt" to changing conditions.

Finally, there are also subtle differences between spagyrics and general alchemy. The lofty goal of alchemy is to gain wisdom and understanding of matter and perfect it on all levels, but the object of spagyrics is much more directed to the present human condition and the problems of everyday life. The spagyricist seeks to produce a specific medicine or compound that can be used to cure particular ailments by healing people of systemic imbalances or "diseases." In a sense, spagyrics is medical alchemy, the art of healing on all levels at once. Historically, Paracelsian spagyrics is the precursor of the iatrochemistry ("healing chemistry") of the 1600s from which our modern commercialized practice of medicine was born.

The Three Essentials in Plants

Since the Three Essentials are present on all levels of reality, we would expect to see them expressed in the plant kingdom. A spagyric medicine is prepared by deliberately "opening up" the plant and separating it into all three of its primordial components of Sulfur, Mercury, and Salt. It is the work of the alchemist to separate and recombine these three basic principles as often as necessary until they are in perfect proportion and harmony with each other. In the following paragraphs, we will examine exactly how each of the Three Essentials manifests in plants.

Beginning with the "oldest" part of a substance, which is its most basic essence of Sulfur, we look for the soul of the plant. In general, Sulfur or soul is the energetic essence of something, the individual qualities that differentiate one object from another. It is the inner blueprint, the eternal part that cannot be destroyed but burns through time. This is the "thing itself" at the most basic level that carries all the characteristics of the substance. In plants, Sulfur resides in the essential oils, which are the most concentrated aspects of a plant's chemistry and properties, and the carrier of scent, which is the most etheric attribute of the plant kingdom. Essential oils, which burn slowly like a fuel, are the expressions of the Sulfur of plants.

In general, Mercury is the spirit, mind, light, or animating life force of something. Mercury is the spirit and vital force of light, the spark that animates a being with life. In plants, Mercury is found in the "spirit" or alcohol, its "volatile juice" derived by fermentation or added as part of the processes of extraction. In lab work, Mercury is the intermediary life force that brings the Sulfur and Salt together, acting from the middle to connect the other two levels and to keep balance overall.

Salt is the form that locks the other two principles of Sulfur (soul) and Mercury (spirit) in manifestation, allowing the more subtle levels of being to exist and act in the physical world. In this sense, the Salt level is a purified container for higher levels of energy and gives it a physical form. In plants, the Salt level resides in the mineral components and hard structural tissues (stalks, roots, leaves) that are reduced by fire to ashes.

The spagyric operation, which begins by the destruction and breaking up of the plant, is not complete until all three basic parts of Sulfur, Mercury, and Salt are reunited in a higher or purer manifestation that is actually closer to the truest signature or inner "star" of the original plant. In order to accomplish this, the spagyric work, like the Great Work of alchemy, always takes place simultaneously on all three levels of reality (the physical, the mental, and the spiritual). To make a spagyric compound, it is not only necessary to perform the mundane laboratory operations but also be involved with the proper mental attitude, as well as appeal to spiritual powers operating Above. The motto of the alchemist in his laboratory is *Ora et Labora* ("Pray and Work"). Like the alchemical laboratory, the spagyric laboratory is considered a sacred space where the product is prepared in a place that Paracelsus would call "in the stars." Every effort is made to protect that space from profane or earthly influences.

Planetary Influences in Spagyrics

Paracelsus followed the teachings of the Emerald Tablet in all his work and in accordance with the Doctrine of Correspondences, he taught that the astral energies of each visible planet travel to earth from that planet and affect the things on earth in predictable ways. Each planet's archetypal energy affects some plants on earth more than others, depending on the inherent astrological and planetary signatures of the individual plant. This two-way current of interaction follows the principle of "as Above, so Below" and "as Below, so Above," and is termed "sympathy."

Sympathy governs most of the basic signatures or characteristics of the living things on our planet. Each of the seven visible planets (Saturn, Jupiter, Mars, Sun, Venus, Mercury, and the Moon) affects plants, animals, and humans in specific ways because of this underlying sympathy. For instance, each planet rules an organ or organ system in the human body and by extension, its diseases. Similarly, each planet rules herbs and plants that support the organ or balance it with the corresponding planetary archetypes. We will examine these planetary archetypes more closely in the next chapter. For now, we are interested in practical ways to work with the energies of the planets to make alchemically active products.

All aspects of spagyric processing, including the harvesting of the plant, cutting and sifting, drying, and wetting of the herb with alcohol, to the inclusion of its salts and other separately extracted materials, should take place during the times ruled by the proper planet, using charts which were originally devised by Paracelsus's teacher, Trithemius. In this way, the forces Above and the forces Below create a living synergy that is greater than the sum of the plant's chemical constituents and can be effectively used as a powerful medicine.

There are three types of planetary charts used in spagyrics. The charts are used to determine the proper time to create or process a spagyric compound.

The simplest planetary chart is the Mercury-Level Chart in which a single planet rules each day all day. A Mercury-level preparation is directed toward disturbances and depletions of the life force, and to attune a spagyric to the Mercury level, a highly refined alcohol is used for extraction, which is elevated before use in a process called spiritualization. Spiritualization is a method of circulating the material worked on, making it volatile and then condensed in cycles, so that it opens up, becomes more subtle and can receive the universal life force, and then closes again and holds that life force. Grapes have the ability to produce more alcohol than any other plant and because of this, grapes are considered alchemically to be the plant with the highest life force. An old alchemical saying is that "all plants aspire to be grapes." Pure grape alcohol magnifies the life force of the Mercury extract, and is the recommended alcohol used by alchemists. Mercury-level products should be prepared on the day of the corresponding planet given in the chart in figure 8 (below).

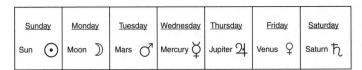

Sunday	Monday	Tuesday	Wednesday	Thursday	Friday	Saturday
Sun ☉	Moon ☽	Mars ♂	Mercury ☿	Jupiter ♃	Venus ♀	Saturn ♄

Figure 8. Mercury-Level Chart. (D. W. Hauck)

To attune a spagyric medicine to the physical or Salt level, a concentrated extract is made with all the mineral components extracted and included in the remedy. To accomplish this, all the plant matter that would have normally been discarded is burned to an ash. From that ash is extracted the clear or white Salt that contains important physical characteristics of the plant such as minerals and alkaloids. These operations must be performed at the time of day indicated in the Salt-Level Chart. This chart divides the day into seven equal periods, and a corresponding planet rules each period. A salt-level preparation is directed to specific bodily complaints and is created during the corresponding planetary day and time cycle from the chart in figure 9 (below).

Period	Sunday	Monday	Tuesday	Wednesday	Thursday	Friday	Saturday
midnight to 3:25 A.M.	Mars ♂	Mercury ☿	Jupiter ♃	Venus ♀	Saturn ♄	Sun ☉	Moon ☽
3:26 A.M. to 6:51 A.M.	Sun ☉	Moon ☽	Mars ♂	Mercury ☿	Jupiter ♃	Venus ♀	Saturn ♄
6:52 A.M. to 10:17 A.M.	Venus ♀	Saturn ♄	Sun ☉	Moon ☽	Mars ♂	Mercury ☿	Jupiter ♃
10:18 A.M. to 1:42 P.M.	Mercury ☿	Jupiter ♃	Venus ♀	Saturn ♄	Sun ☉	Moon ☽	Mars ♂
1:43 P.M. to 5:08 P.M.	Moon ☽	Mars ♂	Mercury ☿	Jupiter ♃	Venus ♀	Saturn ♄	Sun ☉
5:09 P.M. to 8:34 P.M.	Saturn ♄	Sun ☉	Moon ☽	Mars ♂	Mercury ☿	Jupiter ♃	Venus ♀
8:35 P.M. to midnight	Jupiter ♃	Venus ♀	Saturn ♄	Sun ☉	Moon ☽	Mars ♂	Mercury ☿

Figure 9. Salt-Level Chart. (D. W. Hauck)

To attune a spagyric preparation to the Sulfur level, the essential oils are extracted separately using steam distillation and other alchemical methods. It is crucial that none of these methods of extracting the oils use solvents, harmful chemicals, or substances with improper signatures. This would contaminate the subtle attributes of the plant's innermost being. Normally, highly refined salts and pure alcohol, representing Salt and Mercury, are included in Sulfur-level preparations. By separating, purifying, and recombining all of the physical and subtle aspects of the plant in a way that is a continuation of its natural growth process, a medicine is created that contains all of the plant's attributes in its natural proportions and relationships, but in a living form elevated far past what is possible in nature. The Sulfur-Level Chart changes each hour (beginning at sunrise) and each planet rules several periods in a single day. A sulfur-level preparation is directed toward deep-seated disturbances of the soul and the astral body and is prepared during the specific hours of the day that relate to the corresponding planetary influence shown in the chart in figure 10 (see next page).

Once a spagyric medicine is prepared, there are three ways in which it may be used. The first method uses planetary sympathy to *support* an afflicted organ or bodily system. Such "sympathetic" spagyric preparations focus on a particular systemic problem by finding that organ's or system's ruling planet to alleviate the symptoms. The second method uses planetary antipathy to *oppose* the progress of disease in the body. This is the traditional allopathic approach of using a substance that produces opposite symptoms to those exhibited by the disease or complaint. Both sympathy and antipathy are straightforward methods, and once planetary archetypes are fully understood, they can be used by almost anyone. The third method of using spagyric compounds is as *constitutional* tonics. In this case, a detailed study of the patient must be made using the astrological and psychological aspects in addition to the physical complaints or symptoms. From this information, an attempt is made to create a specific tonic containing the correct mixtures to enhance the healing response from the person's own body.

Hour	Sunday	Monday	Tuesday	Wednesday.	Thursday	Friday	Saturday
1st	Sun ☉	Moon ☽	Mars ♂	Mercury ☿	Jupiter ♃	Venus ♀	Saturn ♄
2nd	Venus ♀	Saturn ♄	Sun ☉	Moon ☽	Mars ♂	Mercury ☿	Jupiter ♃
3rd	Mercury ☿	Jupiter ♃	Venus ♀	Saturn ♄	Sun ☉	Moon ☽	Mars ♂
4th	Moon ☽	Mars ♂	Mercury ☿	Jupiter ♃	Venus ♀	Saturn ♄	Sun ☉
5th	Saturn ♄	Sun ☉	Moon ☽	Mars ♂	Mercury ☿	Jupiter ♃	Venus ♀
6th	Jupiter ♃	Venus ♀	Saturn ♄	Sun ☉	Moon ☽	Mars ♂	Mercury ☿
7th	Mars ♂	Mercury ☿	Jupiter ♃	Venus ♀	Saturn ♄	Sun ☉	Moon ☽
8th	Sun ☉	Moon ☽	Mars ♂	Mercury ☿	Jupiter ♃	Venus ♀	Saturn ♄
9th	Venus ♀	Saturn ♄	Sun ☉	Moon ☽	Mars ♂	Mercury ☿	Jupiter ♃
10th	Mercury ☿	Jupiter ♃	Venus ♀	Saturn ♄	Sun ☉	Moon ☽	Mars ♂
11th	Moon ☽	Mars ♂	Mercury ☿	Jupiter ♃	Venus ♀	Saturn ♄	Sun ☉
12th	Saturn ♄	Sun ☉	Moon ☽	Mars ♂	Mercury ☿	Jupiter ♃	Venus ♀
13th	Jupiter ♃	Venus ♀	Saturn ♄	Sun ☉	Moon ☽	Mars ♂	Mercury ☿
14th	Mars ♂	Mercury ☿	Jupiter ♃	Venus ♀	Saturn ♄	Sun ☉	Moon ☽
15th	Sun ☉	Moon ☽	Mars ♂	Mercury ☿	Jupiter ♃	Venus ♀	Saturn ♄
16th	Venus ♀	Saturn ♄	Sun ☉	Moon ☽	Mars ♂	Mercury ☿	Jupiter ♃
17th	Mercury ☿	Jupiter ♃	Venus ♀	Saturn ♄	Sun ☉	Moon ☽	Mars ♂
18th	Moon ☽	Mars ♂	Mercury ☿	Jupiter ♃	Venus ♀	Saturn ♄	Sun ☉
19th	Saturn ♄	Sun ☉	Moon ☽	Mars ♂	Mercury ☿	Jupiter ♃	Venus ♀
20th	Jupiter ♃	Venus ♀	Saturn ♄	Sun ☉	Moon ☽	Mars ♂	Mercury ☿
21st	Mars ♂	Mercury ☿	Jupiter ♃	Venus ♀	Saturn ♄	Sun ☉	Moon ☽
22nd	Sun ☉	Moon ☽	Mars ♂	Mercury ☿	Jupiter ♃	Venus ♀	Saturn ♄
23rd	Venus ♀	Saturn ♄	Sun ☉	Moon ☽	Mars ♂	Mercury ☿	Jupiter ♃
24th	Mercury ☿	Jupiter ♃	Venus ♀	Saturn ♄	Sun ☉	Moon ☽	Mars ♂

Figure 10. Sulfur-Level Chart. (D. W. Hauck)

Making Spagyric Compounds

The first step in making a spagyric compound is to have a clear idea of the properties you are seeking and how the preparation will be used (medicinal tincture, general tonic, culinary use, aromatherapy, massage, and so on). Next, choose an herb with the desired signature and properties according to a reference source of herbal signatures or properties. If you grow your own herbs, the times of planting, harvesting, and processing should all be alchemically correct. That is, the plant seeds should be placed in the ground, picked, and processed on the day and hour ruled by the relevant planetary chart above. Before any spagyric operations are begun, it is necessary to wash the plant material to remove dirt, mold, and insects. If you plan to use the herb whole (such as bay leaves), also remove stems and broken or discolored leaves. Be sure the material is thoroughly rinsed and excess water removed by shaking or using a salad spinner.

Normally, the first step in the spagyric process is to begin drying the herbs. This can be accomplished by hanging whole bunches from strings (with leaves down) or suspending plant pieces in a mesh bag in direct sunlight or in a very warm room. Commercial food dehydrators may also be used if the temperature is kept below 105°F (40°C) to avoid scorching. Drying time will depend on the thickness of the stems and leaves and on the ambient temperature and aeration. To test if drying is complete, break a piece of stem to see if it snaps easily without bending. Normally, the leaves will become more pastel and less vibrant in color. The dried material should be hermetically sealed in clean, sealable storage bags; screw jars (such as jelly jars); or in canning jars. The containers should be properly labeled and stored in a cool yet dry environment out of direct light.

Properly collected and prepared plants can also be obtained from a limited number of commercial sources. The minimum requirements are that the plant material be organically grown without chemical additives and free from contaminants such as dirt or insects. The plants should be processed (dried and crushed) as soon as possible after harvesting and the product housed in clean, cool storage areas. Many natural food stores now carry dried herbs that meet these basic requirements.

There are many ways of preserving the life force of plants in spagyric preparations that are easy to use and store. There are spagyric creams, toothpastes, soaps, seasonings, and scores of liquid remedies. Infusions are a simple way of extracting the active principles of herbs through the action of hot water. The preparation of infusions is similar to the way tea is made, and this method is used to extract the volatile components of the dried or green aerial parts of herbs and plants like flowers and leaves. Infusions may use single herbs or a blend and are consumed hot or cold. This is the most common and cheapest method of extracting the medicinal components of herbs. Decoctions are a step beyond infusions in that the material is harder to extract and the plant parts must be boiled longer. After cooling down and separating the remaining solids from the liquid, decoctions can be taken hot or cold. Syrups are infusions or decoctions thickened or flavored with sugars.

Essential oils are the volatile oily components of aromatic plants, trees, and grasses. They are found in tiny glands located in various parts of plants, such as the flowers (like neroli), leaves (like eucalyptus), roots (like calamus), wood (like sandalwood), or in the resins (like frankincense). Essential oils are extracted by four main methods: steam distillation, expression, solvent extraction, and enfleurage. In steam distillation, the oil is extracted by the action of hot steam and then selectively condensed with the water from which it is separated. In the second method (expression), the oil is extracted by pressure or centrifugation. In the third method (solvent extraction), the oil is dissolved in a volatile solvent that when evaporated leaves a heavily natural wax substance from which the oil is separated. Enfleurage is a longer process involving the dissolution of the oils in animal fat and its separation using alcohol.

Ointments are insoluble mixtures prepared like hot infused oils, except that the herbs are simmered in waxes or fats containing no water. The result is a solid mixture of wax or fat with the medicinal constituents of the plant. Creams are soluble mixtures of oils or fats with water. Since water and oils are not mixable, it is necessary to add an emulsifying agent that avoids their separation. Creams are stable emulsions of oils that allow the skin to breathe.

Tinctures and elixirs are preparations that capture the deepest essences of plants. Most of the volatile components of medicinal plants and herbs are soluble in alcohol. The preparation of a tincture begins by immersing dried or fresh parts of plants in a "menstruum," which is what the alchemists called the dissolving alcohol used. The active principles are easily extracted in concentrations that far exceed those that can be achieved by infusion or decoction. Elixirs are a more complete form of extract that includes the plant salts. Elixir literally means "from the ashes," and making an elixir involves adding the purified ashes (or Salt) from the extracted material to the tincture to resurrect the "higher body" of the plant.

Tinctures and elixirs are more alchemically active than other types of preparations and for that reason, there are a few general rules in the preparation and use of tinctures that do not generally apply to them. First, no tincture at any time during processing or administration should touch metal, especially aluminum. The archetypal powers of the metals quickly overcome the delicate energies of tinctures. Aluminum is considered an "energy sponge" and the man-made metal is held in very low esteem by alchemists. Another point to remember is that the storage temperature of tinctures should never reach more than 105°F (40°C), or the hidden "spark" that animates the tincture might be driven away or destroyed. Sometimes, in a process known as "reanimating the Mercury," life force is projected into the tincture from the alchemist to try to restore the animating spark. In the alchemical view, tinctures prepared according to the art of spagyrics are considerably stronger than any chemical extract because the tincture is able to retain life force.

Experiment 4: Making a Tincture

Preparing alchemical tinctures from plants is not complicated, although it can be time-consuming. Always keep in mind that the phrase "haste makes waste" was originally a motto of the alchemists. Spagyric work is slow and careful, giving time to allow feelings and intuitions to catch up with thoughts that are guiding the process. Remember that the alchemist is an integral part of any alchemical experiment. His or her purity, attention, and concentration affect the quality of the product.

The extraction apparatus in making a tincture can be anything from a simple mason jar to a sophisticated laboratory distillation extractor. We will perform a simple sealed-jar extraction to more easily grasp the basic steps involved. The first thing to do is find the proper menstruum, the liquid that will extract the essence of the plant we are working with. Tinctures are generally made using pure natural ethyl alcohol distilled from fruits and cereals. Never use methyl alcohol, methylated spirits, isopropyl alcohol, or any other kind of non-potable spirit to make tinctures, as these will produce poisonous compounds! Ideally, naturally fermented grape wine is used for the menstruum, and even then, the alchemist distills the wine several times further to increase its potency. Absolute grape alcohol (200 proof or 100%) is the best menstruum. The next best option is the 180-proof drinkable alcohol (such as "Everclear" and "White Lightning"), which can be obtained from most liquor stores. Vodka may also be used, since it is considered "transparent" (does not add odor or color to the tincture).

Commercially prepared alcohol and even alcohol prepared by distilling lacks an essential ingredient, Celestial Fire, which is driven off by the heat of distillation. The Celestial Fire is one of the four grades of fire with which the alchemist works and is carried by the element of Air. The acquisition of this spirit, which becomes a kind of living intelligence in the experiment, is achieved by pouring the alcohol into an open bowl or bottle and warming it very gently. The acquiring of Celestial Fire is not difficult, and all that is usually required is to open up the alcohol and let it breathe. The alchemist assists by meditating to bring the celestial spirit into the alcohol while opening the soul of the alcohol. In fact, since body heat is sufficient at this stage, all you need to do is cradle the open flask in your arms or lap during meditation. The enlivening spirit enters from Above, as the alchemist opens and activates the soul of the liquid from Below. The dormant soul of the distilled wine is now resurrected and quickened by the intervention of spirit. This is called "Animating the Mercury" and is the final crucial step in preparing the menstruum. Obviously, attempting to use a dead menstruum in spagyrics would be senseless.

In this experiment, we will be extracting the essences of Lemon Balm (*Melissa officianalis*); however you can use any herb as a source for your tincture by following the general steps outlined here. Lemon Balm or "Melissa" was a favorite of Islamic alchemists and has been grown in the Mediterranean for many centuries. Women there wore sprigs of Melissa around their necks to show they already had lovers and were faithful to them. It is used in potions, cooking, liqueurs, perfumes, and tonics. The alchemist Avicenna recommended the sweet-smelling herb for heart problems, and Melissa is used today as a tranquilizer (prescribed for psychiatric problems) and treatment for cold and flu symptoms, and as an antiviral for cold sores. Melissa's element is Fire, and its ruling planet is Jupiter.

Begin the extraction in a convenient planetary hour of the ruling planet, which for Melissa would occur immediately after sunrise on Thursday and reoccurs that day in the eighth, fifteenth, and twenty-second hour after sunrise. At the selected hour, start with meditation or prayers that these mysteries may be revealed to you and that a sacred place may be created in your heart and laboratory. When you feel purified, take an ounce (52 grams) of the dried herb in your hand and begin grinding it between your palms or in a mortar and pestle. This is the beginning of the maceration operation when the material is ground to a powder. The finer the powder, the more Sulfur will be extracted. During this phase, focus on the idea that you are releasing the divine power in the herb as well as within yourself. It is important that you spend some time with the herb in close physical contact, as well as in contact with your personal energy field and the planetary counterparts in your psyche and body. If it is necessary to machine grind the herb to a powder (with a coffee grinder or other appliance), make sure your personal connection with the plant is already well established. You can tell by how much empathy you have with the plant. Can you see it clearly in your mind's eye? Can you smell its aroma even when it is not nearby? Can you taste it with your mouth closed?

Place the powder in a clean jelly jar or small mason jar. Slowly, with focused intent, pour about 4 ounces (120 cc) of the selected menstruum (alcohol) over the herb until it is saturated with fluid and the jar is not over two-thirds full. Tightly seal the jar. If a metal lid is used, it must be completely covered in plastic wrap, since the solution should never come in contact with metal during processing.

Wrap the sealed jar in cloth or foil, since it should not be exposed to light during the initial incubation period. Place the jar in an incubator or other warm location, such as near a radiator, furnace, or water heater. The fluid inside will evaporate as it warms up and condenses again, since it is not capable of escaping. This inner circulation or maceration (literally, "chewing") is responsible for the tincturing process and the fluid will become darker with each passing day. Each time this inner distillation repeats, the soul of the Melissa is regenerated by minute degrees closer to perfection. In alchemical terms, the coloration (or tincturing) is the extraction of the Sulfur or soul essence from the Salt plant matter by the Mercury (spirit or alcohol) medium.

Shake the jar vigorously once or twice a day. You may remove the covering to check the contents periodically. Continue this process for two-to-three weeks, until the color of the tincture is dark. Remember, this is your "Philosophical Child" and must be treated with love and respect. Let no one else handle the jar. Each time you handle it, treat it as a physical representation of your own inner soul. It is the attitude of the alchemist, even more than the operation itself, that makes the process divine. This attitude is literally transferred to the matter being acted upon, just as if it were a patient receiving magnetic or spiritual healing. When the final product is then consumed, we are taking into ourselves a veritable consumable talisman.

After the color of the liquid has darkened to the color of tea, let the jar cool and then open it. If you open the jar when it is warm, some of the volatile essences will escape. Press out any remaining liquid from the mass of plant matter. Filter the solution again until it is clear from even the minutest particles or physical debris. This liquid (the tincture) contains the Sulfur or soul of Melissa (its essential oils and vegetable fats) along with its Mercury or spirit (alcohol and small amount of water). Save the filtered dead plant material for use in making the elixir.

Tinctures can be used as flavoring in cooking and mixed drinks, but most tinctures are taken for medicinal purposes. To use, take four-to-ten drops under the tongue twice a day. The spirit of the alcohol delivers the essence of the herb in a very purified form. You will experience that as a rush of energy in your head and chest.

Experiment 5: Making an Elixir

The remains of the plant material you save from making the tincture is an essence-depleted mass, which is known as the feces and phlegm or the *Caput Mortum* (literally, the "dead head"). Place this material in a heatproof bowl or pot and cover with a wire screen. Metal contact is not a concern now, since the tincture has been removed. Ignite the material and let it burn. Because of the smoke generated, it is often best to do this initial burn outside on a barbecue grill or on the ground or under a kitchen exhaust fan. Use a pot cover to smother the flame, if necessary. You may need to put the pot on a flame to boil off the liquid. When all the liquid is gone, the herb mass will begin to roast and finally incinerate. Let the dead plant matter burn itself down to ashes and cool.

Take the ashes from the initial combustion and grind into a fine powder. Then place the ashes in a covered crucible or heatproof dish and heat in the oven at the highest temperature possible. Heat until the ashes have turned grayish white. It may be necessary to remove the ashes and grind them into a still finer powder. The finer the ash particles, the easier it is to get the whitest or purest ashes. The alchemists discovered that if you heat the ashes for prolonged periods (over a week) at high temperatures (above 1100°F. or 600°C.), the ashes turn snow white and finally transform into a deep red color. Gray-white ashes are sufficiently pure for most alchemical work. Store the purified Salt ashes in a clearly labeled container.

The next step is to mix the tincture extract and the Salt. This act should be performed during the correct planetary hour on the planetary day ruling the herb, which for Melissa is on Thursday at the times already noted in the previous experiment. For a weak elixir, used to evelate mood and clarify the mind, you can simply mix a teaspoon (1–2 grams) of the Salt and 10 to 20 drops (1–2 ml) of the Melissa tincture in a glass of distilled water. For a stronger medicinal elixir, pour the entire extract over the purified Salt. If the tincture is still living, there should be a slight fizzing sound. Shake vigorously, and then tightly seal the jar or bottle.

Put the bottle in an incubator or by a heat source and let it digest. Shake three times daily. During this time the Salt will completely absorb the extracted essence. After three weeks, pour off any remaining liquid, leaving the Salt residue in the flask. Stopper the flask and let it sit for another few weeks in an incubator or in a warm spot out of direct light. Finally, open the jar and let the material dry up and granulate. Scrape this regenerated Salt out of the jar after it has dried, then grind it to a fine powder and store in a clean dark-glass jar. The elixir powder is ready for use; it can either be kept dry or mixed with ethyl alcohol in dark-glass bottles.

It is extremely important to understand the sacredness of the elixir operation. This is nothing less than the regeneration of the plant in a new incarnation, the resurrection of the dead salts through the sacrifice of life force by the tincture. If the connection is strong enough between the alchemist and the plant, then a corresponding change is possible that makes the elixir magically regenerative for the alchemist. Some alchemists combine this aspect of spagyrics with cabalistic or astrological invocations, similar to what is done magically for talismans, to intensify the rejuvenating effects even further. The elixir is the basis of stories of alchemists who lived for hundreds of years.

5

Climbing the Ladder
of the Planets

Figure 11. Archetypes of the seven planets grow in the earth as the
seven metals, which are transformed through the four grades of Fire.
(Basil Valentine, *Occulta Philosophia*, 1603)

THE IDEA THAT OUR SPIRITUAL EVOLUTION is intertwined with the planets is an age-old tenet of alchemy known as the Ladder of the Planets. According to Hermes Trismegistus, whom the Greeks viewed as the author of the Emerald Tablet, the planetary forces are present in everything around us, including our individual personalities. Our spiritual return to the stars, or the gaining of cosmic consciousness, is accomplished by climbing the philosophical ladder of the visible planets from Saturn through Jupiter, Mars, Venus, Mercury, and finally, the Moon and Sun. That is to say, we reach enlightenment by conquering—understanding and controlling—the archetypal energies represented by each planet as it is expressed in the heavens, and correspondingly, within our own bodies and personalities. Before we can return to our true home in the stars, we have to sever the chains of the planetary forces.

Figure 12. The metals grow to perfection in the bowels of the earth guided by the Three Essentials (Sulfur as Fire, Salt as the Stone, Mercury as Water) above.

The planets therefore represent powerful primordial forces embedded in the structure of the universe that express themselves on all levels of reality. The highest and purest signatures of these forces can be found in the planets themselves, in their physical structure, and in the myths and feelings mankind has intuited about them. In the following chapters we will take a short journey up the Ladder of the Planets to become familiar with the planets and expand on their archetypal expressions on their corresponding metals.

Saturn

Saturn is the first step on the Ladder of the Planets. Of all the visible planets it is farthest from the Sun (888 million miles) and represents the galactic starting point on our journey in from the stars. To the observer on earth, Saturn looks like a slow-moving, yellowish-gray star. It is most easily spotted during the twilight hours, when the sky takes on a deep blue color. Saturn reaches its peak visibility high in the northern sky in the dead of winter. It is the coldest planet and also the slowest moving. While the other planets dance merrily around the warm Sun, lumbering Saturn—the second largest planet—takes thirty years to complete its distant orbit. With strong binoculars, you can make out the planet's dark core and mysterious, shimmering triple ring of rocks trapped by its powerful gravity. Saturn has ten moons, some of which are the size of small planets. Its largest moon, Phoebe, is bigger than earth. Had Saturn been able to attract more mass to its core, it would have transformed into a star and our galaxy would have had two suns. But now ancient Saturn sleeps, having lost its bid to become a star.

According to alchemical philosophy, it is up to mankind to return to Saturn to redeem the planet and complete its transformation into light. But this time the "star" into which Saturn will transform will be completely new "matter," on a higher level of reality than has yet been achieved in our galaxy. In other words, the dark matter of Saturn will be perfected or "spiritized" and reborn. The evolution of consciousness in the human species is the seed of light that will transform our whole galaxy. When that seed arrives at Saturn, the Great Work will be completed. Saturn stands for the cosmic law that limits or defines manifestation. It is the limit of the parameters of existence and the foundation of all.

Saturn marks the boundary on the Ladder of the Planets between the personal and the transpersonal. The ancients considered distant Saturn the first or oldest planet whose orbit encompasses all the other visible planets. Saturn is the last planet that can be seen with the bare human eye. For any of the more distant planets (Uranus, Neptune, and Pluto), we need a telescope. It represents the boundary between our cozy solar system and the chaotic forces of the universe. For that reason, Saturn acquired a dual reputation as both a protector of the status quo and the initiator of profound transformation. Saturn was considered the place where created matter first manifested and represented its most primitive or primordial state.

Saturn's symbol is Father Time (Chronos) with his distinctive hourglass and sickle, who personifies the forces of age, death, and transformation, as well as the attainment of deep wisdom. In myth, Saturn (as Chronos) was imprisoned by his father in a deep cave while still a child. Chronos conspired with his mother to overthrow his father and ended up castrating him with a sickle. Chronos then became king of the Titans and ruled just as ruthlessly as his father. When he heard a prophecy that his own children would dethrone him, he ate them at birth. But his wife fed him one child in the form of a stone, which he later vomited out to become Jupiter (see figure 13, opposite). Thus, Jupiter (or Zeus) escaped being eaten by his father and eventually overthrew Chronos and all the chthonic ("heavy or dark") powers, whom he banished to the darkness of the underworld. Sometimes Saturn is depicted with a peg leg to indicate his wounds and incompleteness in the larger divine scheme.

The black crow is the messenger bird of Chronos and also symbolizes the beginning stage of alchemical transformation, which is the Black Phase (the *Nigredo*). This is a period of a state of "darkness over light" and "matter over mind." The cipher for Saturn (and lead) can be interpreted as a downward-pointing sickle with a horizontal line through the handle $-\hbar-$ that represents the earthly plane of manifestation. The lunar crescent blade is completely beneath the

Figure 13. Chronos (Saturn) vomits forth the stone of Jupiter fed to him by his wife Rhea. (Michael Maier, *Atalanta Fugiens*, 1618)

cross of earth, which symbolizes the soul suffocated beneath the earth, trapped in the darkness of the body.

In Chaldea, a region of southern Mesopotamia settled around 1000 B.C., astrologers referred to Saturn as the Sun of Night or the Black Sun of winter who journeyed into the underworld so that spring might come again. Babylonians considered it the Lord of Death, the ghost of the dead sun and oldest spirit in the universe. The season of the planet in the heavens is mid-winter, appearing in the heavens as cold and death reign on earth below. The Roman Saturnalia festivals, which lasted for three days through the winter solstice, celebrated death and atonement as a precursor to the sun's rebirth in spring. Sometimes the celebrants made a human sacrifice to help get things going, although in later periods, dolls and candles were used. The tradition of sacrifice goes far back to the agrarian rituals of the Barley King, a human leader who was beheaded with a sickle in the middle of the fields, so his blood would flow into the ground and fertilize the land for another year. Saturn became associated with the end or "death" of the week (Saturday) and heralded the sun's rebirth and beginning of the new week on "Sunday." For pagans, it was their entry to the dark world below; for the medieval Church, it represented the Gates of Hell.

The archetypal energies of Saturn are associated with fate and the passage of time. Its archetypal properties are predestined structure, stability, and firmness. Its negative attributes expressed in individuals are stubbornness, darkness, materialism, depression, passivity, coldness, heaviness, morbidity, gloominess, and coldness.

However, Saturn has a dual aspect and there is also a feminine or nurturing aspect to the planet's archetypal energy. Since it was connected to both death and life, Saturn carried both destructive and creative potential. In fact, the word Saturn is from the Latin *serere* meaning "to sow or plant." The ancients considered Saturn a source of infinite transformative energy that could manifest changes in physical reality. Saturn's astrological sign, Capricorn, is the tenacious mountain goat that persistently and patiently moves forward to reach great heights by remaining firmly grounded in matter. To individuals, Saturn brings the challenges of material life that transform the soul. The positive qualities evoked by Saturn are patience, diplomacy, practicality, seriousness, the work ethic, endurance, self-discipline, and an understanding of cause and effect.

The occult knowledge and fertilizing energy of Saturn are found in its threatening darkness and spring forth from the unconscious mind. But Saturn is perhaps the only planetary archetype that can control the forces of darkness, and give form and function to the otherwise amorphous, chaotic, and ambiguous influences of the universe. Saturn establishes order and sequence. It is not so much a cold, cruel, restrictive force as it is a chance to embody and make something real that only exists in the uncreated state, hidden in the darkness. Saturn is truly the Guardian Planet at the threshold of both death and rebirth, the bridge to the outer planets and stars, as well as to completely other levels of being.

For that reason, Saturn was the most important planet to the alchemists, and they thought of it as the beginning and end of the Great Work. Within the darkness of Saturnine energies are all possibilities for change and healing. An early cipher for Saturn was "Rx," which is our modern symbol for prescription drugs. Alchemists wrote it on a slip of paper and prescribed it as a cure. Their patients actually *ate* the piece of paper with the sigil of Saturn, which the alchemists had "animated" with magical intent.

Jupiter

Jupiter is the second step on the Ladder of the Planets. It is the largest and most impressive planet in our solar system, but it is mostly gas. It has four moons, which are all more active and larger than our moon. The planet's name is the root of the word "jovial" or cheerful, and the energies of Jupiter are expansive, even joyful, but lacking in depth. Still, Jupiter is considered the great "bene-factor" of the solar system and thus represents the principle of divine grace.

Jupiter's light and expansive presence in the solar system balances the heavy and contractive influence of Saturn. Esoterically, the Great Red Spot that floats around on the surface of the planet represents the necessary attitude of revolt, the deep-seated anger that enabled the son of Saturn to overthrow his father and become the ruler of Mount Olympus. Jupiter thus represents the light and energy with-out which the soul would remain imprisoned within the Saturnic darkness of matter. Hermetically, tin is linked with the planet Jupiter. The alchemical symbol for both Jupiter and the metal tin –♃– represents the lunar crescent rising above the cross of the four elements and becoming receptive to the light of spirit.

Jupiter and Saturn have a similar chemical makeup and are dozens of times larger than any of the other planets. Their cores are thought to be made of pure hydrogen metal. Together they form the Olympian throne of our solar system with the court of the lesser planets (and gods) spread before them. The biggest planet in our solar system is the rightful home for the chief-god Jupiter, who was the heavenly father of the Romans (Zeus of the Greeks). Jupiter was associated with the element Water and was worshiped as a rain god, which is another reason he was associated with thunder (his voice) and lightning (his weapon). In Rome, he was commonly known as Jupiter Pluvius, the "Heavenly Father Who Rains." His function was to fertilize the soil with his seminal moisture. His wife was the Great Mother, Juno (Hera of the Greeks), who was the Virgin Mother of the god Mars.

The mythological attributes of Jupiter are expansion, fluency, joviality, abundance, prosperity, growth, and success. In India, Jupiter takes the form of Indra, the god of fire and lightning, who in Scandinavian tradition is represented by the god Thor. Jupiter represents active, masculine energy and authority and is said to convey an aristocratic demeanor over those born under the astrological sign. In direct opposition to Saturn, it produces a state of mind over matter. This is a world of creativity, music, divination, good luck, wealth, sexuality, and moving out of the darkness of the Black Phase (Nigredo).

Astrologically, Jupiter is primarily linked with Sagittarius, the centaur with his bow and arrow. The centaur is a half-man, half-horse and symbolizes the person who has grown above his instinctive state and who has gathered social values and wisdom. Sagittarius aims high and possesses high ideals, beliefs, and optimism. With the combination of growth and a positive attitude, it is not surprising that Jupiter is the planet of healing, regeneration, and rejuvenation.

Mars

The third stop on the Ladder of the Planets is Mars. Mars is considered the brother of Earth, and the two planets share many characteristics. They have the same axial tilt (twenty-four degrees) and the same axial rotation, and therefore they both experience nearly identical daily cycles and seasons of the year. Both have polar ice caps, water, similar surface features, and an atmosphere, although because Mars is much smaller than Earth, its lesser gravity enables it to retain only vestiges of its atmosphere. Like Earth, Mars has active volcanoes, such as the great Nix Olympica, the biggest volcano yet discovered in the solar system. Mars also has two moons. Originally, the glyph for Mars was a circle with a cross on top, symbolizing matter over spirit, but over the years that small cross became an arrow that represents the aggressive, thrusting nature of its planetary energy. Today we find the symbol for Mars –♂– in common usage, representing the masculine gender.

March (the month of Mars) is the period when the sun enters the sign of Aries (from *Ares*, the Greek word for Mars). This is the time of year when day and night are equal, the point where the celestial equator intersects the ecliptic during the spring equinox. It is here that we begin a new solar cycle of the zodiac, and Aries (with his ruler, Mars) is the sign that provides us with the energy to do this. In alchemy, this is the period when the Great Work begins and the fire and energy we generate during this period is what propels us through the next twelve solar months of transformation. Mars requires about two years to make a complete cycle through the zodiac, and it remains in each sign about two months.

Mars, as the powerful God of War and exoteric ruler of Aries, is considered by many esotericists to be the cosmic troublemaker. In fact, the other Roman gods did not like Mars, and in Greece, he was not much cared for either. In their myths, Venus was always coming to Mars's rescue. Esoterically, the red planet governs the animal soul, passions, and the survival instinct. Martian qualities reinforce the ego and individuality, strengthen will, and help surpass previous limitations.

In older astrological systems, Mars was considered a "malefic" indicator, bringing ill health and problems. It was thought that our circumstances were the result of planetary influences outside of ourselves and during the warlike transits of Mars we could expect to suffer. Only recently have astrologers begun to see in Mars a

redeeming value. It is Mars that provides us with the energy to
act, to begin a new project, or follow a life's dream. Through Mars
(as action and energy), we create our karma, and through Saturn
(limits and lessons), we fulfill it or make it manifest. It is through
Mars the Warrior that we can mobilize the forces within us to
reverse course, move toward the goal of divine liberation, and find
the true peace that passes understanding.

In modern astrological analysis, wherever Mars is by sign and
house position in your birth chart, you will find your source of
energy. Since Mars can be both our undoing as well as our salva-
tion, it is important to take note of not only its placement but also
any aspects that other planets make to it. This will show you if
your energy is blocked or flowing freely.

Venus

The next rung on the Ladder of the Planets is Venus. Venus has the
slowest rotation about its axis (244 days compared to 24 hours on
Earth) of any planet, and is twice as close to the sun as Mars. About
the same size as earth, Venus is constantly enveloped in thick sulfuric clouds and has a dense and sultry atmosphere with a surface
temperature of around 450°F. Like Mars and Earth, Venus is
thought to have active volcanoes.

Although its true face is never seen, Venus is the brightest planet
in the sky and appears as both the "evening star" and the "morning
star." Esoterically, the veiled planet represents refinement of the
senses, the arts, mystical love, desire, and earthly relationships. The
character of both the planet and goddess Venus is passive, receptive,
magnetic, feminine, relating, able to adapt to others, kind and
gentle, and able to enjoy the company of others. The symbol for
Venus – ♀ – represents spirit over matter and is the common symbol
for the female gender.

Venus is associated with two astrological signs. Taurus represents the sensual part of Venus, while Libra is focused on relating
and connecting with persons and subjects. In earthy Taurus, the
attracting and beautifying power of Venus is displayed more in pos-

sessions and money, while in Libra the trend is toward art and harmony in all things. While Venus is the undisputed exoteric ruler of Taurus, Vulcan, the alchemist's creative God of the forge, is the esoteric ruler. The enlightened Taurus, with Vulcan, sees through the veil of matter into the energetic principle that underlies, interpenetrates, and sustains all manifestation.

Venus is the Roman Great Goddess (Aphrodite to the Greeks), and both Greeks and Romans emphasized her sexual aspect. Roman temples to Venus were actually schools of instruction in sexual techniques taught by harlot-priestesses known as *venerii*. Their techniques were meant to teach spiritual grace (called *venia*) through exercises similar to Eastern Tantrism. The romantic city of Venice was named for the goddess, and our word "veneration" literally means to "pay homage to Venus."

In mythology, Venus was the mother of Cupid, and she was married to the god of alchemy and metals, Vulcan. Despite her happy marriage, she could not resist being attracted to Mars, the god of war, and they ended up having many secret romantic trysts. In her Nature Goddess aspect, Venus is associated with animals of the forest and was once known as the "Lady of the Animals." Adonis, the Horned God who appears as both hunter and the sacrificial stag he hunts, fell in love with Venus when he saw her bathing nude in a stream in the forest. Our word "venison" actually means "son or follower of Venus." Overall, Venus is the goddess of love, beauty, art, balance, harmony, peace, and acceptance of natural law.

In many ways, Venus is a goddess of both birth and death—the Goddess of Generation involved in the complete cycle of being. She exhibits both life-giving and death-giving characteristics. The religion of Venus, just as in the Hermetic tradition of alchemy, promised a "sacred marriage" (the Conjunction) through which the initiate could escape the cycle of rebirth and be reborn on a whole new level of reality. Death was thus seen as a transformative event and became associated with ecstatic sexual climax. In his alchemical masterpiece, *Metamorphoses*, Ovid described how he wished to die in this way: "Let me go in the act of coming to Venus; in more senses than one, let my last dying be done!" Sexual imagery in

alchemy almost always refers these deeply transformative Venus energies to the Venus metal copper and the mysteries of Conjunction.

Mercury

The next stop on the Ladder of the Planets is Mercury. It is the
closest planet to the sun and revolves around it in eighty-eight
days, thus making it the fastest-moving planet in our solar system.
From Earth, it is never seen more than twenty-eight degrees from
the sun and most of the time is not visible to the naked eye because
it is so close to the sun's radiant light. However, when Mercury is
visible, either in the early morning or late evening, the tiny planet
is one of the brightest objects we can see in our solar system. Like
Venus, Mercury has a slow axial rotation (fifty-nine days), and its
surface looks very much like the moon. Mercury and the moon
have the most reflective surfaces of any planets and each reflects
exactly the same amount of sunlight (7 percent). Mercury has a
very irregular and eccentric orbit and sometimes even appears to go
backward in the heavens. Esoterically, the swiftest planet governs
the intellect, reasoning, writing, and speech.

Known to the Greeks as Hermes and the Romans as Mercury,
the namesake of the metal Mercury was considered to be the messenger of the gods and also the patron god of alchemy. His alchemical symbol –☿– represents the union of all three levels of reality,
the marriage of spirit and soul to produce the new body of the
Philosopher's Child.

As Hermes, one of his duties was to conduct souls of the dead to
the underworld, and perhaps this is why Hermes was also believed
to have magical powers over sleep, dreaming, and altered states of
consciousness. The god is often depicted with winged sandals and
a winged hat to connote the ability to move and deliver information
quickly. He symbolizes contact, communication, transportation,
flow, swiftness, playfulness, and flexibility.

Mercury the god is in fact considered neutral or androgynous.
This is because Mercury, which is responsible for the mind and the
nervous system, reflects and registers everything in its environment

and does so in a non-personal or non-polarized manner. It is the powerful presence of the Sun (masculine polarity) and Moon (feminine polarity) that gives Mercury the many nuances of meaning it then communicates to the self and others. The concept "Messenger of the Gods" has deep meaning, for without the interaction or connection between the personality and the soul, there would be no intelligent life force present to interact with. It is the archetype of Mercury that creates this link. When Mercury withdraws from the energetic human structure we see troubles arise such as dementia or other mental difficulties.

Mercury rules two signs, Gemini and Virgo. Gemini is the third sign in the zodiac and it is here that the life force that began in Aries (beginnings, impulse to life) and progressed through Taurus (stability, preserving) begins the process of establishing a sense of reality through discrimination. It is through the juxtaposition of figure and ground that the mind begins to discern separate parts within the cosmic soup and establish a construct of what we consider reality or *maya*. According to medical astrology, Mercury rules the blood circulation, the breath, transfer of nervous signals, thinking processes, lungs, arms and hands, and the senses as organs of communication. The urge or impulse of Mercury is to know, to communicate with the mind and intellect. It registers the endless flow of energy in its continual process of construction and reconstruction (yin into yang into yin again represented by the alchemical Uroboros).

Mercury has a higher octave and it is the planet Uranus. Uranus embodies the force we call the intuition. In order to gain access to the intuition that can reveal insights and knowledge beyond the linear progressions of facts or data, we must first develop a strong vehicle to contain it. In other words, all the insight in the universe will not do us any good if there is not a well-balanced mind present to receive it.

The Moon

The ancients considered the Moon a planet and made it the sixth rung on the Ladder of the Planets. It lies only about 240,000 miles from Earth, and because of its "captured orbit," always shows us the same face. Since the Moon does not have its own light and shines only by the reflected light of the sun, the Earth casts shadows on its face that make it appear to change shape in a twenty-eight-day cycle. The Moon that circles the earth is not at all similar to moons that circle other planets. While most moons are tens of thousands of times less massive than their planets and are made of the same minerals, our Moon is only eighty times less massive than the earth and composed of entirely different minerals. For these reasons, most astronomers consider our Moon another planet and view earth-moon as a double planetary system. Oddly, the alchemists were exactly right in believing the Moon was another planet.

Since moons are celestial globes that do not have their own orbit but circle around planets, the symbolic meaning of the Moon is receptivity and protection, reaction and reflection. The Moon's monthly phases are related to the rhythms of ebb and flow, both in the tides, human hormones, and the female menstrual cycle. *Meno* is a Greek word meaning "moonpower" and is connected to our words "menstruation" and "menopause." Thus the Moon is related to cycles and changeable emotions, femininity, and motherliness. In many areas of the world, including India, planting and agriculture are still governed by the thirteen-month lunar calendar, because it is believed this cycle most closely matches the cycle of growth and decay on our planet.

In mythology, the Moon is associated with the virgin goddess Diana and the multibreasted symbol of fecundity Artemis. Egyptian priests called the Moon the "Mother of the Universe," and Luna became the queen of alchemy. Its symbol is a caricature of the Moon (☽).

In Tantric alchemy, the Silver (or Moon) Chakra is at the forehead. Tantra is a form of Hindu alchemy focusing on the purification and control of the life force and sexual energy. There are many parallels between Tantra and Western alchemy, and the two traditions may have sprung from the same Egyptian spiritual teachings. Siddhars are the great masters of Tantra, and they use techniques very similar to the operations of alchemy. The first Siddhar was

Agastyar, who is virtually identical to his Western counterpart, Hermes-Thoth. Like Thoth, Agastyar arrived from a distant land of enlightenment, invented a sacred language (Tamil), and was the father of the arts and sciences.

In both Tantra and European alchemy, the Moon rules the astral body, the subconscious and magnetic feminine energy. Lunar energies govern growth and fertility, and the stomach, womb, and fluids of the body. In both traditions, the Moon Chakra is in the forehead, which in terms of anatomy is often interpreted as the pituitary gland (the bi-lobed master gland in the forebrain).

The Moon is associated with the astrological sign of Cancer and is thought to control fertility, maternity, death, and cyclic decay. Cancers are prudent yet emotional people with a sense of family and domestic values.

The Sun

The Sun is the last rung on the Ladder of the Planets. Our own personal star is the crowning glory and spiritual center of our solar system. At ninety-three million miles away, it takes light from the Sun only eight minutes to reach the earth, compared to over four years from the next nearest star. The Sun emits energy in every conceivable wavelength from X-rays to visible light to radio waves, and this energy is what makes life possible in our solar system. The Sun is the purest body in the solar system; 93 percent of it is composed of hydrogen atoms, which is the simplest form of matter known. It is also in a process of constant purification in which cooler and darker masses known as sunspots rise to the surface. The formation of sunspots is on a remarkably regular eleven-year cycle during which the intensity and number of spots steadily increases. In the period between the purging cycles, the Sun is completely free of sunspots for many months at a time.

The alchemist saw the Sun as the King and consort to the Queen Moon, and in another case of amazing alchemical synchronicity, the Sun and moon appear to be exactly the same size in the sky. Since the moon is physically four hundred times smaller than the ʂun but also four hundred times closer than the Sun, they seem to be the same size from an observer on earth. When a total solar eclipse (or complete alchemical conjunction) occurs, the lunar disc exactly and completely covers that of the Sun.

The solar archetype of the Sun is an image of wholeness and a point for the focus of life. Its symbol implies wholeness and integration $-\odot-$. This ultimate symbol of health, wealth, and happiness permeates everything we do, whether we are aware of it or not. Gold has to do with the core, the essential energy, the most important part of something.

In Tantric alchemy and Kundalini Yoga, the Gold (or Sun) Chakra is the Crown, which in physical terms is often interpreted as the pineal gland (a pinecone-shaped phallic appendage at the center of the brain). Esoterically, this chakra is pictured as a thousand-petaled lotus that floats above the head like a halo. This inverted lotus, rooted in the Above, is said to embrace all colors, all senses, all functions, and is all-pervading in power. It is the Gate of Brahman, the escape hatch to the supraliminal realm where the individual emerges completely from the confines of time and space. Duality disappears, and the alchemist is finally one with the universe in which the divine is experienced directly as a state of being. One achieves a true understanding of all things on all levels.

The Sun and its metal represent the Christ or Osiris consciousness in man, as well as Hercules in his aspect of monumental strength. In astrology, the Sun and Leo represent your deepest identity, the true you, your inner authority, your justified pride and dignity. In the zodiac, the Sun presides over the essential self, ambition, spirit, highest will, energy, power, and organization. The blazing Sun corresponds to ambition, courage, vitality, creative energies, and electric or masculine energy.

Music of the Spheres: The Octave of Creation

To the ancients, the planets represented individual melodies in the Music of the Spheres—archetypal "vibrations" that influence every part of our lives. "Each celestial body," noted Pythagoras in

550 B.C., "produces a particular sound on account of its movement, rhythm, or vibration. All the sounds and vibrations together form a universal harmony in which each part, while having its own function and character, contributes to the whole."

This universal pattern is quite familiar to all of us, and we experience it in our love for music. In what esotericists call the Law of Octaves, energetic archetypal vibrations follow the same pattern as the musical octave. The octave is a seven-stepped process that raises the vibration of the first note on the scale to a new incarnation at a higher vibration. In Western music, there are seven notes (*do, re, me, fa, sol, la, si*) that increase in tone to an eighth note (*do*), which is a return to the first note on a still higher scale. Thus, the entire octave runs from *do* to *do* or from the beginning to the end, which is the beginning taken to a higher level.

The *Law of Octaves* is universal, and it is recognized in many philosophical systems including the I Ching, the Fourth Way, and Gnosticism. In fact, Gnostic sects considered the 8×8 configuration of chessboards imbued them with sacred energy. To play chess for them was a mystical experience. A chessboard is engraved in the Egyptian temple of Kurna, where it is thought to have been used in rituals. The temple is located on the sacred west shore of the Nile and dates from 1400 B.C. In modern chemistry, the Law of Octaves is expressed in the periodic table, where every eighth element repeats the characteristics of the first.

The Ladder of the Planets is another example of the *Law of Octaves*. The overall pattern of harmony in the universe is a seven-stepped formula for transformation embedded in our solar system. Just as the first seven notes of the musical scale represent our progress through the planets, the eighth note is a return to the first note at a higher vibration. The eighth note is the beginning of a whole new octave of creation that represents our leaving behind the grosser materiality of the planets and experiencing the more subtle matter of the spiritual universe.

On the Ladder of the Planets, the planet Saturn is the eighth note, the *do*—the one note that is both beginning and end, the alpha and omega of the transformation. That is why the alchemists considered Saturn and our *return to Saturn* as the most important part of the Great Work of alchemy.

A Space Odyssey

The alchemists considered the Ladder of the Planets the key to understanding the Great Work and Saturn the key to accomplishing it. They created hundreds of arcane treatises and complicated diagrams on the subject. Yet none of these mystical tomes caught the essence of the ancient teachings more dramatically than a motion picture directed by a modern alchemical artist by the name of Stanley Kubrick, whose film, *2001: A Space Odyssey*, is an ingenious journey of transformation on the Ladder of the Planets of the alchemists.

Most people who have seen *2001* do not have a clue about what it means. When it was released in 1968, dazed moviegoers wandered out of theaters scratching their heads, quizzing each other about what it all meant. Despite disappointing initial sales, the film became a smash hit because those same puzzled moviegoers kept going back to see the film over and over. *2001* was the first theatrical release in which repeat business was the major factor in its success. Something in the visually stunning film attracted people at a deeper level than just a sci-fi story about a neurotic computer.

The real star of the film—and source of all its mystery—is the rectangular black monolith that appears throughout the movie. Whenever it shows up, there is a profound transformation in the plot and characters. The mysterious monolith (literally "One Stone") is the Sorcerer's Stone of the alchemists. It now appears that Kubrick intended his film to be a vehicle of transformation for the general public.

Filmmaker and Hermetic scholar Jay Weidner, who co-authored *Mysteries of the Cross of Hendaye: Alchemy and the End of Time* and *Monument to the End of Time: Alchemy, Fulcanelli and the Great Cross*, was the first to recognize what Kubrick had in mind. In an article published in 1999 (see www.sacredmysteries.com/kubrick. htm), he wrote:

In a secret that seems to never have been seen by anyone, the monolith in the film has the same exact dimensions as the Cinerama movie screen on which it was projected in 1968. This is only apparent if one sees the film in its wide-screen theatrical format. Kubrick himself created the first drawing of what the monolith would look like, including its dimensions. Completely hidden—from critic and fan alike—is the fact that Kubrick consciously designed his film to be the monolith. Like the mysterious monolith, the film projects images into our heads that make us consider wider possibilities and ideas. Like the monolith, the film ultimately presents an initiation, not just of the actor on the screen, but also of the audience viewing the film. The transformative monolith is the Stone of the alchemists, and Kubrick is revealing that he understands the Great Work. Using powdered silver nitrates, glued onto a strip of plastic that is then projected onto the movie screens of our mind, Stanley Kubrick has proven himself to be the ultimate alchemist-artist of the late twentieth century.

Dawn of Man: The Black Phase of Alchemy

The theatrical version of *2001* opens in utter blackness to eerie, swirling sounds, almost as if it were the beginning of time. Suddenly, we hear the stirring music of "Thus Spake Zarathustra" by Richard Strauss. Zarathustra, known as Zoroaster to the Greeks, was a sixth-century B.C. Persian prophet. His philosophy of renunciation of all worldly illusions and strict dedication to the spiritual evolution of humanity was popularized by nineteenth century existentialist writers such as Friedrich Nietzsche and Søren Kierkegaard.

As Strauss's masterpiece plays, the sun and moon move into conjunction, which is a merging of planetary energies the alchemists saw as a celestial marriage. The darkened moon covers all but a sliver of the earth, which slowly emerges as if the moon were giving birth to it. The sun rises majestically above both, like a proud father. Such dramatic celestial alignments occur throughout the film whenever some magical transformation is about to occur.

The next scene in the film is a red sunrise over a barren plain.

The title "Dawn of Man" appears on the screen. There will be three chapters in the film that correspond to the three stages of alchemical transformation. This first chapter is the Black Phase (Nigredo), during which the inferior aspects of the subject at hand are destroyed or sacrificed.

The beginning of the long Black Phase of humanity is depicted as a typical day in the life of the proto-human apes that lived on the earth millions of years ago. Unaware of both the outer universe and their inner selves, they forage for food, are attacked by predators, and spend their time fighting over a watering hole with another clan. Night comes as the tribe huddles together against the growling sounds of animals on the prowl.

The next morning, the ape men awake to find an imposing black monolith standing upright in the middle of their camp. It is a flawlessly crafted object the likes of which they have never seen. The lead ape man hunches closer to the monolith and timidly brushes his fingers along its perfectly smooth surface. Something numinous has occurred, and this is a profound moment in human history. The scene ends from the viewpoint of the ape man, who is looking up at the top of the monolith, which is centered in perfect alignment with the sun and moon above it. The sun and moon are just parting from another conjunction, in which the ape man, the monolith, and the heavenly bodies are all lined up together. We are witnessing the dawn of consciousness in our species.

The next scene shows the ape man leader sitting in a pile of animal bones and suddenly realizing that the thighbone he is holding can be used as a weapon. The birth of knowledge over instinct takes place, as the ape man realizes he can kill animals by using the bone as a club. Next, we observe the members of the tribe no longer scrounging for seeds and leaves but gorging themselves on warm raw meat from an animal they have just killed. And at the next confrontation with the competing clan at the water hole, the lead ape man strikes the other clan leader on the head and kills him instantly. The stunned and frightened members of the competing clan hastily retreat, as the ape men, now armed with clubs, take turns beating the already dead body on the ground. In this violent and cowardly moment, the ape men lose their innocence, for man has killed his brother.

Howling in victory, the lead ape man throws his bone club high into the air. Spinning end-over-end, the thighbone slowly morphs into a spaceship rising up from earth. In this one audacious moment, Kubrick tells us that all of history is irrelevant. He dismisses civilization as if it were insignificant in relation to a greater process going on in the universe. Except for our tools becoming larger and more sophisticated, not much has really changed in the human soul. We are still in the Black Phase of alchemical transformation.

As we watch the evolved thighbone-spaceship emerge from the atmosphere, the sun and earth are shown in a blazing conjunction. The spaceship then passes in front of a distant and lonely moon. The planetary forces are still present, still working in the background, but they are out of balance by our presence. We have assimilated the sun's masculine spirit on earth, and it has led to great technological advances, but our lunar feminine soul has been pushed away in the process. The key to transformation, as any alchemist knows, is the union of solar and lunar forces, the sacred marriage of the sun and moon. Instead, there exists an estrangement between them, and correspondingly, between our own spirits and souls.

Like the alchemical trickster Hermes, Kubrick fools us into feeling a certain amount of pride in human accomplishment. There are so many wonderful feats of the human spirit shown, and the triumphant engineering and intriguing gadgets contrast sharply against the ape men's meager existence. It is hard not to feel proud about our species' advancement, but this technological wonderland has some very basic flaws. We have lost the connection with our essence in the world of nature. Instead, we are immersed in a soulless, technocratic world of human design, full of manufactured food, contoured plastic furniture, and impersonal devices for remote communication. Even the characters appear wooden, emotionless, shallow and arrogant. According to alchemy, the end result of the Black Phase is that the "soul departs from the body."

The air of human smugness will become almost unbearable by the end of this part of the movie, whose signature theme is the beautiful but pretentious Viennese waltz ("Blue Danube" by Johann Strauss). The music and revolving Ferris-wheel space station are subtle reminders that mankind is just going in circles, caught in an artificial social structure that we believe is all there is. We are still unaware of the bigger picture, the unlimited potential of the light of human consciousness and its mysterious connection to the stars.

The icon of smug joviality is Heywood Floyd (played by William Sylvester), the lone passenger in the spacecraft, which docks at the revolving space station. Floyd is on a secret mission to investigate the discovery of an alien artifact buried just five meters (sixteen feet) beneath the surface of the moon. The object is emitting a weak radio signal that was detected during an electromagnetic survey. However, the astonishing discovery is something the military-industrial complex decides to keep secret. "I'm sure you are aware of the extremely grave potential for social shock and disorientation caused by this information," Floyd blandly explains at a meeting on the lunar base. "We can't release it without proper conditioning." Everyone nods in silent accord.

After the meeting, Floyd boards a transport vehicle and travels to the site of the discovery. The exposed monolith stands before them as imposing and enigmatic as the first one that appeared to the ape men. This time, however, the humans react with utter disregard for the importance of the discovery. Without the slightest display of awe or wonder, they begin snapping photographs of themselves in front of the black stone, like tourists in a national park. Just at that moment, the sun rises over the horizon and rays of light hit the monolith for the first time in millions of years. The monolith responds with a high-pitched signal that pierces their helmets and makes them cringe in pain. The second part of the film ends with a shot from the horizon of the moon showing the distant earth above and behind the sun, as all three bodies takes their places in another powerful alignment.

Discovery Mission: The White Phase of Alchemy

The second chapter of the film begins with the title "The Discovery Mission—18 Months Later," and we find ourselves on a behemoth interplanetary spaceship. Of course, the ship is just another "bone" thrown into the air by ape men; we are really continuing the story of the relationship between man and his tools, only now the story ends with the discovery of man's soul. This is the second stage of alchemical transformation, known as the White Phase (Albedo), in which the true essences of the substance at hand are revealed.

There are only two active astronauts on board, Frank Poole (played by Gary Lockwood) and David Bowman (played by Keir Dullea). Three others are in hibernation, sealed in sarcophagus-like containers. The astronauts are just as soulless as the people shown earlier. They register no emotion; they are always logical; they always agree. The only presence that seems to have a soul is HAL, the ship's computer, whose initials stand for "Heuristic Algorithmic Learning" system.

But the infallible supercomputer starts to suffer from existential angst. Unlike the humans on board, HAL begins to question the meaning of the mission and the reasons for its own existence. Before long, HAL suffers a sort of nervous breakdown, becomes paranoid about its human operators, and starts killing off the astronauts. The underlying message here is that we are putting too much faith in our machines. If you go up in the alphabet to the next letters in HAL, it spells IBM.

Bowman ends up the lone survivor on the giant ship and finally kills HAL by shutting down its circuits. As HAL suffers through the throes of disconnection, a video buried deep in its memory banks begins to play. The video shows Heywood Floyd explaining that an extraterrestrial artifact discovered on the moon was emitting a strong signal toward Jupiter when it was exposed to sunlight. (It should be noted that in the original script and Arthur C. Clarke's novelization of the movie, the destination planet was Saturn not Jupiter, but the special effects department was unable to come up with a convincing model of Saturn and its complicated rings. Kubrick reluctantly agreed to substitute Jupiter in the film version only.)

In alchemical terms, Saturn is the planet that symbolizes the beginning and end of the Great Work. We have worked our way up the ladder to the light of solar consciousness and knowledge, but now we must return to the beginning of the Great Work to probe the darkness beyond Saturn, beyond the perimeter of our solar system, and beyond even who we think we are.

Beyond the Infinite: The Red Phase of Alchemy

The third chapter of the film, "Beyond the Infinite," begins with ominous, almost psychedelic music. Not a single word will be spoken for the rest of the film, because the ensuing experiences are beyond logic and words. This is the third stage of transformation, the Red Phase (Rubedo), in which the substance at hand is perfected through union with cosmic (or divine) forces.

The chapter begins with astronaut Bowman exiting the ship in a space pod and approaching the monolith orbiting the gigantic planet. When Bowman nears the monolith, he is suddenly drawn into the Stargate, a warp in space that leads to other dimensions. Traveling at the speed of light, everything is blended together in a vertical wash of brilliant, living colors. The rift of color then takes on a horizontal orientation, as new dimensions of time and space open up. Beautiful streaming formations that look like giant sperm and ova create even more complex embryonic clouds of swirling matter. Finally, he "arrives" somewhere, and seven glowing octahedrons appear to guide him the rest of the way. Undreamed-of-landscapes start sliding by in wild chaotic hues. We see Bowman in the pod and realize he is close to experiencing visual overload (as are some members of the audience).

Bowman is the first human through the Stargate, the first man to tap into the power of the hidden but universal Stone of transformation represented by the monolith. Astrologically, Bowman is the "man with the bow" represented by the constellation Sagittarius. The starry figure of Sagittarius is shooting his arrow at a hidden point in the sky, and astronomers now realize his arrow points to an enormous black hole at the center of the Milky Way galaxy. It is also where our own Bowman is shot like an arrow through the Stargate. According to ancient teachings, this hidden point in the heavens is the "Black Sun" or "Sun behind the Sun," the true source of all matter and energy.

Once past the Stargate, Bowman's space pod ends up sitting incongruously on the floor of an opulent hotel suite. The set is a combination of modern and French baroque styling, and all the lighting comes up from the floor. In other words, the light is coming from below, from Bowman's mind, which has "cracked" open and is spilling its contents around him. The only sound is incomprehensible mumbling voices coming from his subconscious mind. His movements in the odd room are determined by what he thinks. He visualizes himself standing outside the pod in the room, and in the next instant he stands outside the pod looking back at it. This is Hermetic space, where thoughts have wings and possess the power to instantly transform reality.

Continuing the transformation initiated by the monolith, Bowman works through material in his own mind—all the baggage he brought with him, all the trappings of civilization that must be exposed for the habitual illusions they are. Things start to change when Bowman drops a wine glass while eating a gourmet meal and the glass breaks to pieces on the floor. He turns in his chair and stares at the broken glass for some time. It is a sign that his illusions are starting to shatter, and he is coming to the realization that he is trapped in a jail designed by his own consciousness.

With each level of purification and transformation, Bowman is getting physically older, a process that mirrors the alchemy of everyone's lives. Finally, he sees himself lying helpless in bed and becomes that. Now extremely aged and hairless, he is tightly wrapped in a golden blanket and looks like a big chrysalis or larva. His metamorphosis is nearing completion, and the monolith suddenly appears at the foot of his bed. Bowman raises his hand feebly and points at the ominous black Stone as if he finally understands it. Those last few seconds of true understanding are all it takes to trigger Bowman's quantum leap in consciousness. His decrepit body turns into pure light until he is enveloped in a circular vessel of glorious white light so brilliant that it is hard to see what is happening inside. There appears to be a standing white bird and other alchemical symbols forming within the vessel as Bowman's soul it transmuted.

Immediately, an embryo of light starts to form in the vessel and turns into a living human fetus. This is the Starchild, the alchemical rebirth of Bowman's soul on a new level of reality. The final step in the Great Work is to redeem matter itself, to manifest the light of consciousness in a whole new embodiment, what the great alchemist Paracelsus called the Star (or Astral) Body.

The Starchild has been created through the purification and union of the universal forces within us, or as the alchemists would put it, through the "fusion of the planets." The Stone is complete and the work is done. In the last scene of the movie, we once again see our familiar moon and earth, but now the Starchild is orbiting between the two, about to make contact with all of mankind.

Each position on the Ladder of the Planets (Saturn, Jupiter, Mars, Venus, Mercury, Moon, Sun) corresponds to a note on the Octave of Creation. These archetypal vibrations are embedded in our solar system, our planet, our bodies, and our souls. This same pattern of transformation is expressed correspondingly in the seven metals (respectively lead, tin, iron, copper, mercury, silver, gold), and the alchemists saw the archetypal energies of the metals as the Ladder of the Planets within us. We will directly experience the powers of the metals and learn how to transmute them within ourselves beginning with the next chapter.

6

Saturn's Child: The Base Metal Lead

WHILE WE HAVE ALREADY DISCUSSED the planetary archetypes, it is worth reminding ourselves at this point exactly how the alchemists looked on the relationship between planets and their metals. They believed that the metals had the same "virtue" as the corresponding planet, that a single spirit infused both the planet and the metal. In other words, the planet was a celestial manifestation and the metal a terrestrial manifestation of the same universal force.

This means that the metals are the purest expression of the planetary energies in the mineral kingdom, which is the basis for material reality on earth. The next stage of evolution on our planet is the plant kingdom, and the alchemists assigned a metal and its corresponding planet to describe the characteristics of every known herb, flower, and plant. Similarly, on the next level in the evolution of matter in the animal kingdom, all creatures carry their own metallic or planetary signatures, which are expressed in their behavior. In human beings, the alchemists referred to the sum total of the cosmic signatures of the metals as a person's "temperament." Originally, that word referred to the metallurgical process of "tempering" or mixing different metals to produce certain characteristics in an alloy.

Lead and Its Secret Fire

Although the alchemists considered lead the lowest of the base metals, they treated it with a great deal of respect, as they did its corresponding planet Saturn. Lead was said to carry all the energy of its own transformation, and it was that hidden energy that the alchemists sought to free. To the alchemists, the ancient metal was a powerful "sleeping giant" with a dark and secret nature that encompassed both the beginning and end of the Great Work.

Lead is the heaviest of the seven metals; it is very tied to gravity, form, and manifested reality. It is also a very stubborn metal known for its durability and resistance to change. Lead products dating from 7000 B.C. are still intact, and lead water pipes installed by the Romans fifteen hundred years ago are still in use today. Alchemists depicted lead in their drawings as the god Saturn (a crippled old man with a sickle), Father Time, or a skeleton representing death itself. Any of these symbols in their manuscripts meant the alchemist was working with the metal lead in the laboratory or a leaden attitude in his accompanying meditation.

Lead is a boundary of heaviness for matter. Metals of greater atomic weight are too heavy and disintegrate over time (by radioactive decay) to turn back into lead. So radioactive decay is really a Saturnic process that introduces a new characteristic—that of time—in the metals. All the hyper-energetic metals beyond lead are trapped in time and inexorably return to lead. There is no natural process more unalterably exact than radioactive decay. Atomic clocks, the most precise timekeeping devices we have, are based on this leaden process. Geologists measure the age of radioactive rocks by how much lead they contain, and the age of the earth is estimated by taking lead isotope measurements. In many ways, lead carries the signature of Father Time.

Native lead, which is lead metal found in a chemically uncombined state, is actually extremely rare. It is found in the earth's crust in a concentration of only about thirteen parts per billion. Lead does not form crystals easily, and thus the pure mineral form is very rare and extremely valuable as rock specimens. Such elemental lead can also be found in very unusual "metamorphosed" limestone and marble formations that are equally rare.

Surprisingly, lead is in the same group in the periodic table as gold, and when it occurs in nature, it is always found with gold and silver. In fact, the chemical symbol for lead (Pb) is from the Latin word *plumbum*, which means "liquid silver." We derive our words "plumbing" and "plumb bob" from the use of lead in those applications. In the smelting of silver, lead plays an important role by forming a layer over the emerging molten silver and protecting it from combining with the air and splattering out. The volatile molten lead covering is gradually burnt away, until only the pure silver metal "peeks out" (in the smelter's terminology) in a stabilized form. Thus, lead protects and even sacrifices itself for the nobler metals.

The planet Saturn and its metal have the same symbol –♄– in alchemy. The Hermetic interpretation is that the symbol is basically the cross of the elements that depicts the division between the Above and Below or spirit and matter. The lunar crescent of the soul is below the cross, representing the manifestation (or entrapment) of soul below in matter.

Despite these associations with the noble metals, lead itself never makes it to such heights. The silvery luster of fresh cut lead quickly fades, as if it were "dying" before one's eyes. Furthermore, alchemists considered lead to be "hydrophobic" or against the life nourishing archetype of water. Lead ores lack the slightest water content and tend to form machinelike structures.

The most common ore of lead is galena, which also contains the noble metals silver and gold. Galena is lead sulfide, a favorite of rock collectors because of its distinctive cubic shapes, characteristic cleavage, and high density. In fact, the structure of galena is identical to that of natural table salt. The two minerals have exactly the same crystal shapes, symmetry, and cleavage, although galena crystals are thousands of times larger. Some galena may contain up to 1 percent silver and often contains trace amounts of gold. The large volume of galena that is processed for lead produces enough silver as a by-product to make galena the leading ore of silver as well.

Galena definitely has the signature of lead. Its color is silver gray with a bluish tint. The luster ranges from metallic to dull in the weathered faces, and the isometric crystals are opaque to light. The massive crystals of galena almost always take the form of a cube or octahedron, and the cleavage is perfect in four directions always forming cubes. Because of the perfect cleavage, fractures are rarely seen and the dark crystalline structure is nearly perfect.

Lead is also found in other sulfuric minerals like calcite and dolomite, as well as lead oxidation minerals such as anglesite and cerussite, which is found in the oxidation zone of lead deposits usually associated with galena. Some formations show cerussite crusts around a galena core as if the act of oxidation was frozen in time. Cerussite is lead carbonate and also a favorite of rock hounds. Its very high luster is due mostly to the metallic lead content, and just as leaded crystal glass sparkles more brilliantly because of its lead content, so too does cerussite. Cerussite has one of the highest densities for a transparent mineral. It is over six and a half times as dense as water. Most rocks and minerals average only around three times the density of water. Cerussite is famous for its great sparkle and density, and its amazing twinned (or double) crystals. The mineral forms geometrically intricate structures and star shapes that simply are amazing to behold; sometimes the twinned crystals form star shapes with six "rays" extending out from the star.

When freed from its ores, lead metal has a bluish white color and is very soft—capable of being scratched by a fingernail. With its dull metallic luster and high density, lead cannot easily be confused with any other metal. It is also malleable, ductile, and sectile, meaning it can be pounded into other shapes, stretched into a wire, and cut into slices. However, lead is a dark, sluggish, base metal. Of the seven metals, it is the slowest conductor of electricity and heat, the least lustrous or resonant. Its Saturnine signature of heaviness is expressed not only in its being the heaviest metal but also in its tendency to form inert and insoluble compounds. No other metal forms as many. Although it tarnishes upon exposure to air like silver, lead is extremely resistant to corrosion over time and seems to last forever. Lead pipes bearing the insignia of Roman emperors, used as drains from the baths, are still in service. The surface of lead is protected by a thin layer of lead oxide, and it does not react with water. The same process protects lead from the traditional "liquid fire" of the alchemists—sulfuric acid. In fact, lead bottles are still used to store the highly corrosive acid. Lead is so inalterable, that half of all the lead in the world today is simply recovered from scrap and formed directly into bullion for reuse.

Lead is truly a destroyer of light. It is added to high-quality glassware (lead crystal) to absorb light reflections and make the glass clearer. Lead salts in glass are not changed by light but change light itself by absorbing it. Incoming light in lead crystal meets with high resistance, but once it is within the glass, light is immediately absorbed or dispersed without any reflected light escaping. Sheets of lead are also impermeable to all forms of light, even high-energy X-rays and gamma rays, which make lead the perfect shield against any form of radiation and is why it is used to transport and store radioactive materials.

Lead is an extremely poor conductor of electricity and blocks all kinds of energy transmission. Indeed, one of the signatures of lead is its ability to "dampen" or absorb energy. Unlike other metals, when lead is struck, the vibrations are immediately absorbed and any tone is smothered in dullness. Lead is an effective sound-proofing medium and tetraethyl lead is still used in some grades of gasoline as an antiknock compound to "quiet" the combustion of gasoline.

Thin lead sheets are used extensively in the walls of high-rise buildings to block the transmission of sound, and thick pads of lead are used in the foundations to absorb the vibrations of street traffic and even minor earthquakes. Lead sheets are widely used in roofing to block solar rays, and lead foil is used to form lightproof enclosures in laboratory work. Ultimately, lead corresponds to the galactic Black Hole that absorbs all forms of radiation and light.

Lead reacts with more chemicals than any other metal; however, instead of producing something new and useful, lead "kills" the combining substance by making it inert, insoluble, and unable to enter into further chemical reactions. Its salts precipitate out of solutions heavily and copiously. Lead has the same impact in the plant kingdom. It accumulates in the roots and slows down the "breathing" process in plants. Young plants are adversely affected by even the smallest amount of lead in the soil.

Lead is poisonous and accumulates over time in the bones of the human body, where it cannot be flushed out. It has also been found in high concentrations in gallstones and kidney stones. The old alchemical graphic for lead—a skeleton—was grotesquely appropriate. The symptoms of lead poisoning (known as "saturnism") are lack of energy, depression, blindness, dizziness, severe headaches at the back of the head, brain damage, attention deficit disorder, learning disabilities and mental retardation, antisocial behavior and anger, atrophy of muscular tissue and cramping, excess growth of connective tissue resulting in a rigid appearance, rapid aging, coma, and early death. Rats fed only five parts per million of lead had a life span 25 percent shorter than normal rats. Children are especially vulnerable to lead poisoning, and it is believed to be an important factor in stillborn fetuses. Children with more than just 0.3 parts per million of lead in their blood suffer a significant slowing of brain function and corresponding drop in IQ. Lead in paint has caused mental retardation and premature aging in hundreds of children who ingested old flaking paint from the walls of their homes. Lead paint was used extensively until the poisonous effects were documented in the 1960s. Because of its lasting durability, lead paint is still used outdoors in advertising and for the yellow lines on highways and curbs. The subtly controlling aspect of those applications is another signature of lead and of "leaden" people in general.

Not surprisingly, lead has found use as an insecticide and was even once considered for use as a military weapon. Lead metal reacts violently with fluorine and chlorine to form the highly poisonous gases lead fluoride and lead chloride. Lead is also used in all kinds of ammunition—another appropriate application of lead's esoteric signature as Father Time and the Grim Reaper. There are many research studies linking lead exposure to anger and violence, especially in adolescents. One recent study of all counties in the United States conducted by Colorado State University revealed that the murder rate in counties with the highest lead levels were four times higher than in counties with the lowest lead levels.

More benevolent uses of lead are in storage batteries, covering for underground and transoceanic cables, waste plumbing, shielding around X-ray equipment and nuclear reactors, solder, pewter, fine lead crystal glass, and flint glass with a high refractive index for achromatic lenses.

Even the elemental metal carries the seed of its own redemption. The alchemists knew that Fire is lord over lead, for the metal has a low melting point and is easily separated from its ore by roasting in an open flame, and the metal itself melts in a candle flame. Lead expands on heating and contracts on cooling more than any other solid heavy metal. (Silver is the opposite and is considered an antidote to lead.)

Perhaps owing to its dual nature, lead carries deep within its structure the fire of its own transformation. Many lead salts reveal a whole rainbow of brilliant colors, with the solar colors of yellow, orange, and red predominating. This is why lead has been used in paints for so many centuries. Finely divided lead powder is pyrophoric ("fire containing") and easily catches fire or erupts spontaneously into flames. When made into a fine powder, lead metal must be kept in a vacuum to keep from catching fire. Otherwise, it ignites and burns down to a bright yellow ash, revealing its deeply hidden solar signature.

The wonder of lead is that hidden deep inside the gray, dead metal is a tiny, eternal spark that is the seed of its own resurrection. In the eyes of alchemists, this makes lead the most important metal despite its unattractive darkness. Dull lead and gleaming gold are really the same things, only at different stages of growth or maturity.

The Secret Fire inside lead is really the alchemical basis for transforming lead into gold, and correspondingly, gives mankind hope for its own spiritual transformation. That tiny spark of light in the darkest part of matter makes resurrection part of the structure of the universe. Deep down inside, the metal lead also yearns to be transformed. It wants to rise in the air and fly, leave matter and form behind, and be free as Fire. Lead unites two contrasting forces: rigid heaviness and revivifying inner fire. Archetypically, the lead process is concerned with death and resurrection. Greek myth says that after death our soul is put on a scale, and the weights of the scale are made from lead, the metal that carries Saturn's signature.

Lead is used in magical rituals, spells, and amulets to promote contact with deep unconscious levels (the underworld) and deep meditation, to control negativity, and break bad habits and addictions, and for protection, stability, grounding, solidity, perseverance, decisiveness, concentration, conservation, and material constructions (buildings).

Correspondences of Lead

Planet: Saturn

Signs: Capricorn and Aquarius

Day: Saturday

Musical note: Do

Gender: Female

Gemstone: Garnet

Chakra: Muladhara (root)

Organ: Gallbladder and spleen

Element: Earth

Experiment 6: The Call of Lead

Pick up a hunk of lead and the first thing you notice is its weight— its connection to gravity. It is that connection to something beyond matter and light, the very form of the universe that is the physical basis for this experiment. During the winter months, preferably on some clear night in late January or early February, go outside and find the planet Saturn in the northern sky. Relax and try to focus all your attention on the golden sphere. Relax completely with an open and quiet mind. Become empty and let the planet influence you. Do this until you feel a real connection with the distant planet. Continue gazing upon Saturn and place a piece of lead metal in your hand. You should be able to feel a strange resonance building. That eerie, cold vibration is not your imagination. It is what alchemists refer to as the "call of lead." You are experiencing the metal's true signature or living correspondence with its planetary twin.

The strange connection between lead and Saturn has been documented by modern scientists, who have shown that lead compounds react differently depending on Saturn's position in the sky. For instance, solutions of lead nitrate produce the greatest weight of crystallization (or manifestation) during February, when Saturn rules the sky, and the least during June, when Saturn is barely visible. Lead compounds also exhibit different properties when Saturn aligns with other planets. As an example, lead sulfate solution rises 60 percent higher on strips of filter paper during conjunctions of Saturn with Mars than at other times. It is also known that the ease of making lead solutions (the "solubility coefficient" of lead) varies with the position of Saturn relative to the other planets. NASA is even considering a series of astrochemical experiments to see if the Saturn-lead effects become more pronounced in outer space.

The Lead Temperament

Surprisingly, because the metals are such perfect expressions of archetypal energies, we can actually learn quite a bit about people by studying the properties of metals and the behavior of planets. That same correspondence exists in the human temperament. For instance, the leaden person is someone who has, like Saturn, lost his bid to become a star. He or she has accepted a mere physical existence and believes the created world is all that counts. The black crows of Chronos (the Greek god of time associated with Saturn by the Romans) bring black moods, depression and despair to us, but they also alert us to illusion and fakeness in our lives. The positive characteristics of the saturnine person are patience, responsibility, somberness, structure and realism, and true knowledge of history and karma.

Because the lusterless metal is so "dead" and resists interaction with other substances, it is used as containers for acids, like automobile batteries, and is used as a lining in pipes that carry corrosive substances. Similarly, the lead-tempered person is like an acid-proof container that stores up caustic feelings and anger. Phrases like "acid tongued" and "vitriolic" have their origins in this alchemical process of storing negative emotional energy.

On the psychological level, lead is symbolic of a person's inertness and unwillingness to change. There is a denial of all higher or spiritual energies, and the alchemists often portrayed the leaden person as lying in an open grave or hopelessly chained to matter in some way. A feeling of being trapped in material reality is symptomatic of a leaden attitude. Leaden people are stubborn, unyielding, and often control other people by making them wait. They must always be right, rarely accept blame or admit to being in error, and have no real regard for the truth of a situation. They may be religious but not spiritual. They tend to be suspicious of genius and inspiration, which they will often attribute to fantasy. They feel threatened by freedom of thought and expression, and sometimes use ridicule or try to "push people's buttons" to control it. They tend to be very uncreative, judgmental, and smug.

On the other hand, leaden people are grounded, earthy, and practical. They are good friends during times of bereavement—stalwart supports at funerals and deathbeds. Such people secretly crave stimulation, excitement, and new ideas. They gravitate to people who supply energy and entertainment in their lives. This craving for stimulation often makes them focus on nervous energy instead of higher inspiration. Therefore, Saturn's children can be very reactive and excitable instead of lethargic, as they try to escape from their prison of matter.

As soon as bright, fresh lead metal is exposed to air, it forms a dull gray oxide layer called the "litharge" that resists any further chemical interaction. In alchemy, air is associated with spiritual energy, and lead reacts to it by instantly forming a barrier or blocking it. Likewise, one of the distinguishing characteristics of someone with a lead temperament is his or her lack of interest in spiritual ideas. There is also a general lack of interest in life in general, and leaden people often seem lazy, lethargic, or unresponsive.

In the individual, lead absorbs the inner light or insight necessary for personal growth and blocks all outside "radiations," such as attempts at spiritual instruction by others. Because psychological lead absorbs both the deeper vibrations of intuition and higher spiritual energies and aspirations, the person with a lead temperament is uninspired, unimaginative, and lacks that creative spark so necessary for positive change. Before long, the lead person starts to feel trapped in his or her dull environment and seeks out excitement, death-defying feats, lively people, and challenging conversation. Their favorite color is often red, and unconsciously, they are seeking the alchemical element of Fire. Fire is one of the Four Elements that represents activity, energy, creative thinking, and transformation. Fire is the tool alchemists use to begin the transmutation of lead into gold as well as transform leaden consciousness into a golden awareness of higher reality. In the laboratory, the changes in the metal and in the alchemist take place simultaneously. Otherwise, there can be no real transformation.

The alchemists transmuted the lead temperament using the Fire operation of calcination, which we will examine and apply to personal transformation in Chapter 14: Personal Purification.

Healing with Lead

Physically, lead and Saturn rule the bones, teeth, spleen, and slow chronic processes such as aging. The therapeutic effects are contracting, coagulating, drying, and mineralizing. Saturn-ruled plants like spinach, potatoes, wheat, horsetail, and mullein enhance the structures of life. They give a sobriety of disposition, enabling one to see limitations. These plants give steadiness, solidity of purpose, subtlety, diplomacy, patience, and an ability to work better on the physical plane.

Saturnic or leaden energies are needed for those who have a hard time finishing projects or for those with plenty of ideas but who never realize them. Alchemists seeking to produce physical effects found in saturnine elixirs the essential vibratory rate that enabled materialization. They believed that each metal had its own vibratory rate or frequency from the lowest in lead to the highest in gold. Generally speaking, any other elixir mixed with a Saturn elixir will be grounded, which makes it of great value when working on physical or bodily phenomenon. Its physical therapeutic properties become refrigerant, antipyretic, sedative, styptic, and astringent.

For instance, if one mixed a saturnine elixir with a mercurial one, the alchemists believed it would release knowledge contained in secret magical manuscripts or in ancient Hermetic traditions, because the Saturn-Mercury vibration contained all hidden knowledge of an esoteric nature within it. Alchemical oils were mixed in the same way; for example, to treat leukemia, alchemists would prescribe an equal mixture of lead oil and gold oil.

The alchemists made an Oil of Lead that was good for "growth of bones after breaking, strengthening the skeleton, osteoporosis and atrophy of the bones, stimulation of the spleen, drying tissue, reducing secretions and discharges, stopping bleeding, reducing fever, increasing patience, and stopping visions and an overactive imagination." They also suggested it for hallucinations due to neurological disorders that had delirious after-effects such as encephalitis and post-traumatic stress syndrome. In the "like cures like" philosophy of homeopathy, lead is used to treat sclerosis, the hardening of bones and arteries, which is the hallmark of old age and signature of lead. The homeopathic name of lead is *Plumbum metallicum.*

7

Jupiter's Rule: The Courtly Metal Tin

NATIVE TIN IS KNOWN AS *STANNUM*, which is the Latin word for tin and also gives the metal its chemical symbol (Sn). The alchemical symbol is ♃, which shows the lunar principle of soul above the cross of the elements or emerging from the darkness of matter.

Tin is a shiny, silvery white metal that is malleable, somewhat ductile (easily drawn out and shaped) and sectile (easily cut with a knife), and seems like a perfected form of lead to the casual observer. In fact, the Romans called tin *Plumbum album* or "white lead." Tin resists weathering and does not oxidize, and tin utensils buried underground or lost at sea in sunken ships shone like new when rediscovered after hundreds of years. "Tinkers" were Gypsy craftsmen who wandered from neighborhood to neighborhood in Europe repairing tin kettles and utensils or melting them down and recasting them. Native or elemental tin is extremely rare in nature and is found with gold and copper deposits. The metal was considered "semi-noble" in ancient times and was used for jewelry in Babylonia and Egypt. The Romans used it to make mirrors, and it was used as coinage in Europe at one time.

Tin has a highly crystalline structure, and due to the breaking of these crystals, a "cry" is heard when a tin bar is bent. Unlike lead, tin has pleasing acoustic effects and is used in the making of bells. Common gray tin has crystals with a cubic structure, but when heated or frozen it changes into white tin, which has a tetragonal structure. After further heating or freezing, white tin disintegrates into a powdery substance. This powder has the ability to "infect" other tin surfaces it comes in contact with by forming blisters that spread until all the metal "sickens" and disintegrates. This transformation is encouraged by impurities such as zinc and aluminum and can be prevented by adding small amounts of antimony or bismuth to the metal. The sickness of tin was called the "tin plague" and was the scourge of tin roofs during Europe's frigid winters. The mysterious effect was first noticed as "growths" on organ pipes in European cathedrals, where it was thought to be the work of the devil to disfigure God's work.

Tin metal has only a few practical uses and most tin is used in alloys. Bronze is an alloy of 5 percent tin and 95 percent copper, and the development of bronze by humans marked a new age of advancement known as the Bronze Age. Most solder is a combination of tin and lead; pewter is also an alloy of tin and lead. Other tin alloys are used to make tin cans and tin roofs, and tin has significant use as a corrosion fighter in the protection of other metals. Tin resists sea and soft tap water, but is attacked by strong acids, alkalis, and acid salts. When heated in air, tin forms tin oxide, which is used to plate steel and make tin cans. Other uses are in type metal, fusible metal, babbitt metal (the metal used for ball bearings), and die-casting alloys. Tin chloride is used as a reducing agent and mordant in calico printing. Tin salts sprayed onto glass are used to produce electrically conductive coatings, which are used for panel lighting and for frost-free windshields. Window glass is made by floating molten glass on molten tin to produce a flat surface. A crystalline tin-niobium alloy is superconductive at very low temperatures, and shoebox-sized electromagnets made of the wire produce magnetic fields comparable to conventional electromagnets weighing hundreds of tons.

The distribution of tin on earth follows an ecliptic at an angle of 23.5 degrees to the equator that is an exact track of the orbit of Jupiter slicing through the planet. Even stranger, these jovian forces seem to form tin veins that zigzag through the rocks in a lightning-bolt pattern. This is no haphazard effect, but an astonishing confirmation of Jupiter freeing the metals from their Saturnine prison on earth. Goethe was just one great alchemical philosopher who believed this. "A remarkable influence proceeds from the metal tin," he wrote. "This has a differentiating influence, and opens a door through which a way is provided for different metals to be formed from primeval rocks."

Tin ore minerals include oxide minerals like cassiterite and a few sulfides such as franckeite. By far the most tin comes from cassiterite or tin oxide. Reduction of this ore in burning coal results in tin metal and was probably how tin was made by the ancients. Cassiterite is a black or reddish brown mineral that has ornately faceted specimens with a greasy, high luster. It is generally opaque, but its luster and multiple crystal faces cause a sparkling surface. Cassiterite has been an important ore of tin for thousands of years and is still the greatest source of tin today. Most aggregate specimens of cassiterite show crystal twins, with the typical twin bent almost at a sixty-degree angle to form a distinctive "Elbow Twin." Other crystalline forms include eight-sided prisms and four-sided pyramids. Cassiterite is sometimes found in nature associated with topaz and fluorite gemstones.

Tin has a surprising affinity for silica and shares its crystalline structure. In the jovian ring on our planet where native tin is found, the metal lies in silica veins of quartz and granite. In the body, high concentrations of tin and silica are found in the boundary layer of the skin, and tin reacts with silica acid in many of the "shaping" processes of growth. In the Middle Ages, sick people were served food on a tin plate and drinks in a tin vessel to help them regenerate and recover their strength. Today, we know that tin acts as a bactericide and pesticide.

Tin carries the preserving qualities of Jupiter. Flowers last longer in tin vases, and food has been preserved in tin cans (actually a thin layer of tin on iron) for over a century. Beer (ruled by the jovial Jupiter) is said to taste best from a tin mug.

Correspondences of Tin

Planet: Jupiter
Sign: Sagittarius and Pisces
Day: Thursday
Musical note: Re
Gender: Male
Gemstone: Amethyst
Chakra: Svadhisthana (genital)
Organ: Blood
Element: Water

Experiment 7: The Call of Tin

Jupiter is usually an easy planet to find in the night sky. Look up in your newspaper or online, the rising and setting times and position of Jupiter for your location. Then go outside one night and gaze on the planet while holding a piece of tin metal or something containing pure tin on its outer surface, such as babbitt metal or an uncoated tin can. Become empty and let the planet influence you. Do this until you feel a real connection with the distant planet. You should be able to feel a resonance building between you and the distant orb. You are experiencing the metal's true signature or living correspondence with its planetary twin and confirmation of the Hermetic axiom of "As Above, so Below." Record your impressions and feelings during this meditation.

The Tin Temperament

Psychologically, the focus of the tin temperament is on sensuality and there is a greater interaction with others than seen in the leaden person. Still, most of the control at this level comes from unconscious impulses. As tin is transformed, a person is dominated by dreams and powerful undercurrents of emotion. Only by fully integrating the contents of the personal unconscious, can tin be successfully transmuted into a higher metal. Repressed feelings form knots or blockages in our bodies that cause symptoms of armoring reminiscent of the "tin man." These blockages have both a psychic and a physiological reality, and often it is necessary to seek outside assistance or achieve great inner objectivity to remove them.

Jupiterian or "jovial" energies are expansive and cheerful but tend to be lacking in depth. That is true of the tin temperament too. Jovial people are often inflated, expansive, and can be seen as overly spiritual. They tend to talk endlessly about obvious or mundane things and can be perceived as thoughtless, shallow, and even licentious. They are judgmental and often blame others for their mistakes. They have access to spiritual forces but are unable to control them because of lack of depth and presence. Finding one's soul mate, working relentlessly with alchemical techniques, learning to relax deeply, and meditating to find one's genuine identity, are methods of transforming the tin temperament.

Tin is used in magical rituals and spells to promote abundance, prosperity, success in business and in legal matters, stimulation, energy, healing, regeneration, and rejuvenation, and to attract what you desire. Standard amulets and talismans for tin are usually made of pewter and charged with Jovian energy. Such energy is said to be transmitted by lightning and the thunderbolt, and in Tibetan ceremonies, the dorje (meaning "thunderbolt") is the stylized magical instrument of these powers.

The alchemists transmuted the tin temperament using the water operation of dissolution, which we will examine and apply to personal transformation in Chapter 14: Personal Purification.

Healing with Tin

Jupiter rules growth, the metabolic system, the liver, the tongue, saliva, and the enrichment of the blood from food. Jupiter's therapeutic effects are antispasmodic and hepatic. Jupiter-ruled plants like asparagus, eggplant, grapes, lemon balm, and olives, preserve the body and promote healthy growth and are the natural healing herbs of the planetary system. They affect the mind in such a way as to promote an understanding of ritual from the highest point of view, and religious leaders, doctors, lawyers, and so on will find great benefit from Jovian elixirs. They also attune one to the wealth vibration and open up channels for growth and expansion, materially as well as spiritually. Jupiter-Mercury combinations produce insight into the philosophical principles of any system and their part in the cosmic scheme and provide an intuitive understanding of the great spiritual masters.

The alchemists made an Oil of Tin that was used to treat the liver (jaundice, hepatitis, cirrhosis), certain types of eczema, liquid ovarian cysts, inflammatory effusions, pleurisies, acne, water retention, and certain types of obesity. This oil was said to be excellent for someone "losing shape." The oil was also used as a sweat inducer, wormer, antispasmodic, cathartic, and laxative.

The polar (opposite) metal to tin is mercury, and Oil of Tin was said to be an excellent antidote for mercury poisoning; likewise mercury was said to balance the bad effects of tin. Tin and mercury oil combined are said to provide deep insight and cure lightheadedness and certain phases of manic-bipolar disorder.

The homeopathic form of tin is called *Stannum*, a remedy which is said to strengthen and regenerate muscle and brain tissue. It is also a remedy for the joints and connective tissue of ligaments and cartilage. *Stannum* is allegedly beneficial in liver disease and is used for congestion, hardening of tissues, encephalitis, and other illnesses where the fluid balance is upset.

8

Mars's Challenge: The Angry Metal Iron

IRON IS THE SECOND OLDEST METAL known to man (after lead) and was known in prehistoric times. Genesis says that Tubal Cain, seven generations from Adam, was "an instructor of every artificer in brass and iron." Iron was smelted by the Egyptians at least as far back as 1500 B.C. and iron artifacts from Asia have been identified from around 3000 B.C. A remarkable wrought iron pillar nearly twenty-five feet high, dating to about 400 A.D., remains standing today in Delhi, India. Corrosion to the pillar has been minimal despite its exposure to the wet weather since it was erected.

Our word "iron" comes from the Anglo-Saxon word "iren," although that word is derived from earlier words meaning "holy metal," because it was used to make the swords used in the Crusades. The chemical symbol for iron, Fe, comes from the Latin word for iron (*ferrum*). The root of the Latin word means "to create, to form, to bear forth." The alchemical cipher for iron is ♂, which is also the symbol for the male generative force. In iron we recognize the male and active character of the war god Mars, building and conquering in a new and sometimes hostile world. As we have only recently learned, it is the massive amounts of iron oxide on its surface that gives the planet Mars its red color, though that correspondence would hardly have surprised the ancients.

Iron is a relatively abundant element in the universe. It is found in the sun and many types of stars in considerable quantity since iron nuclei are very stable. Iron is a vital constituent of plant and animal life on earth, and is the key component of hemoglobin in the blood. The pure metal is not often encountered in modern commercial applications but is usually alloyed with carbon or other metals. The pure metal is very reactive chemically and rapidly corrodes, especially in moist air or at elevated temperatures. However, as an oxide and in other ores, iron is the most abundant metal on earth, forming up to 5 percent of the planet's crust.

Native iron is quite often a misnomer as natural pure iron is not necessarily "native" to earth, since it rarely occurs on the earth's surface by terrestrial processes. It is mostly found in the form of meteorites that have crashed into the earth's surface. All natural iron, whether it is native or meteoric, is actually an alloy of iron and nickel. The two elements are combined in varying percentages from less than 6 percent nickel to as much as 75 percent nickel, although iron is by far more common than nickel. Iron is steel gray or black with a metallic luster, and is somewhat malleable and strongly attracted to magnets. Iron filings cause spectacular sparks in flames and react explosively in a burning mixture of potassium chlorate and sucrose.

Iron has an unusual relationship with carbon and readily combines with it to form a nobler and stronger metal known as steel. European alchemists noticed this effect when they accidentally dropped bits of charcoal into molten iron. The iron hungrily "devoured" the charcoal to produce what we now call cast iron. While pure iron is soft and malleable, the new metal was hard and brittle. By controlling the amount of charcoal introduced, it is possible to produce steel, whose characteristics lie between the extremes of pure iron and cast iron. Nearly all iron produced today is used in the steel industry, which transforms iron into steel in carbon-based, forced-air blast furnaces. This process is one of the most significant industrial processes in history and originated in England around the year 1773. In the process, iron oxide is reduced with carbon and becomes coke. Because of this process, iron (and steel) is the most common metal in human civilization, even though native iron is extremely rare.

Iron also has an affinity for other metals, each of which adds different qualities to pure iron to produce unique forms of steel. The alchemists viewed these secondary metals as earthly spirits or "brothers of iron" and named them accordingly. Cobalt was associated with the "kobolds" or mischievous gnomes who live deep in the earth and help or hinder miners according to their whims. The alchemists considered cobalt an earthier and earlier form of iron. Nickel was associated with the "nixies" or underwater spirits. The alchemists viewed it as the "watery brother" of iron, which expressed itself in the shiny liquid surface of the pure metal and in the sea green compounds it produced, such as Green Vitriol. Manganese is the "fiery brother" of iron and produces red to flaming violet salts. Added to iron, it produces extremely hard and "dry" steel. Steel almost as hard as diamonds is produced by adding tungsten and vanadium to iron. Shiny chromium is iron's "sister" and restores the shiny liquid look of pure iron to steel.

In terrestrial deposits, iron is found with gold, platinum, and sulfide ores. In meteorites, iron is associated with silicon minerals and some other minerals that are only found in meteorites. The meteorites that contain iron-nickel crystals are fascinating in their possible origins and diversity. It is postulated that another planet similar to earth (a rocky planet) broke apart early in the formation of the solar system and is responsible for the iron-nickel debris that rains down upon the earth on a daily basis. Since it is known that the earth has a substantial amount of elemental iron and nickel in its core, this lends credence to this theory and gives us much to think about. However, many believe the meteor debris to be left over primordial material that the earth and the other planets were built from. Meteorites are very diverse and even novice collectors can distinguish samples from different meteorites by their unique character. Often these meteorites have inclusions of large crystals of other minerals or the iron has a unique crystal pattern that is characteristic.

Heavy dark iron oxides such as hematite, marcasite, magnetite, and siderite are the primary iron ores. Along with iron meteorites, they tend to exhibit distinctive radial and spherical crystalline spiraling, which is very significant in an esoteric sense. These signatures show the fundamental role that the iron archetype plays in the formation of matter in general.

Several noted astrologers believe that iron is the mechanism by which the ether penetrates the planet and human body and brings life force to dead matter. In *The Nature of Substance*, Rudolf Hauschka writes: "The spiral tendency always arises when time enters space and develops toward a center. The fact that this dynamic shows up so clearly in iron ores points to the fundamental role played by the iron process, for it transforms spherical forces quite unrelated to the laws of earth into radial forces working toward a center. One can say that the function of iron is to help cosmic, weightless elements to enter the sphere of gravity. Iron is the only substance which makes visible in an archetypal picture the incarnating force during its spiral descent, for a path followed by meteors is indeed a spiral, the result of interacting radial and spherical forces."

The most valued iron mineral is olivine, which is actually a general term for several silicon minerals in which iron and magnesium are always present in varying degrees. Olivine is also known as "chrysolite" and "evening emerald" (or peridot). Chrysolite is light yellowish green olivine; evening emerald is a name given to olivine's darker gemstone variety, peridot, which is the birthstone of August. The most attractive peridots have an iron percentage of less than 15 percent. When iron is present predominately, the mineral is not as attractive (heavier and darker than the higher magnesium varieties) and rarely qualifies as a gemstone.

Olivine minerals have a high melting point and are the first minerals to form crystals in magma or lava containing high iron and magnesium content. In fact, olivine minerals make up most of the molten magma in the earth's mantle and are the most common rocks by volume on the planet, although on the surface and in the crust they are not nearly as common. Olivine is also found in many iron meteorites—not just as small grains but as significantly sized crystals sometimes occupying over 50 percent of the meteorite's volume. Thinly cut slices of these meteorites are extremely attractive with the polished steel gray of the iron and the embedded grains of gemlike green olivine. The effect produces the closest mineral equivalent to stained glass artwork.

Marcasite, also known as fool's gold or pyrite (iron sulfide FeS_2), is an ore of sulfur that has bonded with iron. It is so common in the earth's crust that it is found almost everywhere. Its beautiful golden luster has often been mistaken for gold nuggets, and it is frequently found in gold deposits. Like gold, pyrite carries the esoteric signature of the sun—a flattened round variety called a "Pyrite Sun" is popular with collectors. Strangely, pyrite's structure is exactly the same as the lead sulfide ore galena. The only difference is that the single sulfur atom of galena is replaced by a pair of sulfur atoms in pyrite. This pair of atoms disrupts the intense fourfold symmetry of the more "ancient" galena. In other words, in the evolution of the metals, the existence of iron has freed the lead archetype of its stubborn materiality and form.

Iron and steel are used in rituals, magical spells, talismans, and amulets to promote energy, strength, determination, willpower, assertiveness, and aggressiveness. They are also used in fertility rites, new beginnings and undertakings, and for speed, power, and courage. The wearing of iron jewelry is thought to bring these same characteristics.

The social implications of the use of iron are a little disturbing to think about. Throughout its history, iron has always served man's will in his weaponry or in the industrial conquest of nature. In classical mythology, the Age of Iron is the final and worst age of the world, marked by selfishness and degeneracy. The negative expression of iron is in the coldhearted struggle for material possessions in a world in which only the fittest (or the richest) survive. From any objective assessment of modern civilization, that seems to be the direction in which we are heading. If the predominance of the iron archetype in our culture continues, we can only expect a further rationalization of nature and mechanization of life. Some spiritual groups, such as the druids, were aware of the dangers of the iron archetype and actually forbade its use in their culture.

Alchemists too were aware of the hidden signatures of iron and the social implications of the Iron Age. In *Alchemy*, Titus Burckhardt quotes several alchemists describing the Iron Age as "an active descent of the Spirit into the lowest levels of human consciousness, so at this stage of the Work, the Spirit appears submerged in the body and as if extinguished in it. This is the outermost Coagulation, and the threshold of the final completion—the transformation of the body into the Spirit-become-form." The incarnating and "fixing" function of iron is predominant on two planets in our solar system (Earth and Mars), and in some ways we could share a common origin and a common fate. "We came to know the Mars process as the force that makes incarnating possible," writes Rudolf Hauschka. "Thus there must always have been a stronger than usual bond between Earth and Mars, even before the Earth became a solid body."

Correspondences of Iron

Planet: Mars

Sign: Aries and Scorpio

Day: Tuesday

Musical note: Mi

Gender: Male

Gemstone: Bloodstone, hematite

Chakra: Manipura (solar plexus)

Organ: Liver

Element: Fire

Experiment 8: The Call of Iron

During the early spring, preferably sometime in March, go outside and find the red planet Mars in the night sky. Relax and try to focus all your attention on the tiny red sphere. Relax completely with an open and quiet mind. Become empty and let the planet influence you. Do this until you feel a real connection with the distant planet. Continue gazing upon Mars and place a piece of iron in your hand or a small cast iron pot or other object, but not something made of steel or chromed. You should be able to feel a resonance building. It is what alchemists refer to as the "call of iron." You are experiencing the metal's true signature or living correspondence with its planetary twin. See how your feelings compare to how the alchemists felt about this powerful metal.

The Iron Temperament

Mars and iron rule the aggressive impulses within us, both individually and collectively. Within us, our iron temperament governs the characteristics of anger, uncontrolled and aggressive self-assertion, lust for power, ego identity, willpower, passion, creativity, and courage. It is our challenge to transform the Mars within into the expression of divine qualities, rather than the selfish fulfillment of the senses. Mars reinforces the ego and individuality, strengthens will, and helps surpass previous limitations. The red planet governs the animal soul, passions, and the survival instinct.

In psychological terms, the iron temperament is the seat of our will to power to control others, and our concerns about providing for material needs in the world. By transmuting iron, we learn to assert ourselves without dominating or submitting to others. We gain insight into our behavior and become aware of the forces of the soul within. The iron temperament makes us determined and hard, but like the metal, the iron temperament is inflexible and brittle and cracks or breaks if bent. Iron also loves air and the iron temperament seeks higher inspiration or fresh spirit.

The paradox of iron is that it is only through iron that we can marshal the energies necessary to transmute iron. That is born out in the signature of the most revered arcanum, the ancient chemical of transformation, Green Vitriol, which is a combination of natural iron and sulfuric acid. It is the Vitriol within us that will transform us. Without it, all is lost to illusion and complacency.

The alchemists transmuted the iron temperament using the air operation of separation, which we will examine and apply to personal transformation in Chapter 14: Personal Purification.

Healing with Iron

Physically, Mars rules the blood, adrenal glands, genitals, and the immune system. Martian herbs like chives, cumin, leeks, and nettles strengthen the blood and immune system, and they make one more aware of the functions of the organs and body. Their physical therapeutic properties are stimulative, caustic, and tonic. Martian elixirs release the action potential of the soul of something.

When mixed with other herbs, Martian herbs activate the potentialities of the other herbs, to a great degree making them more forceful in application and generally more active. Mars herbs are wonderful tonics when mixed with Sun herbs. The combination gives great physical energy, tones the muscles, and increases sexual potency. They also provoke self-reliance, spontaneity, and independence. If the alchemist is involved in magical evocation, a mixture of a Mars, moon, and mercurial elixirs are said to assist in manifesting the desired result because the planetary energies combine energy and the powers of transformation.

Spagyrically, iron is associated with the life force in blood and the energy obtained from meat, as well as beets, dark green vegetables, whole grains, dried fruits, nuts, apple syrup, and seaweed. Plants containing a lot of iron, like urtica, equisetum, kelp, and spirulina, are thought to provide energy.

In the human body iron is found in the blood (providing energy and clear thinking) and the liver (associated with positivity and willpower). In medical astrology, Mars is connected with the red blood cells, the adrenal glands, the muscles, the male reproductive organs, fever, and inflammation (and other complaints of too much Fire). The iron in blood makes it red and fuels metabolism. When we inhale, the iron molecule hemoglobin binds with oxygen and distributes it throughout our body; when we exhale, it unites with carbon dioxide and carries the by-products of our combustion back to our lungs where they are expelled. Thus, iron is intimately responsible for the process of breathing, which is how bodily energies are controlled in both Taoist and Tantric alchemy. Manganese, the "fiery brother" of iron, performs the same function in the chlorophyll of plants in combining with carbon dioxide that iron performs in the blood with hemoglobin in combining with oxygen. These two "breathing" metals are very similarly constructed.

In most applications in the plant and animal kingdoms, iron acts as a carrier of life force and rejuvenator, but when iron becomes too predominant (as in the modern world), it becomes destructive to life and tends to rigidify and mechanize living systems. "The Mars impulses at work in iron," notes Rudolf Hauschka, "are the carriers of the forces of embodiment, but these forces lead to mummification if they become too active and overwhelm the system."

The alchemists made an Oil of Iron that they believed was regenerative, "purifying the blood, healing wounds and cuts, soothing the gall bladder, stimulating the pancreas, stopping bleeding ulcers, strengthening bone marrow, increasing the organism's sensitivity, enhancing instincts, and enhancing passion." The known biological effects of iron are that it is antiakathisic, antianemic, anticheilitic, and antimenorrhagic. Exemplary homeopathic iron remedies are *Ferrum phosphoricum* and *Ferrum metalicum*.

9

Venus's Embrace: The Loving Metal Copper

COPPER IS A REDDISH BROWN METAL with a bright metallic luster. It is in the same group in the periodic table as gold, and like gold, it is remarkably ductile. It is also very malleable and sectile (it can be pounded into other shapes and cut into slices) and is an excellent conductor of heat and electricity. Molten copper is a sea green color, and copper tarnishes with a green color and burns with a blue-green flame with flashes of red, which alchemists sometimes described as Venus, the metal's archetypal planetary source, dressed in a blue cloak over a red gown.

Venus and copper have been associated for eons, and both are associated with love and intercourse; for example, the Venus moon sometimes appears during a lunar eclipse when the earth's shadow causes the moon to take on a distinctive copper color. During this period, which can last over two hours, planting actions like sowing and lovemaking are said to be especially fertile.

The discovery of copper dates from prehistoric times, and copper beads dating back to 9000 B.C. have been found in Iraq. Copper pottery dating from 4900 B.C. has been unearthed in Egypt. In fact, native copper has been mined for so long that it is now all but depleted. The name for the metal comes from the Latin word *cuprum*, meaning the island of Cyprus, which was one of the main copper mining areas in the ancient world. Actually, the island took its name from the Assyrian word for copper (*kipar*).

Part of the reason for copper being used so early is that it is so easy to shape. Methods for refining copper from its ores were discovered around 5000 B.C., and Phoenicians and Sumerians made all their tools and weapons from copper. Then, around 3100 B.C., Egyptian alchemists discovered that when copper is mixed with other metals, the resulting alloys are harder than copper itself. Both brass (a mixture of copper and zinc) and bronze (a mixture of copper and tin) are harder than copper. The discovery of bronze changed the evolution of mankind, and the Bronze Age began around 2100 B.C.

The origin of the glyph for copper and Venus ($♀$) is the symbol for the life force used by the Egyptians. Known as the *ankh*, it depicts a circle over a cross, denoting the emergence of the solar archetype from the cross of the elements or the triumph of spirit (life force) over matter. Copper is a necessary chemical in venous blood that carries toxic substances to the excretory system. In sea creatures (such as snails, mollusks, crabs, and squid), copper (as hemocyanin) takes the place of hemoglobin as the chemical of the blood and respiration. Copper is abundant in the female sex organs, and some studies suggest copper in the body is used up during sexual intercourse. Copper is also present in gallstones, which medieval physicians blamed on lack of sexual activity.

Unlike lead ore, copper ore has a great affinity for water, and soluble copper salts (such as copper sulfate and copper chloride) contain as much as 35 percent water. In fact, its ability to absorb water and change its form and color is one of the attributes of copper and makes it an important chemical of life. Copper veins run extensively throughout the planet, and it combines readily with other elements to form alloys or transform substances into complex salts. In fact, copper is so ready to combine and enter into deep transformation with other substances that the alchemists called the metal *meretrix metallorum* ("harlot of the metals").

Copper shows a special love for sulfur, and geologists agree that copper and sulfur have been locked in the bowels of the earth since primordial times. Copper sulfate is one of the most beautiful and useful compounds formed by copper. It was known as "Blue Vitriol" to the alchemists. It dries into a white powder when exposed to air but rapidly returns to its beautiful blue crystals when exposed to water. This is an exception to the normal behavior of copper, since the metal rarely shows crystal faces or forms whole crystals in its salts.

Copper has many applications in the modern world, including in wiring, electrical components, pennies and other coins, tubing, and so on. Most modern copper production is from sulfide ores containing little copper but quite a bit of iron, and copper smelters present major environmental challenges. Complex procedures are used to create a form of copper sulfide appropriate for final reduction with a copper oxide. The resulting crude copper is purified using an electrolytic procedure involving plating onto pure copper cathodes. This purification step leaves an "anode slime" that contains useful amounts of silver and gold.

Copper is used in rituals, spells, and amulets to promote love, sensuality, friendship, positive relationships of any kind, fruitful negotiations, and peace, and the metal has always been associated with beauty and harmony in the world. Egyptian women used the powdered copper ore malachite to beautify their eyes, and copper pigments make wonderfully colorful paints and ink. Other colorful copper ores include azurite, dioptase, and bornite, whose colors range from green and blue to purple and red. Much of the wonderful colors in birds are made possible by the presence of copper in feathers, and some birds (such as the alchemically symbolic peacock) have up to 6 percent copper in their pigmentation.

Combining copper with zinc produces brass, which is an important and sacred metal in many parts of the world that brings the signatures of gold within reach of the common person. In modern alchemy, zinc is associated with the planet Uranus, and both were discovered at about the same time. In astrology, Uranus is associated with the sign of Aquarius and connected with renewal, moderation, revolution, originality, and progressivity. The god Uranus granted man the divine flame (electricity, intuition, sudden insights, cosmic consciousness) and the feeling for cosmic rhythms. Medical astrology places the potential and the rhythmical processes of the nervous system under zinc and Uranus. Brass and zinc are used in rituals, spells, and talismans, to promote originality, flashes of insight, renewal, inventions, advanced technology, cooperation within a like-minded group, humanism, and freedom of thought.

Correspondences of Copper

Planet: Venus

Sign: Taurus and Libra

Day: Friday

Musical note: Fa

Gender: Female

Gemstone: Adventurine, malachite, emerald

Chakra: Anahata (heart)

Organ: Kidneys & throat

Element: Water

Experiment 9: The Call of Copper

Pick up a piece of copper and the first thing you notice is its surprising feeling of warmth and moisture. It is that connection to something archetypal and nourishing that makes up the signature of this metal. It is easy to connect with copper, just as its planet (Venus) is easy to see in the sky. It is so brilliant it is often mistaken for a bright star or even a UFO. The best time to see it is in the early evening or morning when it is close to the horizon. In fact, Venus has been called both the "Morning Star" and the "Evening Star" and is associated with magical energies. It is the "first star I see tonight" upon which one makes a wish that will come true by means of the sympathetic Venusian energies. On some clear night or morning, go outside and find the planet Venus. Relax and try to focus all your attention on the brilliant white sphere. Relax completely with an open and quiet mind. Become empty and let the planet influence you. Do this until you feel a real connection with the distant planet. Continue gazing upon the planet and grab a piece of copper, a fistful of pennies, or even a copper cooking utensil. You should be able to feel a warm resonance building. That deep and soothing vibration is not your imagination. It is what alchemists refer to as the "call of copper." You are experiencing the metal's true signature or living correspondence with its planetary twin.

The Copper Temperament

The veiled planet Venus represents refinement of the senses, the arts, mystical love, desire, and earthly relationships. She was considered to be the feminine goddess of love and beauty just as her counterpart, Mars, was thought of as the masculine god of war and strife. These two archetypes complement each other perfectly and work as a polarity, manifesting a tension of the masculine and feminine, which offers a complete picture of human existence on the material and emotional levels. In the Depth Psychology pioneered by Carl Jung, these archetypes are often thought of as the anima (feminine soul) and animus (masculine spirit). It is believed that until a person can bring both of these forces into conscious awareness and learn to balance and accept them fully, he or she cannot be a complete individual. If we repress or deny one of these forces within ourselves we can contribute to a submerged, destructive energy (the shadow) that will manifest in self-defeating behaviors such as strong aggression or extreme passivity.

Venus represents the psychological function of judging and evaluating experience through the inner, subjective, feminine impulse in both sexes. Without the Venusian archetype, we would have to rely totally on our objective senses and the concrete mind to evaluate others. Even our intuition would not be able to function correctly without the channel of Venus to bring our insights to conscious awareness.

The copper temperament is associated with the powers of touch and speech, balanced feelings and ascending mind. The idea expressed here is the creation of the feeling intellect, the union of the female and male aspects of consciousness in a new state of truth-based intuition. In developing his or her copper temperament, the true heart of the initiate is actualized. In alchemical terms, this is the marriage of the sun and moon, the solar and lunar ways of knowing, the coming together of the forces of spirit and soul. While there is less self-serving attachment to other people, there is also greater caring and responsiveness exhibited at this level. There arises a giving, optimistic person in place of the previous manipulative one. As the transmutation of copper continues, the alchemist begins to exercise free will, unencumbered by buried emotions, addictions, impulses, and instincts.

Copper needs to work with the element of Earth, but too much Earth here produces someone who is materialistic and overly practical, and could produce a "user" mentality or mimic the "take everything I can" attitude of Iron.

In alchemical astrology, Neptune is considered the "higher octave" of Venus. Neptune represents unconditional love—a love that embraces all creation, is totally accepting and without discrimination or judgment. While many of us strive to attain unconditional love of others and ourselves, we must first travel with Venus and copper in order to learn personal love. Until we have had the experiences that Venus brings us through relationships, either with people or things, we cannot reach the expanded consciousness that the transpersonal planet Neptune promises.

The alchemists transmuted the copper temperament using the Earth element operation of conjunction, which we will examine and apply to personal transformation in Chapter 15: Becoming an Alchemist.

Healing with Copper

For many centuries, European apothecaries carried the Powder of Sympathy, which was a form of copper vitriol. Whole books were written about its amazing power to heal wounds, including titles by physicians and noblemen (such as the *Discourse Touching the Cure of Wounds by the Powder of Sympathy* written in 1658 in the court of Charles I). The powder was not applied directly to the wound, but blood or bandages from the wound were placed in a bowl of water containing a handful of copper vitriol powder. The copper solution never touched the wound but healed by "sympathy" or through "etheric conductivity." In any case, patients immediately reported a cooling effect that diminished pain and resulted in rapid healing of the wound.

Copper metal was also applied directly to afflicted areas. For instance, to alleviate the symptoms of influenza, a medieval physician would prescribe rubbing the forehead with copper metal twice daily. It was also said to strengthen the blood and clean the arteries. Copper metal or powdered copper was also rubbed on sore joints to ease the pain of arthritis, neuralgia, and rheumatism—a tradition carried on today in the therapeutic wearing of copper bracelets.

Copper metal kills germs, fungi, and algae, and a copper coin dropped into a vase of flowers or aquarium will keep the water fresh longer. Florists provide copper salts in small plastic bags for this purpose. Even brass doorknobs have been shown to kill the germs of infected guests. Biologically, copper is antiarthritic, anti-inflammatory, antispasmodic, and has been used to control pain, lower cholesterol and high blood sugar, as well as treat schizophrenia. It stimulates the *veinous stasi* in the human organism, and it removes the affections of its key organ, the kidneys, and also the thyroid. It is excellent in post-traumatic problems such as after accidents and surgery, and in convalescence. Copper is also useful in controlling the bad effect of an excess of its metal in polarity: iron.

Using copper pans and utensils in the kitchen reduces the risk of passing germs on to food, and copper pans distribute heat evenly and cook foods faster and more thoroughly. However, as we have noted, copper is a notorious "harlot" when it comes to combining with substances, so be careful what you cook in copper pans. In some cases, poisonous substances could be formed. The alchemists used copper pans and cauldrons to infuse their extracts and tinctures with Venus energy and were aware of the possible combinations and salts that could be formed.

The alchemists believed that deficiencies of copper in the body caused thyroid problems, sexual dysfunction, poor circulation, cramps, aneurysms, multiple sclerosis, epilepsy, and even mental illnesses. There is some modern evidence that copper deficiencies can result in gray hair, wrinkles, crow's feet, varicose veins, and saggy skin. Since the liver is rich in copper, liver extracts were often used to treat such maladies.

Experimenters have discovered that copper wire or tubing twisted into an open circle (ends overlapping but not touching) and placed around a tree or plant enhances growth and prevents disease. Similar copper "relaxation circuits" are used to balance the body's natural energy. Copper plough tips do not dry out soil as iron ploughs do, and some farmers use fine copper filings to "charge" the soil or produce more powerful compost. Other researchers use copper chromatographic techniques to test the quality of compost material. In some Wiccan rites, copper objects are used in ritual copulation ceremonies to ensure the fertility of the land.

Physically, Venus rules the face, skin, and the kidneys, and copper's therapeutic properties are softening of tissues, easing of kidney ailments, and purging of the stomach. Venus-ruled plants like apples, strawberries, pears, cinnamon, peppermint, and alfalfa affect celestial form and magnetic qualities and give an ability to attract. In medical astrology, the skin, kidneys, veins, and pancreas are the Venusian body parts. The female body needs more copper during pregnancy to support the placenta and nourish the fetus. To support the Venusian body parts, such practitioners recommend consuming food that contains a lot of copper, such as lettuce, apricots, persimmons, tomatoes, nuts, and black cherries.

Standard medical tests using copper chloride solution are used to detect a variety of diseases in the blood, while alternative healers have discovered that herbs containing copper metal seem to react to human blood samples by mimicking the shapes and arrangements of corpuscles. Homeopathic copper is used to treat leg cramps and children's growing pains in general, as well as convulsions, diabetes, and to stimulate the kidneys. Homeopathy uses copper under the name *Cuprum metallicum*.

Copper's "ally and alloy"—zinc—also exhibits healing properties. A zinc pendant or mineral supplement can calm down a surplus of nervous energy, and zinc is used to treat nervous stress, restless legs, nervous asthma, hyperventilation, stammering, nervous heart complaints, epilepsy, cramps, agitation, and Alzheimer's disease. Homeopathy works with the remedy *Zincum metallicum*.

The Venusian signature gives refinement of senses and the ability to appreciate beauty. Artists, actors, and others in the public eye will find these elixirs a great aid to performing their work. Venus herbs also enhance the taste perceptions, promote affection, give an amiable disposition, and make one more psychically sensitive to astral influences. For those who feel a lack of charm, or some of the softer human qualities, a Venusian elixir will stimulate the right vibration in your aura. Venusian elixirs also promote harmony and balance within our being and in our dealings with others. Venusian elixirs are said to give access to that realm of the astral that is intimately connected with the working and forces of the most intimate magic of nature. They are a great aid to alchemists who wish to make herbal alchemy their life work, as they open up the human consciousness to the secrets of the plant kingdom. Naturalists will find these elixirs most illuminating, as they will give conscious contact with the various "deities" of long past nature religions.

The alchemists' Oil of Copper was said to contain the soul of copper metal. They recommended it for blood pressure abnormalities, glandular problems, low energy, impure blood, kidney problems, infectious diseases, liver problems, skin infections, myocardial infarction, leukemia, Wilson's disease, cancer, thyroid gland abnormalities, reproductive organ problems, and chronic problems with dry or irritated mucous membranes. On the mental level, copper was said to increase one's personal magnetism and attraction to the opposite sex, increase psychic abilities, and give insight into the plant kingdom and nature in general.

Colloidal Copper

A colloid (pronounced "koloid") is a mixture in which one substance is divided into minute particles of pure elemental metal and dispersed throughout a liquid such as distilled water. Colloidal copper is produced electrically and charges the copper particles so they stay suspended in the solution. The electrical charge in colloids is a function of the total surface area of the particles. A one-inch metal cube has a surface area of six square inches but divide it into molecular-sized particles and the area increases to over five million square inches—each particle with a tiny electrical charge. Generally, metals in colloidal suspensions have no toxic effects.

One property of a colloid that distinguishes it from other solutions is that colloidal particles scatter light. If a light passes through a colloid, the light is reflected by the colloidal particles and the path of light can be seen by the naked eye. When a beam of light passes through a normal solution (such as a solution of table salt), there is so little scattering of the light that the path of light cannot be seen and can only be detected by certain sensitive instruments.

Colloidal copper is used to treat a variety of conditions, including restoring gray hair to its natural color, encouraging the growth of elastic fiber in the skin, increasing skin flexibility, and acting as an antiwrinkle agent.

10

Mercury's Magic: The Living Metal Quicksilver

MERCURY IS TRULY UNIQUE. It is the only metal that is liquid at room temperature and is the heaviest natural liquid on the planet. According to alchemical theory, all the metals began in the liquid state deep in the earth, but only mercury was able to retain its original innocence and life force and resist taking on a final form; for that reason, the ancients called it *Mercurius vivens* (the "living mercury"). This silvery liquid metal (also known as quicksilver) was known to ancient Chinese and Hindus before 2000 B.C. and has been found in sacred tubes in Egyptian tombs dating from 1500 B.C. It was first used to form alloys with other metals around 500 B.C. Because of mercruy's germ-killing properties, the Greeks added mercury to healing ointments (to the benefit of those afflicted with wounds and skin infections), and in the Middle Ages, Paracelsus used it successfully to treat syphilis. However, when the ancient Romans applied mercury compounds for long-term use in cosmetics, many beautiful women eventually died of its cumulative poisonous effects. Today, many popular brands of eye makeup still contain low levels of mercury.

Mercury the metal is named after Mercury the planet. The chemical abbreviation, Hg, is from the Latin word *hydrargyrum* (meaning "watery silver"). The alchemical symbol for mercury is ☿, which represents the androgynous state on all levels created by the union of the symbols for copper (or Venus) and iron (or Mars) in the Below and the union of the symbols for silver (or the Moon) and gold (or the Sun) in the Above. In 1807, English chemist John Dalton proposed using an eight-spoked wheel as mercury's symbol, which is similar to ancient Oriental ciphers for mercury (and the Wheel of Life).

Many of the typical mineralogical characteristics of the metals simply do not apply to mercury because it is a liquid: there is no hardness (since it cannot be scratched), no malleability, and no ductility. There is no crystal structure, no fracture, and no cleavage. Paradoxically, mercury is a comparatively poor conductor of heat yet is extremely sensitive to it and expands and contracts in a linear relationship to temperature (which is why it is used in thermometers). It is a fair conductor of electricity in its natural state but becomes one of the best conductors (between copper and gold) when frozen. In ancient times, mercury was transported in tightly sewn sheepskin bags and later in iron or glass bottles. The alloys of mercury are called "amalgams," and the ease with which mercury amalgamates with gold makes it of primary importance in the recovery of gold from its ores.

Amalgamation is one of the primary signatures of mercury, and it moistens and dissolves metals the way water dissolves salts. For this reason, the alchemists believed it was the key to the transformation of the metals. Mercury dissolves gold, silver, copper, tin, lead, zinc, cadmium, and all the alkaline metals, but does not affect iron or any members of the iron family (such as nickel and aluminum). The alchemists thought this was because iron and mercury have diametrically opposed signatures—iron representing the mechanical processes of consolidation and structuring and mercury representing the living processes of growth and mobility. The struggle for pre-eminence between the forces of iron and mercury are played out on all levels of planetary, social, and individual behavior. This archetypal process is most obvious in the two cultures of our civilization: science and the humanities. Science (and its partners in the military-industrial complex) seeks to aggressively and mechanically control nature and human behavior, while the humanities (expressed in art, literature, and religion) seek more reflective and passive methods of living in harmony with nature and giving freer expression to human behavior. Alchemy makes a point of combining both cultures into one holistic approach to the human condition.

Like iron, aluminum is considered antipathetic to mercury and more in line with mechanical systems than the "living" approach of mercury. Methods of producing aluminum are very technological and use massive amounts of electricity, and ubiquitous aluminum products (such as aluminum cans and other throwaway products) leave their antinature signature throughout the world. Lightweight and cheap aluminum carries the signature of the common man seduced by the modern technological world. Esoterically, aluminum dulls the senses and cuts off Hermetic inspiration. Cooking in aluminum pans has been linked with Alzheimer's disease, and aluminum utensils and containers quickly combine with lab chemicals to form poisonous compounds. Alchemists truly despise this metal, and no alchemist would even consider using aluminum in serious laboratory work.

Because of its signatures of life and growth, mercury has long been associated with twisted serpents (such as in the Staff of Hermes, the medical caduceus, Asian fighting dragons, shamanic serpents, and even the structure of DNA). All these symbols allude to the fact that the metal mercury somehow carries the life force. An interesting chemical synchronicity in this regard is the burning of pellets of mercury and ammonia compounds. The mercury pellets expand into very long dancing "snakes," which entwine and gyrate like living serpents on fire. This effect is the basis of the "Snakes in the Grass" novelty sold at fireworks stands.

Mercury is extremely dense, yet has a high surface tension that causes it to form tiny little perfect spheres in the pores of rocks. Most ores of mercury release their precious metal when they are roasted in an open fire. The hot mercury oozes out between the crevices of the rocks and drops into ashes of the fire, from which it is later separated. The ancient Chinese also crushed mercury ore and mixed it with vinegar to extract the mercury.

Cinnabar (mercury sulfide) is the primary ore of mercury. It is a beautiful scarlet red, semiprecious mineral that is used as a high-grade paint pigment known as vermillion. The word "cinnabar" is from the Persian word for "dragon's blood." The affinity between mercury and sulfur in cinnabar was considered a fundamental and magical principle in nature by early metal workers and alchemists. Cinnabar was mined by the Romans for its mercury content, and it has been the main ore of mercury throughout the centuries. Some mines used by the Romans are still being mined today. Cinnabar shares the same trigonal symmetry class with quartz but the two have different crystal habits. The mineral does not often show well-formed, single large crystals, and crusts and small crystal complexes are more common. The crystals tend to be unusual six-sided trig-onal scalahedrons that appear to be composed of two opposing three-sided pyramids. The cleavage of cinnabar crystals is perfect in three directions. Cinnabar is often found with deposits of quartz, stibnite, mercury, pyrite, dolomite, and realgar.

Calomel (mercurous chloride) is a minor ore of mercury. It is somewhat rare and is never found in large quantities. Most often it is a secondary mineral that forms from the alteration of cinnabar or other mercury minerals. Calomel is deposited from hot under-ground solutions, and it is usually found as coatings on other min-erals. The yellow or white luster is very high and attractive and some specimens show a nice fluorescent red under ultraviolet light. The crystal habits are small pyramidal or hornlike crystals usually seen as coatings or crusts on other minerals. Calomel has significant healing properties and is used in mercurochrome, but its cousin mercuric chloride is a violent poison and corrosive sublimate.

Mercury is used for making thermometers, barometers, diffusion pumps, and many other laboratory instruments. It is also used for mercury switches and other electrical apparatus, as an electrode in some types of electrolysis, for making batteries (mercury cells), in pesticides and antifouling paint, and in dentistry (for silver-amalgam fillings). In mercury-vapor tanning lamps and streetlights, mercury atoms are electrically excited to emit a blue-green light that is at the highest energy and frequency in the visible light spectrum. The violet and ultraviolet light mimics sunlight and produces vitamin D and tanning in the skin just like the sun.

Strangely, mercury exhibits a "breathing" pattern when heated almost to its boiling time, at which point it starts sucking in oxygen and produces a yellow-red oxide (HgO). Upon further heating, the process is reversed and the mercury expels the oxygen like a "metallic lung." It was this odd characteristic of mercury that led chemist James Priestley to discover the element of oxygen. In other chemical reactions, mercury acts as a catalyst that speeds up reactions and unites and harmonizes chemical polarities. The power of mercury to contain and balance diverse substances makes it useful in working with explosive substances. Mercury fulminate is a combination of mercury and nitric acid that makes a detonator used in explosives. Mercury is also used in the making of nuclear bombs. In fact, in nuclear experiments carried out in the 1990s, scientists allegedly discovered an isotope of mercury called "red mercury" that is the densest matter ever found (21 grams/cc). Details have been lost in a wave of secrecy, but the properties of red mercury make it ideal for a suitcase-sized, non-radioactive neutron bomb, as well as a possible source of nearly endless energy. To add to the intrigue, rumors have circulated that natural deposits of red mercury have been discovered in Grenada and Iraq—certainly fodder for conspiracy theorists. One thing is certain: the mysterious and paradoxical allure of mercury continues into modern times.

Mercury has always had a dual nature and was often referred to as a two-headed figure known as the "Rebis" (see figure 14, opposite). While mercury is a symbol of the life force, it is also intimately connected with the forces of death and decay. Mercury metal is very poisonous and volatile and should only be handled under well-ventilated laboratory conditions. Dangerous levels are readily attained at room temperature, and the threat increases under warmer conditions. Containers of mercury should be tightly sealed and spillage should be avoided. Small amounts of mercury spillage can be cleaned up by the addition of sulfur powder, but the

Figure 14. The mercurial Rebis ("double thing") tames the dragon of the First Matter by uniting opposites on all levels. (Basil Valentine, *L'Azoth des Philosophes*, 1613)

resulting mixture must be disposed of carefully. For these reasons, experimenting with mercury is not recommended.

Organic mercury compounds are especially dangerous. Methyl mercury is a lethal pollutant from industrial waste found in rivers and lakes. Mining and the utilization of mercury in commercial products have increased the organic mercury content of oceans and rivers by at least four times. High concentrations have been detected in shellfish, tuna, and swordfish, as well as other aquatic species. It has been estimated that industrial waste has increased the levels of mercury in the overall environment to ten times its natural level. An increase in soil concentrations is making mercury detectible in nearly every kind of food. In addition, pesticides, paint, some batteries, fungicides, fabric softeners, air-conditioning filters, furniture polish, barometers, antiseptics, thermometers, floor wax, and antimildew agents, all contain mercury as an active ingredient.

Symptoms of mercury poisoning begin with concentration and attention problems and progress to anxiety, agitation, excessive emotions, impaired motor function, impaired memory, depression, hallucinations, tremors, slurred speech, and mental retardation. This syndrome is known as erythrism and was first diagnosed among hat makers in the nineteenth century who used a mercury compound to kill bacteria in felt and fur hats to keep them from rotting. It became known popularly as "Mad Hatter's Disease" and was indicated by unusual red pigmentation and orange-red hair.

Because of the dangers of mercury, silver replaces it in mercurial rituals and talismans. Magical spells invoking mercury archetypes deal with improving communication, trade, commerce, transport, progress, change, travel, mental clarity, learning, thinking, memorizing, test results, writing and speaking, and powers of persuasion.

Correspondences of Mercury

Planet: Mercury

Sign: Gemini and Virgo

Day: Wednesday

Musical note: Sol

Gender: Androgynous

Gemstone: Opal and lapis lazuli

Chakra: Vishudda (throat)

Organ: Brain

Element: Ether (water, earth, air)

Experiment 10: The Call of Mercury

Mercury is difficult to see in the night sky because it is a small, extremely fast silvery sphere that likes to stay close to the sun. Mercury even appears to go backward (retrograde) in the sky, a fact which terrified medieval observers and was thought to mark the beginning of a period of bad luck. Try to find mercury in the night sky (you may have to consult your newspaper or an astronomy book). Relax and try to focus all your attention on the fleeting sphere. Relax completely with an open and quiet mind. Become empty and let the planet influence you. Do this until you feel a real connection with the planet of quicksilver. Continue gazing upon mercury and find something containing mercury in a glass container, such as a thermometer or a glass mercury switch (which you can purchase at an electronics supply store for less than a dollar). Put the object in the palm of your hand. See if you can feel a resonance building between the liquid metal and the planet. The "call of mercury" you are experiencing will probably not emanate from your hand, but you will feel something in the long nerves in your arm, in your throat ganglia, or behind your forehead. Try to find words to describe the signatures of mercury you are feeling. Warning: Do not attempt to hold or touch liquid mercury. Mercury contains the signatures of both life and death, so do not take a chance on how it will react to you.

The Mercury Temperament

As Mercury is transmuted, a sense of trust and sublimity arise in individuals, and they sense a presence of unlimited sustenance and potential within them. In changing from mercury into silver, the impression of this Presence becomes even more solidified, and gradually, a powerful vibration or resonance with the divine begins here. It is at this level that fermentation begins.

Personal mercury is said to be transmuted in the throat chakra, which is the boundary between Above and Below in the body as well as the boundary between the personal and the transpersonal. It marks the beginning of the worlds of spirit, a new world of divine communication, movement of spiritual energy, and inspiration. Mercury (as Hermes) at this stage unites mind, spirit, and matter, but gives primacy to intellect and understanding.

Psychologically, the forces of Mercury in a person's temperament yearn for Sulfur, just as metallic mercury seeks union with sulfur. Sulfur here is divine passion and not worldly emotions. The wrong Sulfur at this stage produces someone who is spiritually unyielding and suffers from a superiority complex. It produces someone who uses spirituality for personal or practical control of others.

The alchemists worked the mercury temperament using the operation of fermentation, which we will examine and apply to personal transformation in Chapter 15: Becoming an Alchemist.

Healing with Mercury

Mercury governs the intellect, reasoning, writing, and speech, and rules the vocal organs, throat, lungs, and lymph glands. Its therapeutic effects are mental clarity, greater adaptability, better functioning of the nerve synapses, and regulation of bodily rhythms. Mercury-ruled plants like carrots, celery, parsley, licorice, and valerian affect the thinking and reasoning processes and give mental resourcefulness. Those who feel debilitated because of a sluggish mind will find that Mercurian elixirs quicken all perceptions to a great degree. Mercury herbs also give one the ability to associate one set of phenomena with another with greater ease and make one aware of synchronicities.

When mixed with solar and lunar herbs, Mercurian herbs harmonize the total being, allowing the individual to express essences. They represent the mythological figures of Hermes and Thoth. They affect the throat chakra, which is related to the power of the Word. When mixed with moon herbs, Mercurian herbs give psychic receptivity. When mixed with sun herbs, they increase telepathic sending abilities. For instance, for loss of memory and Alzheimer's disease, mercury herbs are mixed with silver herbs.

By taking the Mercurian herbal tinctures and extracts as a regular regimen, the alchemist opens up to the sphere of magic on the mental plane. This will enable him or her to progress in the Art at a much faster pace. In contacting whatever sphere you are working with, this type of elixir will create a link from your personal microcosm to the greater macrocosmic principle you wish to experience.

Another safe way to use the signature of Mercury in healing is to use it in one of the "potentized" homeopathic forms that are used to treat AIDS, syphilis, bone marrow problems, problems of the central nervous system, and snake bites.

Taking spagyric herbs with the signature of mercury is a lot different from taking preparations that actually contain metallic mercury. At the beginning of this century (before the discovery of alternative drugs), there were over two dozen mercury pills and ointments prescribed by physicians as antiseptics, antibacterials, and fungicides. Pure mercury metal was even prescribed for bowel obstructions, in the hope that the sheer weight of up to a pound of the liquid metal would relieve the problem.

In the East, metallic mercury was the main ingredient in most Tantric medicinal preparations. In his travels through India, Marco Polo observed that many people drank a concoction of mercury and sulfur twice monthly from early childhood with no observable ill effects. They believed the drink gave them longevity. Tantric alchemists in India still take metallic mercury in place of food as an elixir of life, although they caution that the body must be perfectly attuned and strengthened to tolerate the intense cosmic infusion of life force. In Indian alchemy, mercury is called *rasa*, which refers to the subtle essence that is the origin of all forms of matter. The cosmic chaos from which the universe sprang is called the *rasasara* or "sea of mercury." The craft of alchemy is referred to as *rasayana* or "knowledge of mercury."

However, metallic mercury is a poisonous heavy metal and is considered so toxic that a spill from a thermometer can contaminate an entire room. In California, if a blood pressure gauge breaks in a doctor's office and spills a teaspoon of mercury on the floor, "Hazmat" teams evacuate the whole building and work for hours to clean up the spill with special equipment.

Nonetheless, a variety of mercury oils and elixirs have been created and used over the centuries and into modern times. The most
famous of the compounds containing metallic mercury is the
rasayana (Indian alchemy) Oil of Mercury known as Makaradwaja
Oil. The mixture of mercury, silver, copper, and gold is used as a
rejuvenative and tonic for the nervous system, lungs, liver, lymph
system, and the brain. Makaradwaja is used to treat paralysis, hemi-
plegia, nervous disorders, tuberculosis, cancer, and immune defi-
ciency. When combined with animal essences (such as musk,
ambergris, or gorochand), the oil is considered a powerful sexual
tonic. The oil is also used to treat mental dullness, increase awareness and psychic powers, aid in developing verbal abilities, and
enhance the powers of solar and lunar herbs. It is believed to
remove obsessions, fixed ideas, mental viscosity, and deep ("putre-
fying") depression.

Makaradhwaja Oil is made from purified medicinal mercury
which has been processed to absorb in itself the healing essence of
copper. In Indian alchemy, it is said that this mercury has received
five impressions or memories. This mercury is alchemically joined
to purified medicinal sulfur by a salt agent, thus becoming a bright
red "exalted" alchemical cinnabar. On being exposed several nights
to the full moon, it resolves itself into a bloodlike oil by "attracting
the universal spirit of the world in the form of corporified light."
Theoretically, Makaradhwaja is said to work by allowing subtle
energy (prana, tejas, and ojas) to flow into parts of the subtle physiology where it would not normally be able to flow, clearing many
of the blockages that may be present. If taken prior to meditation or
even sleep, it is said that the effects can be seen to permeate the
subtle energy channels (nadis).

According to certain Indian sects, the mercury in the oil allows
the body to digest the otherwise only partly digestible elements of
gold and silver, which are often added to the mixture for this purpose. This is said to allow concentrated "solidified sunlight" to gild
the body's immune system and aura. The most fantastic legends
have grown up around members of the Bhairavi cult, worshipers of
a particularly wrathful form of Lord Shiva. They are said to live

hundreds of years through the alchemical use of Makaradhwaja and other mercury-based compounds. Some are said to have obtained immortality by freeing their minds and overcoming their innate addiction to time. Statues used in rituals in the Bhairavi cult display some of the characteristics of this incredible extension of life force. They are statues of mutated, other-dimensional beings who are supposed to be what successful candidates taking the mercury elixirs really look like.

11

The Moon's Reflection: The Lunar Metal Silver

PURE SILVER HAS A BRILLIANT WHITE metallic luster that tarnishes black when exposed to ozone, hydrogen sulfide, or air containing sulfur. It does not tarnish when exposed to pure air or water. It is a little harder than gold and is very ductile and malleable. It has the highest electrical and thermal conductivity of all metals, and possesses the lowest contact resistance. More than any other metal, silver yields freely to the passage of heat and electricity, passing it on and leaving little for itself. In other words, heat and electricity expand fastest into space through silver.

Silver has been known since ancient times and is mentioned in Genesis. Slag dumps in Asia Minor and on islands in the Aegean Sea indicate that man learned to separate silver from lead as early as 3000 B.C. Silver has always been popular in jewelry and for coinage but only in the past hundred years has the demand for silver been so great. The reason is the use of silver in the photographic film industry, which is based on silver's reactivity to light.

The word silver is from the Anglo-Saxon word *siolfur* meaning "silver." The origin of the chemical symbol for silver, Ag, comes from the Latin word *argentum* meaning "silver." The alchemical symbol for silver is the Moon (☽). Silver was viewed as being the metal nearest to perfection, and to gold. Since the medieval world thought the Moon was the second most important planet in the cosmos, next to the Sun, they assigned silver to the Moon. Luna was the queen of alchemy, and her symbolic color was white. *Luna Philosophorum* was the name the alchemists gave to this living spirit of silver, which they saw as the refined essence of heat and water.

The Moon was associated with the soul and the unconscious self, of which the conscious self is a reflection. Or as Titus Burckhardt put it: "The Moon [and the metal silver] was considered to be analogous to the soul in its state of pure receptivity; whereas the soul transmuted and illumined by the spirit was analogous to the Sun and the metal gold."

Appropriately, silver has a great affinity with light. Silver is used in the making of mirrors, and the lunar metal is the best reflector of visible light known. Many of silver's compounds are extremely sensitive to light, such as silver nitrate in photographic film, in which the crystals of the silver nitrate actually are rearranged through the action of light. A mixture of magnesium metal with silver nitrate solution reacts explosively and gives off a blinding white light.

Silver has other lunar signatures. When melted and hardened again, trapped oxygen is expelled in gas eruptions that leave behind a lunar surface pocked with craters. The moon controls tides of the ocean, the menstrual cycle, and even the ebbing and flowing of human emotions. Likewise, silver metal has a great affinity for the oceans, and most of the silver metal on this planet is dissolved in sea water. Silver nitrate also exhibits beautiful, wavelike patterns (called Liesegang rings) when dropped onto a glass coated with chrome gelatin. The newly formed silver chromate spreads out in concentric circles like mini ocean waves. Chemist Lilly Kolisko demonstrated that 1 percent silver nitrate solution produces a different liquid "picture" (as it rises up filter paper) corresponding to the phases of the moon each night. Such liquid pictures reveal that the new moon and full moon show distinctive patterns that repeat in the silver salt. The pictures also reflect disturbances caused by lunar eclipses.

Native silver is rare and most silver is produced from silver-bearing minerals. It is often associated with deposits of lead and copper. Specimens of native silver usually consist of wire-shaped structures that are curved and intertwined together, making an inspiring mineralogical curiosity. Silver's crystal habits include massive and disseminated grains and plates on the metal's surfaces. "Jack Frost"-type crystal growth as shown on some specimens produces beautiful intricate structures. Whole individual crystals are extremely rare but when present do not exhibit cleavage. Overall, silver metal is the most "organic" of the metals, and its structures tend to resemble living plant structures rather than more mechanical mineral forms.

Silver is used in photography as silver nitrate, silver bromide, and other silver salts. It is also used in dental amalgams with mercury, in coinage, in solder and brazing alloys, in electrical contacts, and in high-capacity batteries. Silver iodide is used to seed clouds to produce rain. Silver dye is used to make brain and nerve structures visible to anatomists. Silver is deposited on glass (by chemical deposition, electrodepositioning, or by evaporation processes) to make mirrors. Silver bells are known for their crisp and pure vibrations. Untarnishable sterling silver is used for jewelry, silverware, labware, and so on, where appearance and cleanliness are paramount. This alloy contains 92.5 percent silver, and the remainder is usually copper.

Silver is used in rituals, magical spells, and talismans to invoke moon goddesses and in "drawing down the moon" ceremonies. The lunar forces are thought to control the female force, cycles, emotional and hormonal imbalances, dreams and intuition, psychic work and psychic abilities, and reflect or neutralize negativity. It is said wearing silver jewelry will improve fertility, emotional balance, and hormonal stability. Silver is also believed to improve the assimilation of food, which is why young children (in their moon years) are traditionally given a silver fork and spoon to eat with. Water charged in silver chalices or cups for six to twenty-four hours is thought to contain the lunar archetype and is used in spells accordingly.

Correspondences of Silver

Planet: Moon

Sign: Cancer

Day: Monday

Musical note: La

Gender: Female

Gemstone: Aquamarine; moonstone; beryl

Chakra: Ajna (third eye or forehead)

Organ: Pituitary

Element: Water

Experiment 11: The Call of Silver

Go outside on the night of the full moon and gaze up at the silver orb. Relax and try to focus all your attention on the surface of the moon. Relax completely with an open and quiet mind. Become empty and let our closest planetary body influence you. Do this until you feel a real connection. Now, pick up a piece of silver jewelry or dinnerware, and hold it in your left hand until it gets warm. You should be able to feel a liquidlike sensation of cool metallic energy. This is what alchemists refer to as the "call of silver." You are experiencing the metal's true signature or living correspondence with the moon itself. Try to remember how this feels in your body. Has the taste in your mouth changed? Has your eyesight altered? How does your skin feel?

The Silver Temperament

Psychologically, the transmutation of the silver chakra produces a lasting mystical state absolutely purified of habitual or egotistical forces. Intuition reaches its highest state of perfection, and one begins to move beyond the limitations of space and time. The feeling is one of intense connection to the cosmos. In the last stages of transmutation, a sublimation of spiritual forces occurs. This lays the groundwork for the formation of a Second Body, a true body of light, in the next and final position on the Caduceus.

The alchemists worked with the silver temperament using the operation of distillation, which we will examine and apply to personal transformation in Chapter 15: Becoming an Alchemist.

Healing with Silver

Silver has been used in healing since 4000 B.C. Many ancient cultures have incorporated the use of silver in their healing practices. The Persians kept their "healing waters" in silver vessels to leach silver atoms into the solution. Egyptians used a form of a silver wrap for wounds. Druids lined their drinking bottles with silver metal for a disinfectant. Medieval royalty held a substantially higher immunity to bacteria than commoners due to the fact that they dined with silverware, ate off silver plates, and drank from silver chalices. Even soldiers were known to swallow a whole silver dollar to ward off infection from wounds. Before refrigerators were invented a silver coin was kept in milk to keep it from going sour. As you can see, the uses for silver are not recent discoveries. The biological actions of silver include being an astringent, a bactericide, and a pesticide.

The therapeutic effects of the lunar metal are sedative, cooling, emetic, and moisturizing. Moon-ruled plants like cucumber, cabbage, watercress, chickweed and clary sage affect the subconscious mind and are useful for hypnosis, breaking bad habits, and working with desires. Lunar herbs are also said to provoke memories of past life experiences and provide a channel through the space-time matrix of consciousness, enabling the alchemist to see clearly through the veil of his or her own thoughts and feelings. If lunar elixirs are impregnated alchemically, karma from the past in the form of bad habits can be reduced. Surprisingly, lunar elixirs also produce an interest in family matters and relationships. They promote sensitivity and imagination, and a fondness for domestic pursuits in general. Lunar herbs can also be a tremendous aid in astral projection. The moon has rulership of the astral plane, and lunar elixirs help us become aware of astral form and function.

Medical astrology places these subjects under rulership of the moon: female reproductive organs, menstruation, the breasts, hormonal imbalances, the stomach, and the watery body fluids like slime, tears, and digestive secretions. Two popular homeopathic medicines derived from silver are *Argentum nitricum* and *Argentum metallicum*.

The alchemists prepared an Oil of Silver they used to treat disorders of the brain and cerebellum, reduce stress, balance emotions, improve memory, treat nervous disorders and epilepsy, and improve both melancholia and mania. It was also used as a physical purgative and mental purifier. It was said to affect the subconscious mind, enable one to see into the past clearly, remove fears and blockages, allow one to unwind, produce "homey" feelings, give a feeling of grace and sensitivity, and enhance imagination.

Colloidal Silver

Colloidal silver is a suspension of submicroscopic metallic silver particles in a colloidal base. It has been documented since 1887 as an effective antibiotic against anthrax spores, and silver solutions were regularly used in the early twentieth century to knock out bacterial, viral, and fungal infections like pinkeye, ringworm, bronchitis, bladder infections, hepatitis, yeast infections, allergies, rosacea, sinusitis, and many more common ailments. In fact, colloidal silver is able to fight over 650 diseases without any known side effects or drug interactions. Today, hospitals put silver solution drops in newborn babies' eyes to prevent infection, and use a cream of 1 percent silver sulfadiazine (known as Silvadene) as a highly effective treatment for burn patients.

However, in recent years the FDA has discouraged the use of silver colloids in the general public because intensive, long-term use of silver preparations can lead to argyria, a condition in which silver salts deposit in the skin, eyes, and internal organs, and the skin turns a permanent ashen gray color. Many cases of argyria occurred during the pre-antibiotic era when silver was a common ingredient in nose drops. Official drug guidebooks have not listed colloidal silver products since 1975.

Experiment 12: Making Colloidal Silver

The ideal voltage for making colloidal silver is 30 volts DC, so three 9-volt batteries (27 volts) make a good power source. All you need to make colloidal silver are the three batteries, three snap-on leads for the batteries, two insulated alligator clips, a foot or so of two-conductor stranded insulated wire, and two silver electrodes. You can get the electronic parts at any electronics store, along with a plastic box to contain the batteries if you wish. The electrode wire should be ten-inch-long pure silver wire (12 gauge, at least .999 fine). Extremely pure (.9999 fine) electrode wire is available from the Crucible Catalog (www.Crucible.org). The wire lasts for many years of production.

It should cost under twenty-five dollars for everything and take less than an hour to construct. Solder or twist-tie your three snap-on battery clips in series (red to black) to provide 27 volts DC. Connect the red insulated alligator clip to the positive (anode) wire and the black insulated clip to the negative (cathode) wire. Cut the silver wire in half, and bend the top ends of the two 5-inch electrodes so they can slip over the top rim of an eight-ounce plastic cup or dinking glass. At least four inches of the electrodes should be submerged in water, and they should be parallel—about an inch apart.

To make alchemically charged colloidal silver, it is best to work during the two "solunar" periods in the day that begin six hours after either moonrise or moonset and last for about ninety minutes. Do not attempt to make silver colloid during the week surrounding the new moon or when the moon is overhead at noontime. After connecting the electrodes and inserting them into the distilled water solution, insert the batteries into their clips to start the process. The process takes six to eighteen hours depending on the conductivity of the solution. Adding just a few grains of sea salt or a little previously made silver colloid and heating the solution a little increases the conductivity and shortens the time needed. The unit produces ionic colloidal silver at the rate of about one ppm (part-per-million) per hour and produces a particle size of about .01 microns.

When finished, detach the electrodes and clean them with a small scouring pad to remove any dark oxides. It is normal to have a tiny amount of dark particles (silver oxide) on the bottom of the glass when the process is over. You can strain them out using a coffee filter. Store the colloidal silver in dark plastic or glass bottles and keep out of the light, and away from extreme temperatures, and magnetic fields. The solution will turn dark when exposed to light, just like photographic film. Stir thoroughly or shake before using. The common dosage is one tablespoon per seventy pounds of body weight, and the shelf life about six months.

12

The Sun's Brilliance: The Solar Metal Gold

GOLD IS A STUBBORNLY PURE METAL when it comes to reacting or even associating with "lesser" elements. That signature explains a lot of the chemical characteristics of gold. Unlike nearly every other metal, there are no plants that contain even trace amounts of metallic gold. There are very few gold ores, because the noblest metal never alloys with the baser metals, but it does alloy with the noble metal silver and makes an amalgam with mercury.

Gold is extremely ductile, malleable, and sectile, and so soft it can be cut with a knife, which makes gold impractical to use for tools. It is also very heavy. A gold bar is twice as heavy as an equal-sized bar of lead. Furthermore, gold embodies an inner equilibrium of forces that makes it pretty much indestructible. Gold never tarnishes like copper or silver or rusts like iron. Whether found buried in the ground, at the bottom of the ocean, in an ancient tomb, or in the ring on your finger, it always looks the same. It cannot be damaged by heat and was considered completely inalterable until around 1100 A.D., when alchemists concocted a mixture of nitric and hydrochloric acids known as *Aqua Regia* ("Royal Water") that could dissolve gold. The immortal metal is endlessly recycled, and all the gold known today is very nearly equal to all the gold that has ever been mined. One ounce of gold can be stretched into a single wire thirty-five miles long, or it can be beaten to just a few atoms thick. It is the most flexible, enduring, and beautiful of all metals.

Gold shows a distinct affinity for sulfur and forms an ore with a rare element called tellurium, which is one of the few elements that easily bonds with gold. In fact, tellurium is rarely found *without* gold. Gold also appears in minerals that are part of a group of tellurium sulfides called the tellurides. However, the amount of gold in these minerals is really miniscule next to the amount of gold found in its native metallic state. Native gold seems to like the company of the purest white quartz and is also found mixed with deposits of pyrite and a few other sulfide minerals. Gold is six times rarer than silver, and it takes about three tons of gold ore to extract an ounce of gold metal.

Around the world, nearly every culture associated their supreme god or goddess with gold. For many centuries only the images of gods graced gold coins, until Alexander the Great began the trend of rulers' images appearing on gold coins around 30 B.C. Even the most primitive societies recognize the sacred properties of gold; for example, the Makuna tribes of modern Brazil believe that gold contains "the light of the sun and stars."

The chemical symbol for gold, Au, comes from the Latin word *aurum* meaning "gold." The alchemical cipher for gold is a rendition of the sun ($\odot$), and gold was considered a kind of congealed light. Sol is the king of alchemy, and his royal purple-red color is revealed in gold colloidal solutions; red is his symbolic color. *Sol Philosophorum* was the name the alchemists gave to this living spirit of gold, which they saw as the refined essence of heat and fire.

Gold was known and considered sacred from earliest times. Gold became popular because it reminded people of the sun with its warm, life-giving properties. Because of its imperishability, the ancient Chinese thought that gold conveyed immortality to its owners. Egyptian inscriptions dating back to 2600 B.C. describe these same associations with gold.

Gold replaced bartering around 3500 B.C. when the people of Mesopotamia started using it as a kind of money because of its eternal value. By 2800 B.C., gold was being fashioned into standardized weights in the form of rings. People started carrying black stones called "touchstones" onto which they scraped a piece of gold to leave a streak. Depending on the brightness of the streak, one could estimate how much gold was in the sample. Around 1500 B.C., Mesopotamian alchemists discovered a process for purifying gold known as "cuppellation," which involved heating impure gold in a porcelain cup called a "cuppel." Impurities were absorbed by the porcelain, leaving a button of pure gold behind. Later alchemists used cuppels to test the quality of their transmutations.

According to alchemists, Nature continually seeks to create the perfection achieved in gold, and they looked at every metal as gold in the making. Alchemists also thought that the objective of every metal was to become gold, and every metal was tested for corrosion and strength and ranked as to how far it was from gold. Many alchemists felt that mercury was the closest metal to gold and that it could be transmuted directly into gold. Their intuition was correct, for mercury can indeed be turned into gold. Gold and mercury are next to each other on the periodic table. Mercury is element eighty (has eighty protons) and gold is element seventy-nine (has seventy-nine protons). In the 1960s, physicists were able to knock out a proton in mercury atoms using neutron particle accelerators, and thereby created minute quantities of gold.

Gold is at the head of the metals, paired with what in the medieval mind was the strongest planet, the sun. The alchemists were obsessed with gold's signature of perfection. Medieval Italian alchemist Bernard Trevisan speculated, "Is not gold merely the Sun's beams condensed into a solid yellow?" Seventeenth-century alchemist John French asked fervently: "Is there no sperm in gold? Is it not possible to exalt it for multiplication? Is there no universal spirit in the world? Is it not possible to find that collected in One Thing which is dispersed in all things? What is that which makes gold incorruptible? What induced the philosophers to examine gold for the matter of their medicine? Was not all gold once living? Is there none of this living gold, the matter of philosophers, to be had anymore?"

Figure 15. The archetypal energies of gold (Sun) and silver (Moon) come together to create the Sorcerer's Stone. (Daniel Stolcius, *Viridarium Chymicum*, 1624)

Gold is highly valued in the everyday world too. It is used as coinage and is a standard for monetary systems in many countries. It is used to make jewelry and artwork, and also in dentistry, electronics, and plating. Since it is an excellent reflector of infrared energy (such as emerges from the sun), the metal is used to coat space satellites and interstellar probes. Chlorauric acid is used in photography for toning the silver image. It is also used in medicine to treat degenerative diseases such as arthritis and cancer.

Chemist Lilly Kolisko performed experiments with gold chloride and showed its chemical behavior coincided with events that altered the strength of the sun, such as the weakening in solar forces during solar eclipses or their increase during the summer solstice. Moreover, she found that both silver and gold salts seemed to be equally influenced by the sun. In the case of silver, it was the forms or patterns that changed, whereas in gold, it was the colors that changed. Silver shapes moved from jagged spikes to smooth rolling forms but the colors remained hues of gray, while the basic shape of gold patterns remained the same but the colors changed from brilliant yellows through violet to reddish purple hues. This work presents an amazing confirmation of how the king and queen, Sol and Luna, work together in creation, with the female principle representing soul and form and the male principle representing spirit and energy. Her work has been duplicated by dozens of other chemists and has been confirmed many times.

The signatures of gold are invoked in rituals, magical spells, and talismans concerning solar deities, the male force, authority, self-confidence, creativity, financial riches, investments, fortune, hope, health, and worldly and magical power. Gold talismans can be very expensive, but you can make one from gold-colored cardboard or write the symbols on it with gold paint or plate an object with gold. Gold jewelry is said to improve self-confidence and inner strength. To charge water with the signature of gold, put a gold object in a glass of water and let it sit in the sunlight for six to ten hours.

Correspondences of Gold

Planet: Sun

Sign: Leo

Day: Sunday

Musical note: Si

Gender: Male

Gemstone: Amber; diamond; topaz

Chakra: Sahasrara (crown)

Organ: Heart

Element: Fire

Alchemists Who Made Gold

Using elaborate mixing and heating techniques, Egyptian alchemists tried making gold by changing the proportions of the Four Elements in the base metals or by attempting to speed up natural growth of lesser metals into gold. Around 100 A.D. Egyptian alchemist Maria Prophetissa used mercury and sulfur to try to make gold. Around 300 A.D., the alchemist Zosimos, whose recipes often came to him in dreams, was working to transmute copper. "The soul of copper," he wrote, "must be purified until it receives the sheen of gold and turns into the royal metal of the Sun." A technique knows as "diplosis" ("doubling") of gold became popular. One such recipe called for heating a mixture of two parts gold with one part each of silver and copper. After appropriate alchemical charging that brought the seed of gold alive, twice as much gold as originally added was produced. Egyptian alchemists believed that the gold acted as a seed in metals, especially copper and silver. According to their view, the seed of gold grew, eating the copper and silver as food, until the whole mixture was transformed into pure gold.

Alchemists from around the world gravitated to Alexandria in Egypt to study the ancient texts, and scribes recorded many instances of them demonstrating their power to make gold. In medieval Europe heads of state, such as Maximilian I (1459–1519), Maximilian II (1527–1576), Emperor Rudolph II (1552–1612), and Margrave Johann of Brandenburg (1513–1571, employed alchemists to supplement their treasuries.

Pope Boniface VIII (1235–1303) was an alchemist who is said to have successfully made gold. He passed his secrets onto Pope John XXII (1245–1334), who was also rumored to have made gold and wanted to keep the secret within the Church. In 1316, he issued a papal Bull forbidding others from pursuing alchemy. After he died, an unusually large horde of unaccounted-for gold was found in his treasury, and his method of transmutation was even recorded in Latin and later translated into French in 1557.

Joh Dee (1527–1608), Edward Kelly (1555–1595), and dozens of other English alchemists were said to have made gold. John Dee even received a license to make gold from Queen Elizabeth. Earlier in 1404, Henry IV had issued a prohibition of alchemy, but in 1440, Henry VI began the practice of issuing licenses to alchemists. In England, laws were passed that a prescribed portion of all gold pieces were to be coined from alchemical gold, and gold coins made of alchemical gold are on display in the British Museum. In fact, all the gold rose noble coins minted during the reign of Edward III are said to be alchemical gold. Rulers around Europe tried to control the production of alchemical gold and often gave alchemists positions in their treasuries. Alchemist Raymond Lully (1235–1315) was responsible for the coining of all Edward III's rose nobles, and Isaac Newton was appointed head of the British mint.

In the 1440s, the French alchemist Jacques le Cor was made Minister of Finance and supervised the coining of gold coins bearing the French Coat of Arms. Both John Dee and Edward Kelly were said to have made gold for the mint of Emperor Maximilian II and some of their alchemical gold coins are on display in the museums in the Czech Republic. All the coins have been shown to be made of high purity gold.

One modern alchemist who is believed to have transmuted mercury into gold was known as Fulcanelli. Perhaps born Jean-Julian Hubert Champagne on January 23, 1877, he began his alchemical work at the age of sixteen and set up a small laboratory in Paris in the early 1900s. In 1916, he took on his first student, a seventeen-year-old boy by the name of Eugene Canseliet. In 1921, he took on the two sons of Ferdinand de Leseps, who set up a laboratory for Fulcanelli at Bourges. In 1922, Fulcanelli accepted two more young men, Jules Boucher and Gaston Sauvage as students.

In 1925, Fulcanelli moved to 59 rue Rochechouart in Paris. It was here that Fulcanelli finally succeeded at make gold. In 1926, the elusive Fulcanelli admitted he found the secret of alchemy, which he entrusted to his students Jules Boucher and Eugene Cansiliet. Soon after some of his research was published in

Mysteries of the Cathedrals, Fulcanelli disappeared and told no one where he was going.

In his book, Fulcanelli revealed that the secrets of alchemy could be found written in plain sight in the bas-reliefs throughout Europe's cathedrals and relates their symbolism to the operations of alchemy. Fulcanelli stated that a specific chemical substance is the gold of alchemy. However, the success of producing it in the laboratory depended on the alchemist's spiritual readiness, as well as certain astrological conditions. He implied that understanding the nature of time is the great secret of alchemy.

In 1954, he summoned his student Eugene Cansiliet to meet him in Seville, Spain, where they set up a laboratory, and Fulcanelli further instructed him in alchemy. Cansiliet later revealed that Fulcanelli looked exactly the same as the last time he saw him over twenty years before, and some of his instruction was in visions and dreams.

Fulcanelli had appeared at least one other time on record. In the summer of 1937, he visited French physicist Jacques Bergier (1912–1978), who was one of the world's leading researchers on atomic energy. Fulcanelli introduced himself as an alchemist and warned Bergier that continued experimentation into the nature of the atom would liberate so much energy that it would be dangerous for the planet. Bergier was impressed with the man's sincerity and they spent the morning talking. Intrigued, Bergier asked him to explain alchemy. Fulcanelli replied:

> You are asking me to summarize in four minutes four thousand years of philosophy and my whole life's work. Furthermore, you are asking me to translate into plain words concepts for which such a language is not intended. All the same, I can say this: you will not be unaware that in present-day official science the part played by the observer becomes more and more important. Relativity and the principle of indeterminacy demonstrate the extent to which the observer today intervenes in all these phenomena. The secret of alchemy is this: there is a way of manipulating

matter and energy so as to create what modern science calls a force-field. This force-field acts upon the observer and puts him in a privileged position in relation to the universe. From this privileged position, he has access to the realities that are normally concealed from us by time and space, matter and energy. This is what we call the Great Work.

When Bergier asked him about the nature of the Philosopher's Stone, Fulcanelli replied:

The vital thing is not the transmutation of metals but that of the experimenter himself. It is an ancient secret that a few people rediscover each century.

Bergier wrote of his encounter in the book *The Morning of the Magicians*. Strangely, Champagne is said to have died in 1932 of mercury poisoning—supposedly from drinking too much absinthe; there are also reports that he is still alive in Spain! His student Jules Boucher died in 1957. Eugene Canseliet pursued his alchemical studies to his death in the late 1980s. To the end, however, his students all agreed that their master had changed mercury into purest gold on several occasions.

Experiment 13: The Call of Gold

During sunrise or sunset, face the sun and try to feel its archetypal presence. If not too bright, gaze into the rising or setting sun and try to see the metallic solar disk of which the Egyptian alchemists spoke. Relax and try to focus all your attention on the golden sphere. Relax completely with an open and quiet mind. Become empty and let the presence at the center of our solar system influence you. Do this until you feel a real connection with the distant sun. Continue facing the sun as you pick up a piece of gold jewelry or a vial of pure gold flakes (such as sold in some novelty shops) and place in your right palm. You should be able to feel an electric warmth building. That eerie, warm vibration is not your imagination. It is what alchemists refer to as the "call of gold"—the resonation of the metal with its "planet." You are experiencing the metal's true signature or living correspondence, and for gold, this is the most perfect expression of all materials. If you can connect with this archetype, you will realize that it a very personal as well as divine presence. As Above, so Below. This is perfection on all levels of your mind, body, and soul resonating with the perfection inherent in the Whole Universe.

The Gold Temperament

For those with weaker wills or loss of contact with the divine presence, gold represents a psychological cure. The solar essences give great ambition, courage, self-reliance, dignity, authority, and the ability to manage oneself and others. The creative principle, no matter how small and insignificant it is within us can be enhanced to a great degree by tapping into the solar archetype. Just as the Sun represents the divine creative force in our immediate solar system, gold represents the same thing in our inner temperament.

For lasting manifestation, the golden temperament needs to be firmly grounded in the world, and the danger at this phase of transformation is that the individual becomes too focused on the workings Above and forgets his or her connection to the real world. Gold and the blazing Sun correspond to personal ambition, courage, and creative energy and vitality, but without a constant effort to remain pure and alive in the real world, the golden temperament can quickly transmute into the leaden qualities of despair, poor self-esteem, lack of confidence, and impurity.

Most important for the golden temperament, however, is to realize that once having reached this plateau, one has certain personal and karmic obligations. The golden attitude of this temperament is what brings the rewards of health, wealth, and happiness through synchronistic responses from the universe. Go against these archetypal powers at this level of achievement and even the slightest deviation from the golden path of righteousness and personal integrity can have disastrous and immediate consequences.

The alchemists transmuted the gold temperament using the operation of coagulation, which we will examine and apply to personal transformation in Chapter 15: Becoming an Alchemist.

Healing with Gold

Chrysotherapy is the name given to healing with gold. The mystical metal has been used for both spiritual and medical purposes as far back as ancient Egypt. Over five thousand years ago, the Egyptians used gold in dentistry and ingested it for mental, bodily, and spiritual purification. The ancients believed that gold in the body worked by stimulating the life force and raising the level of vibration on all levels. In Alexandria, alchemists developed a powerful elixir known as "liquid gold," which reportedly had the ability to restore youth and perfect health.

In ancient Rome, gold salves were used for the treatment of skin ulcers, and today, gold leaf plays an important role in the treatment of chronic skin ulcers. The great alchemist and founder of modern medicine, Paracelsus, developed many highly successful medicines from metallic minerals including gold. In medieval Europe, gold-coated pills and "gold waters" were extremely popular. Alchemists mixed powdered gold into drinks to "comfort sore limbs"; today, it is widely used in the treatment of rheumatoid arthritis. In the 1900s, surgeons implanted a five dollar gold piece under the skin near an inflamed joint, such as a knee or elbow. In China, peasants still cook their rice with a gold coin in order to help replenish gold in their bodies, and fancy Chinese restaurants put twenty-four-karat gold leaf in their food preparations.

The alchemists believed that gold represented the perfection of matter, and that its presence in the body would enliven, rejuvenate, and cure a multitude of "dis-eases." Gold never corrodes or even tarnishes, is completely non-toxic, and exhibits no interactions with other drugs. Gold is the only heavy metal that has a right-hand atomic spin and is therefore easily tolerated by the body.

Physically, the Sun rules the heart and circulation and the distribution of bodily heat and its herbal therapeutic effects are tonic, heating, cardiac, and diaphoretic. While there are no plants or herbs that contain metallic gold, gold the metal is used to treat a variety of degenerative diseases including cancer. Aside from actual injections of gold, gold salts are administered intramuscularly as a treatment for arthritis. Gold has been used to inhibit or prevent the pathogenic progression in rheumatoid arthritis that damages cartilage, bone, and other connective tissues. Gold is thought to create a beneficial balancing and harmonizing effect on the natural rhythmic balancing and healing activity of the heart, improving blood circulation, rejuvenating sluggish organs (especially the brain), and assisting the digestive system.

Sun-ruled plants like almonds, sunflower seeds, chamomile, eyebright, and St. John's Wort affect the soul in its positive phase of manifestation, which presents itself on the personal level as our idea of ourselves as a progressive unified entity. Solar herbs help us realize our evolutionary epoch as an individual among many other individuals, helping to synthesize and synchronize our goals with those of the macrocosm. In this sense they are ego fortifiers—but with a divine purpose.

Solar herbs heal inferiority complexes, bolstering people and giving them a sense of purpose beyond the norm. The Sun represents the Christ and Osiris consciousness in man, as well as Hercules in his monumental strength. For those with weaker wills, Sun-ruled herbs will provide the springboard for more positive action; they also bestow the quality of generosity to our souls. Solar plants, when alchemically charged, will reveal the divine purpose of our solar system, and will let you become aware of the will of God in manifestation. Solar essences give great ambition, courage, self-reliance, dignity, authority, and the ability to manage.

In medical astrology, the Sun rules the physical heart and the eyes as mirrors of the soul. The Sun controls the heart, the circulatory system, and the central energy system of the spine. Because they carry the signature of the vitality principle on the cosmic level, solar herbs can be of seemingly miraculous aid in cases of apathy, lethargy, and unproductivity. The creative principle within us can be enhanced to a great degree as the Sun represents the divine creative force in our immediate solar system.

There are several alchemical oils of gold available, although as with any gold product, one should be aware of the extravagant claims sometimes made for them. Simple Oil of Gold is said to be excellent for leukemia patients as the "highly fixed phosphoric principle will join by the law of affinity with its corresponding human phosphoric principle within the bones." This quote from an old herbal described how gold heals through the alchemical principle of correspondence. The "phosphoric principle" is light (or spirit), and since gold contains the maximum amount of this healing light, it heals by increasing the corresponding light in the human body. Since phosphorous absorbs light and even glows with it, it is the agent in the body that absorbs the spiritual light from the gold oil. Phosphorous delivers this light directly to the marrow of the bones and the marrow produces new blood cells that carry the healing light throughout the body. Thus the gold archetype will establish itself in the blood and do its work of regeneration from within. Similarly, gold oil is used for most heart diseases. Gold oil is also used for teenagers who have a "difficult physical incarnation," as well as several cancers, spinal deformation, venous stasis, vertigo, and general circulation. The Red Oil of Gold is used as a circulation aid, heart tonic, blood purifier, regenerative of brain cells, protector of bones and joints, and to treat rheumatism and arthritis, to cure cancer and syphilis, for uremia and multiple sclerosis, to increase vitality, and to balance metabolism. Psychologically, it is thought to cure a weak will, give ambition, restore courage, and increase creativity.

The formulas for making gold compounds tend to be very obscure and sometimes outlandish. For instance, the recipe for Dr. Anthony's Famous *Aurum Potabile* contains the following ingredient: "Take the urine of a healthy man drinking wine moderately; put it into a gourd which you must stop close, and set in horse dung for the space of forty days." Another recipe for Oil of

Gold calls for "calcinated gold fused into a colorful glass with special alchemical salts elaborated from a phosphoric principle and
combined naturally with the universal spirit which contains corporified light or astral fire. When exposed several nights to the full
moon, this glass dissolves by attraction into an oily thick paste."

If you want to ingest gold by eating the metal, edible gold flakes
are generally available in gourmet cooking stores. The German
schnapps "Geldschlager" also contains gold flakes. Probably the
most effective way of taking gold, however, is in the form of gold
colloid.

Colloidal Gold

If metallic gold is divided into fine particles with sizes ranging from
one to one hundred billionths of a meter, the particles are permanently suspended in solution (it becomes colloidal) and exhibit new
properties due to the larger amount of gold surface area available.
Pure colloidal gold was first prepared in 1857 by the English scientist Michael Faraday and many uses were found for the amazing
solutions of "activated gold."

Historically, colloidal gold has been found useful for glandular
and nervous conditions because it helps to rejuvenate the glands and
stimulate the nerves. It helps release pressure, allowing the nerve
signals to function and reach through to the various organs and
glands. Colloidal gold also regulates body temperature. Gold is a
catalyst for endorphinlike hormones, as well as the antioxidant
enzyme SOD (superoxide dismutase).

Colloidal gold has a balancing and harmonizing effect on all
levels of body, mind, and spirit. It is used to improve mental
attitude and treat unstable mental and emotional states such as
depression, melancholy, sorrow, fear, despair, anguish, frustration,
suicidal tendencies, seasonal affective disorder, poor memory, poor
concentration, and many other imbalances in mind and spirit.
Because of its powerful transformative effects, however, colloidal
gold is not recommended for use by people with bipolar disorder.

Colloidal gold is said to increase life force and libido. It also relieves attention deficit disorder, and improves willpower and mental focus. In the nineteenth century, colloidal gold was commonly used in the United States to cure alcoholism, and today it is commonly used to reduce dependencies on other compounds besides alcohol, such as caffeine, nicotine, and food (especially carbohydrates). According to many studies, colloidal gold increases mental acuity and the ability to concentrate. Recent studies at the University of Utah have shown a 20 percent increase in IQ in people who took daily doses of colloidal gold for only three to four weeks. Colloidal gold is thought to strengthen mental function by increasing the conductivity between nerve endings in the body and on the surface of the brain.

Colloidal gold requires much higher voltage and frequency to produce the correctly sized particles, and it is usually not practical to make it at home like silver colloid. True gold colloids consist of nanometer-sized particles held in constant suspension in the liquid. Many products that claim to be colloidal gold are actually ionic gold, which is chemically reactive and could even damage nerve cells. Ionic gold is easy to identify because it is a clear liquid and looks like water. If it does not have the red-purple signature of gold, then it is not true colloidal gold. Interestingly, the red color of ruby gems is also attributed to the gold content of the stones.

13

The Operations of Alchemy

ACCORDING TO THE ANCIENT HERMETIC TEACHINGS, the operations of alchemy are stages in an eternal pattern of transformation that is part of the fabric of time and space. We have already seen these stages expressed in the Ladder of the Planets, the stairway to stars embedded in our solar system. We have seen it, too, in the relentless pattern of perfection expressed in the transmutation of the metals into gold. The same pattern is within us, as a species slowly moving toward evolutionary perfection and in our personal temperament as well: the inner struggle of our soul buried in matter to unite with spirit in the clear light of higher consciousness. Through all these shifting correspondences on all levels of body, mind, and spirit, the pattern remains the same.

Like the planetary ladder, there are seven steps in the universal process of transformation with which the alchemists worked. They saw these steps as operations to be performed on the matter at hand, whether it be a chemical, a metal, or the human soul. While within these operations there are numerous sub-operations or laboratory processes involved, the seven stages represented by the planets and metals and revealed in the Emerald Tablet were the primary operations.

The alchemists went to great lengths to scramble the order of these operations in order to keep it secret, even from other alchemists, but they did say that the order described in the Emerald Tablet was the only correct or "universal" version. Because of that, it has become common among alchemists to speak of the seven primary operations as the Emerald Formula.

The real secret of the Emerald Formula is that it is meant to come alive in the alchemist and guide his work. That is to say, the true formula can never really be expressed in any linear or fully knowable fashion, but it has a life of its own. Each of the operations comes alive at some point in the experiment, but it does not necessarily follow any strict order. The alchemists were aware of this living quality of their operations and remained extremely flexible and intuitive about the order in which to apply them.

As you read the descriptions of the operations that follow, you will recognize operations that have taken place in you in the past or which you are now experiencing. Often these processes go on for years, so it may be difficult to become aware of them. There are psychological tests one can take to help reveal these stages, because each of the operations of alchemy are now recognized by many noted psychologists as stages in personal transformation. There are also numerous online tests that directly relate to these stages such as the self-scoring Personal Alchemy Quiz (www.AlchemyLab.com/quiz.htm). We will examine the Emerald Formula as it applies to personal transformation in more detail in the next chapter. For now, we will focus on each of the operations in turn to become familiar with their basic characteristics and applications.

The Azoth of the Philosophers

As a visual guide to the operations of alchemy, we will use an alchemical mandala actually used by the alchemists in trying to understand the relationships between the processes of transformation. The "Azoth" (shown in figure 16, opposite) is a meditative emblem that appeared in several different forms during the late Middle Ages. The version we are using is based on an illustration first published in 1659 in the *Azoth of the Philosophers* by the legendary German alchemist Basil Valentine. The word "Azoth" in the title is one of the more arcane names for the First Matter. The

"A" and "Z" in the word relate to "alpha" and "omega," the letters at the beginning and end of the Greek alphabet. Thus the word is meant to convey the idea of the absolutely complete and full meaning of the First Matter and its transformations. In this sense, the Azoth represents not just the chaotic First Matter at the beginning of the Work but also its perfected essence (the Philosopher's Stone) at the conclusion of the Work.

Figure 16. The Azoth of the Philosophers shows the seven operations of alchemical transformation. (Based on Basil Valentine, *L'Azoth des Philosophes*, 1613)

At the center of this striking drawing is the face of a bearded alchemist at the beginning of the Work. Like looking into a mirror, this is where the adept fixes his or her attention to begin meditation at the center of the mandala. The downward-pointing triangle super-imposed over the face of the alchemist represents Water in its high-est sense as divine grace or the gift of life pouring down from Above. Therefore, within the triangle we see the face of God, and the draw-ing clearly implies that the face of God and the face of the alchemist are the same. Of course, this idea was considered blasphemy to the medieval Church, which explains why this drawing was circulated secretly in so many different forms during the Middle Ages. It was not until the Renaissance, when the idea of the divine nature of man gained acceptance that the drawing was first published.

The schematized body of the alchemist is shown in perfect bal-ance with the Four Elements as depicted by his arms and legs. His feet protrude from behind the central emblem, and one is on Earth and the other in Water, indicating he is grounded in the real world. In his right hand is a torch of Fire and in his left hand a feather symbolizing Air. Although he is firmly planted in the world of matter, the alchemist has easy access to the powers of spirit.

The alchemist also stands balanced between the masculine and feminine powers in the background. He is really the offspring of the marriage between Sol, the archetypal Sun King seated on a lion on a hill to his right, and Luna, the archetypal Moon Queen seated on a great fish to his left. "Its father is the Sun," says the Emerald Tablet, "its mother the Moon."

The jovial, extroverted Sun King holds a scepter and a shield indicating his authority and strength over the rational, visible world, but the fiery dragon of the rejected contents of his unconscious waits in a cave beneath him ready to attack should he grow too arrogant. This dragon is created by the fiery nature of conscious-ness any time we forcibly reject part of the contents of our psyche and relegate it to the shadows. We have given this undesirable part life energy in the very act of rejection. The fact that light casts shadows is inherent in masculine consciousness, and it becomes a source of demons that plague us throughout our lives.

The melancholy, introverted Moon Queen holds the reins to a great fish, symbolizing her control of those same hidden forces that threaten the King, and behind her is a chaff of wheat, which stands for her connection to fertility and growth. The bow and arrow she cradles in her left arm symbolizes the wounds of the heart and body she accepts as part of her existence, for feminine consciousness accepts the world as it is, with all its pain and suffering.

In simplest terms, the King and Queen represent the raw materials of our experience—thoughts and feelings—with which the alchemist works. The King symbolizes the power of thought and planning, which are characteristics of spirit. The Queen stands for the influence of feelings and emotions, which are ultimately the chaotic First Matter of the soul. The much-heralded marriage of the King and Queen produces a state of consciousness best described as a feeling intellect, which can be raised and purified to produce a state of perfect intuition, that Egyptian alchemists referred to as "Intelligence of the Heart." This special kind of intelligence or way of knowing is at work in the alchemist for he is born of the sacred marriage of masculine and feminine consciousness.

Between the legs of the alchemist dangles the Cubic Stone, which is labeled *Corpus* (meaning "body"). The five stars surrounding it indicate that the body also contains the hidden Fifth Element, the invisible Quintessence whose "inherent strength is perfected if it is turned into Earth," in the words of the Emerald Tablet.

Where the head of the alchemist should be, there is a strange winged caricature. This represents the Ascended Essence, the essence of the soul raised to the highest level in the body. This image evolved through the decades with this drawing, and at one time or another was shown as a golden ball, a helmet, a heart, and finally as a depiction of the pineal gland (a light-sensitive, pinecone-shaped organ at the center of the brain).

Touching the wings of the Ascended Essence are a salamander engulfed in flames on the left side of the drawing and a standing bird on the right. Below the salamander is the inscription *Anima* (Soul); below the bird is the inscription *Spiritus* (Spirit). The salamander, as a symbol of soul, is attracted to the blazing heat of the Sun, while the bird of spirit is attracted to the coolness of the Moon. This is a visualization of the fundamental bipolar energies that drive the alchemy of transformation. This is similar in meaning to the Tai Chi symbol representing the interplay of the feminine yin and masculine yang energies. In this process, one thing takes on the characteristics of the other as it becomes its opposite. This is the relationship between Mercury and Sulfur in alchemy, and explains why Mercury is sometimes associated with soul and other times associated with spirit. The same is true of Sulfur. The alchemists believed that within this interplay could be found the source of the life force. Carl Jung gave this overall process of one thing changing into its opposite the unwieldy name of "inandromedria."

Spiritus, *Anima*, and *Corpus* (Spirit, Soul, and Body) form a large inverted triangle that stands behind the central emblem of the alchemist. Together they symbolize the Three Essentials behind anything, the celestial archetypes that the alchemists termed Sulfur, Mercury, and Salt.

Operation 1: Calcination

The star-shaped pattern that makes up the body of the alchemist represents what Paracelsus called the "star in man," the hidden process that is going on in our souls, just as it is the hidden process behind the evolution of the *Anima Mundi* or the soul of the universe. The first ray in this inner star is the black ray labeled number one and pointing to the Corpus Stone. It represents the beginning of the Ladder of the Planets and is marked by the cipher that stands for both the metal lead and the planet Saturn. This is the archetypal situation at the beginning of the Work. The square symbol for Salt is also shown in the first ray, which indicates the Work begins in the unredeemed matter of an imperfect incarnation. It could be any substance that needs to be perfected, from lead to the human soul.

Movement through the Azoth is clockwise, and between each step on the Planetary Ladder are a series of circles that show how to proceed to the next step or transform the current situation.

These are the operations of alchemy. The first circle shows a black crow perching on top of a skull. Next to the first circle (between the first and second rays) is the Latin word *Visita*, which means to visit or start a journey. Black crows are symbols of the initial Black Phase (*Nigredo*) of alchemy, during which the subject of transformation is purified by breaking it down.

The scene in the circle represents the first operation of calcination, which works with the element Fire to burn away dross and reveal hidden essences. The word "calcination" (and such related words as "calcify" and "calcium") are from the Latin root *calx*, which means limestone or bone. To calcine something is to burn it until it turns chalky white, reduce it to ashes, or cremate it. After calcination, the substance at hand is no longer affected by common fire.

Fire was very important to alchemists, who were often called "Philosophers of Fire." They believed it was the primary agent of transformation. "All our purifications are done in fire, by fire, and with fire," noted the twentieth-century alchemist Fulcanelli. "Become acquainted with the secrets of fires," counseled alchemist Johann Daniel Mylius (*Philosophia Reformata*, 1622), "and the true achievements of our Medicine, which lead easily to the achievement of the Magistery."

The skull in the first circle is the classic symbol of the process of calcination. Other images at this stage include funeral pyres, hell, bonfires, blazing furnaces (athanors), crucibles, salamanders, the Red Lion fighting other animals, the Sun and Moon roasting over flames, the King being burned alive, cremated, or sitting inside a sweat box. Another calcination image is a yellow lion devouring or struggling with a green snake. The lion represents the fiery principle of Sulfur and the Secret Fire in the alchemist's soul. The green serpent is unrefined or unclean Mercury that must be redeemed during calcination. In the alchemist, this is the false identity or poisoning ego that fights desperately for its survival but must be devoured in the flames of higher consciousness.

In laboratory calcination, a substance is heated over an open flame or in a crucible until it is reduced to ashes. Alchemists considered acids, especially Vitriol, as a kind of liquid fire that also was considered a process of calcination. Vitriol is a thick green substance that forms from the weathering of sulfur-bearing rocks. It is a combination of iron and sulfuric acid that fascinated the alchemists. Sulfuric acid became the fire that drove hundreds of chemical reactions. It is a powerful corrosive that eats away flesh and all metals except gold.

Physiologically, the fire of calcination can be experienced as the metabolic discipline or aerobic activity that tunes the body, burning off excesses from overindulgence and producing a lean and efficient body. Bodily calcination begins in the base or lead chakra at the sacral cup at the base of the spine. On the planetary level, it is the fire of creation, the formation of a livable environment from molten matter and volcanic ashes.

Psychologically, this operation involves the destruction of ego and our attachments to material possessions. Calcination is usually a natural humbling process as we are gradually assaulted and overcome by the trials and tribulations of life. However, it can be a deliberate surrender of our inherent hubris gained through a variety of spiritual disciplines that ignite the fire of introspection and self-evaluation. In society, the calcination is expressed in the lives of revolutionaries, conquerors, and other warriors who try to overthrow the status quo.

Operation 2: Dissolution

The second ray in the star of the Azoth points toward the King, and the operation here is directed toward masculine consciousness and signatures. This is the second rung on the Ladder of the Planets and is marked with the symbol that stands for both the metal tin and the planet Jupiter. This ray is usually white or light blue in color.

The second circle depicts the operation of dissolution and shows the black crow watching itself dissolve before its eyes to reveal its white or purer part. Reflecting back from the pool of dissolution is the white image of the Soul Bird, which is exposed during this operation. This is still the Black Phase of alchemy, and the process of purification continues. In the outer ring next to the circle of dissolution is the word *Interiora*, meaning the operation takes place in the interior or innermost parts.

Images of dissolution include retorts, tears, menstruation, floods, melting, orgies, Mother Nature, water springing from the earth, plants blooming with seven flowers, poisonous toads, the King swimming naked, the King and Queen sitting in a bath together, dark dragons, basilisks (winged serpents), and demons guarding secret treasures. Another image of dissolution is the Sun and Moon surrounded by total darkness with a white bird descending from the sky. One frequent image of dissolution is the Green Lion reaching up to devour the Sun. The Green Lion is the purified Green Snake of calcination, purified and alive during dissolution. But the Green Lion is still imperfect Mercury, although it is now imbued with the soul's sincere desire to ascend. On the chemical level, the Green Lion is the purified Vitriol, the *Aqua Regia* acid that can dissolve even gold.

In the laboratory, the second operation involves dissolving the ashes from calcination in water, acid, or another solution. These ashes are sometimes called the Salt of the Stone (*Sal Salis*), which is the inner matrix that carries all the essences that later become the Philosopher's Stone. In summing up the important transition from the operation of calcination to the operation of dissolution, Daniel Stolcius wrote (*Chemishes Lustgaertlein*, 1625): "The fiery man will sweat and become hot in the fire. Also will he resolve his body and carry it far through moisture."

Psychologically, dissolution represents a further breaking down of the artificial structures of the psyche by total immersion in the unconscious, the rejected part of our consciousness. Within the alchemist, the dissolving water of dissolution can take the form of dreams, voices, visions, and strange feelings that reveal a less ordered and less rational world existing simultaneously with our everyday lives. During dissolution, the conscious mind lets go of control to allow the surfacing of buried material and tied up energy. Dissolution can be experienced as "flow," the bliss of being well used and actively engaged in creative acts without personal hangups or established hierarchy getting in the way. In society, the

process of steady growth through gradual dissolution is exemplified
by monastic, nature-based, or agrarian lifestyles.

Physiologically, dissolution is the continuance of the *kundalini*
experience, the opening up of energy channels in the body to
recharge and elevate every single cell. Dissolution takes place in
the genital or tin chakra and involves changes in the lungs and
spleen. On the planetary level, dissolution is the Great Flood, the
cleansing of the earth of all that is inferior.

Operation 3: Separation

The third ray of the Azoth points toward the torch of Fire and is
marked with the cipher signifying both the metal iron and the
planet Mars. This ray is usually colored red or orange and is also
marked with a smaller symbol denoting sulfur. Iron and sulfur come
together chemically in Vitriol or sulfuric acid, the aggressive and
biting liquid fire of the alchemists.

The third circle shows the operation of separation in which the
black, earthbound Soul Bird splits into two white birds that retrieve
the saved remains of calcination and dissolution. This is the first
coming together of soul and spirit, and the newly acquired vantage
point allows the discernment of what is worthy of being saved from
the previous two operations. Above this circle is the written *Terrae*,
which means "of the earth" and refers to the real or manifested
essences being separated out from the dregs of matter at this stage.

At this stage, the saved elements are pure but opposite and were
often seen at war or struggling with each other. It can be a tortu-
ous time that demands will and determination. To keep the fighting essences alive yet separate, the alchemists made use of ascending
and purifying operations associated with Air. Of this phase, the
Emerald Tablet says, "The Wind carries it in its belly," and the alchemists felt they were applying the element Air in their work during
separation.

"On this third rung of the Ladder of the Wise," noted Mylius in
his *Philosophia Reformata* (1622), "the warring elements previously mentioned and distinguished from each other, are separated

by a rectifying distillation. Therefore, the third step is called Our Separation."

Images for the separation process include filter funnels, piles of sand or dirt, knights wielding swords, the caduceus as a weapon, divorce, dismemberment, surgery, splitting of the Red Sea, breaking apart of heaven and earth, scenes from the apocalypse, and complicated geometric diagrams such as the Squaring of the Circle. Alchemical engravings often show white birds taking flight at this stage, sometimes with images of fire, destruction, and a blackened earth below symbolizing the results of the earlier operations. Another popular image is that of a youthful Hermes (or Mercury) wearing full armor and trying to separate the arguing King and Queen, like a teenaged boy in a family dispute.

Laboratory separation is the isolation of the components of dissolution by filtration or fractional distillation; any impure or unworthy material is then discarded. It is the isolation of the desired components from the previous two purification operations (calcination and dissolution). In the laboratory, the components of the polluted solution from dissolution are separated out by filtration, cutting, settling, or agitation with air. Any dead or unworthy material is then discarded.

Psychologically, this process is the rediscovery of our essence and the reclaiming of dream and visionary "gold" previously rejected by the masculine, rational part of our minds. For the most part it is a conscious process in which we review formerly hidden material and decide what to discard and what to reintegrate into our refined personality. Much of this shadowy material consists of things we are ashamed of or were taught to hide by our parents, churches, and schooling. Separation is letting go of the self-inflicted restraints to our true nature so we can shine through. The process of separation retrieves the frozen energy released from the breaking down of habits and crystallized thoughts (assumptions, beliefs, and prejudices) and hardened feelings (emotional blockages, neuroses, and phobias). This misspent energy is now available to drive our spiritual transformation. In society, separation is expressed as the establishment of clans, cities, and nationalities.

Physiologically, separation is following and controlling the breath in the body as it works with the forces of Spirit and Soul to give birth to new energy and physical renewal. Separation begins in the navel or iron chakra located at the level of the solar plexus. Separation on the planetary level is represented by the formation of land-masses and islands from the powerful forces of Air, Water, Earth, and Fire.

Operation 4: Conjunction

The fourth ray of the Azoth points to the area at the top of the drawing where the right wing of the Ascended Essence touches the salamander wallowing in flames. The ray is marked with the single symbol for both copper and Venus and is usually colored green or yellow-green.

The fourth circle depicts the twin birds of soul and spirit leaving the earth together, lifting a five-spiked crown (the Fifth Element or Quintessence recovered from the preceding operations) into heaven or the realm of spirit. At this point in the Work, only the purest and most genuine parts of the substance to be transformed remain in the vessel. The goal of the conjunction operation is to recombine these saved elements into a whole new incarnation. As the Emerald Tablet says of this stage, "Its nurse is the Earth," and the alchemists felt they were working with the element Earth during conjunction.

Above this circle is inscribed the word *Rectificando*, which means "by rectification" or setting things right, and the wings of the Ascended Essence spread over this operation as if to bless it. It is truly a sacred process. The alchemists often referred to the con-junction as the "Marriage of the Sun and Moon," which symbol-ized the two opposing ways of knowing or experiencing the world. Solar consciousness is intellectual and relies on rational thought; lunar consciousness is feeling based and taps into non-rational sources of information like psychic impressions and intuition. After this Marriage of the Mind, the initiate experiences an increase in intuitive insight and the birth of intelligence of the heart. This newly found faculty produces a sense of reality superior to either thought or feeling alone.

Conjunction is more than a simple marriage however. It is actually an alchemical crucifixion in which the substance at hand (or the alchemist) is nailed (or fixed) on a cross between the Vertical Axis of reality and the Horizontal Axis of reality. In the vertical orientation, conjunction is the attempted union of the forces of spirit Above and matter Below. As can be seen in the Azoth drawing, conjunction is really a turning point from working with the first three operations Below (in matter) and working with the last three operations Above (in spirit).

In the horizontal orientation of left and right, the conjunction is an attempt to balance the masculine consciousness of the King with the feminine consciousness of the Queen. As is presented in the Azoth drawing, conjunction marks the balancing point between the forces of the *Anima* (Soul) on the alchemist's right side, to the forces of the *Spiritus* (Spirit) on the alchemist's left side. In fact, it is the alchemical crucifixion at the center of the vertical and horizontal realities that makes conjunction the most significant operation in alchemy.

Images of horizontal conjunction include the fruitful earth, sexual intercourse, rams and satyrs, double-chambered furnaces (athanors), glue or tape binding opposing entities, two streams coming together in one stream, Janus or double-faced people, people wearing crowns, and the hermaphrodite. Often engravings show the King and Queen in reconciliation at this stage, with Hermes (or Mercury) joining them with an embrace or handshake. In some of these drawings, Hermes is shown with a wry smile or even with two faces. This is a subtle revelation that the conjunction is really a good-natured ruse by the notorious trickster, who knows that both the King and Queen must die or sacrifice their identities in the marriage to produce the Child of the Philosophers, which is all Hermes really cares about.

Images of the vertical conjunction include the Ladder of the Planets, seven stars on an object inclined upward, and rainbows (the seven colors in harmony). Other images are a white bird descending into flames, a bird chained to an earthbound animal, the Red Lion partly disappearing into a sphere, or stylized representations of the union of Fire and Water. Carl Jung suggested that angels coming down from heaven and the landing of UFOs were also images of vertical conjunction, in the obvious sense of the union between the powers Above with the powers Below.

In the laboratory, the operation of conjunction is the recombination of the saved elements from separation into a new substance. Often this was a forced marriage done by fusing or amalgamating metals or by mixing saved components in a new chemical reaction by the addition of a temporary mediator such as an acid or a catalyst.

Physiologically, conjunction is using the body's sexual energies for personal transformation. Conjunction takes place in the body at the level of the heart or copper chakra. On the planetary level, conjunction occurs when primordial life-forms are created from the energy of the sun or lightning.

Psychologically, conjunction is empowerment of our true selves, the union of both the masculine and feminine sides of our personalities into a new belief system or an intuitive state of consciousness. The alchemists referred to it as the Lesser Stone, and after it is achieved, the adept is able to clearly discern what needs to be done to achieve lasting enlightenment. Often synchronicities begin to occur at this stage that confirm the alchemist is on the right track in his or her personal transformation. In society, it is the growth of crafts and technology to master the environment.

Operation 5: Fermentation

The fifth ray of the Azoth points to the area where the left wing of the Ascended Essence touches the standing bird of Spirit. The ray is marked with the cipher for the metal mercury (quicksilver) and the planet Mercury, as well as an identical smaller symbol indicating the heavenly principle of Mercury. This ray is usually colored blue-green or green, symbolizing the living energy of transformation spoken of in the Emerald Tablet or what the Sufis called the "Emerald Vision."

The fifth circle is under the inscription *Invenies*, which means "you will discover." This is the operation of fermentation in which the unexpected mystic substance forms, the ambrosia of the gods, which represents the first lasting solidification of the conjoining of soul and spirit. The circle shows the Soul and Spirit birds nesting in a tree, brooding over their Egg, waiting for the mystical birth to occur.

Fermentation is the introduction of new life into the product of conjunction to completely change its characteristics, to completely raise it to a whole new level of being. The Emerald Tablet tells us to leave the earthly realm by the fire of imagination, "gently and with great ingenuity," into a state that sets our soul afire with higher passion. This is the second or higher application of the Fire element in the tablet, and the alchemists thought of it as working with the heavenly substance of Sulfur.

Like natural fermentation, alchemical fermentation is a two-stepped process that begins with putrefaction, in which the matter is allowed first to rot and decompose and then to ferment or come alive again in spirit. In his *Chemisches Lustgaertlein* (1625), alchemist Daniel Stolcius describes the importance of this uncomfortable phase: "Destruction brings about the Death of the material. But the spirit renews, like before, the Life. Provided that the seed is putrified in the right soil—otherwise all labor, work, and art will be in vain."

Images of the putrefaction phase of fermentation include corpses, graves, coffins, funerals, guardian angels, massacres, mutilation, worms, or rotting flesh. Drawings of this phase occasionally depict a bird descending into a pitch black sky or caught lost in the dark clouds during a thunderstorm. Skeletons or black crows standing on corpses or rotting balls of earth are also seen. Images of fermentation include scenes of sowing and germination, greenness and rebirth. Sometimes the King and Queen are shown with wings or as angels to emphasize their spiritized forms.

Laboratory putrefaction begins with the rotting of the plant material or substance of transformation. The alchemists often added manure to help get the process going. The sign that putrefaction is nearing its end is a milky white fluid that appears like a tunnel of white light in the black, rotting material. The dead material seems to come to life again with an influx of digesting bacteria as fermentation begins. This is the introduction of new life into the product of conjunction to revive and rejuvenate it in a process of spiritization. Finally, out of the utter blackness of putrefaction comes the yellow ferment, which appears like a golden wax flowing out of the foul matter. Chinese alchemists called this substance the golden pill, which marked their intermediary Yellow Phase (the *Xanthosis*), an alchemical transition also recognized by Alexandrian alchemists. The production of the ferment or golden pill is heralded by the formation of an iridescent, oily film the alchemists named the *cauda pavonis* ("peacock's tail").

We see this process most clearly in the making of wine. First, the grapes are "sacrificed" or crushed to release their essences in the juice. Then, putrefaction begins as the juice is allowed to decompose and rot. Next, a white layer of digesting bacteria arises that begins the process of fermentation. This phase is also sometimes marked by the waxy substance the alchemists called the ferment and the oily film known as the peacock's tail. Finally, the new life force "conquers" the original identity of the grape juice and supplants it with a new and higher presence or life. This higher presence is released during the next operation (distillation), which produces the true Spirit of Wine (its alcohol), and which contains the purified essence of grapes.

Psychologically, this process is the death of the feeble (or unstable) child of the conjunction that will eventually result in its resurrection to a new level of being. Fermentation starts with the inspiration of spiritual power from Above that reanimates, energizes, and enlightens the alchemist. Out of the blackness of the alchemist's despair (putrefaction) comes a brilliant display of colors and meaningful visions (the peacock's tail). Fermentation can be achieved through various activities that include intense prayer, desire for mystical union, breakdown of the personality, transpersonal therapy, psychedelic drugs, and deep meditation. Thus, personal fermentation is living inspiration from something totally beyond us. In society, the fermentation experience is the basis of religion and mystical awareness.

Physiologically, fermentation is the rousing of living energy (*chi* or *kundalini*) in the body to heal and vivify. It is expressed as vibratory tones and spoken truths emerging from the throat or mercury chakra. On the planetary level, it is the evolution of life to produce consciousness in matter.

Operation 6: Distillation

The Azoth's sixth ray points to the feather, symbol of Air and indicating the process of spiritualization. This ray is usually colored indigo, although it is shown as white or light gray. It is marked with the symbol for silver and the moon.

Distillation is the sixth of the major operations in alchemy, and it is represented in the sixth circle by a unicorn lying on the ground in front of a rosebush. According to legend, the unicorn runs tirelessly from pursuers but lies meekly on the ground when approached by a virgin. The virgin is the purified matter at hand, which has returned to a state of innocence and potential. Above the circle is the word *Occultum*, meaning secret or hidden, since the essences at the beginning of this stage are invisible.

Distillation is a key process on all levels of alchemy. It involves releasing volatile essences from their prison in matter and condensing them in a purified form. In practical terms, this involves heating a substance until it boils, and then condensing the vapors into a purified liquid. In the Lesser Work of purification in the first three operations, sulfurous and mercurial substances are distilled into a clarified and purer form. In the Greater Work of rebirth, the process takes on an infinite aspect, as substances are continually distilled and circulated in a sealed vessel. Repeated distillation produces an extremely concentrated solution the alchemists called the "Mother of the Stone." In a kind of distillation known as sublimation, the vapors condense directly into solid powder at the top of the distilling apparatus and remain "fixed" there. Distillation is described in the Emerald Tablet as: "It rises from Earth to Heaven and descends again to Earth, thereby combining within Itself the powers of both the Above and the Below."

The alchemical symbol for distillation is the alembic, a hood that fits over the boiling fluid, condensing the rising vapors and directing the purified condensate via a funnel or tube to a collecting vessel. Images include complicated distillation trains with multiple piping into tall vessels, large turning wheels, baptismal fonts, a rain of purified dew, the lotus flower, a five-petaled rose, the Rosy Cross, the unicorn, white doves, and the pelican. The pelican was thought to sacrifice its own blood to feed its young, and it is also the name of a feedback-distillation apparatus. Sometimes this crucial step is represented by flames ascending into the sky or a dragon in flames with its tail in its mouth. Dream images include flying, climbing to the tops of mountains, or confronting mountain lions or eagles.

In the laboratory, distillation is the boiling and condensation of the fermented solution to increase its purity, which is why this is known as the White Phase of alchemy. Psychologically, this agitation and sublimation of psychic forces is necessary to ensure that no impurities from the lower personality are incorporated into the next and final process. The alchemists thought of this phase as working with the heavenly substance mercury to extract and refashion the metals. The ferment, the soft amalgam or balsam resulting from this operation, must be hardened into a stone before it can be made permanent, and the final phase of distillation is a sublimation in which vapor turns solid, or the spirit is made corporeal. Chemical distillation is the boiling and condensation of a solution to increase its concentration and purity. Chemically, it is the boiling and condensation of the fermented solution to increase its purity, such as takes place in the distilling of wine to make brandy.

Psychologically, distillation is the agitation and sublimation of psychic forces and is necessary to ensure that no impurities from the inflated ego or deeply submerged id are incorporated into the next and final stage. Personal distillation consists of a variety of introspective techniques that raise the content of the psyche to the highest level possible, free from sentimentality and emotions, and cut off even from one's personal identity. Distillation is the purification of the unborn Self—all that we truly are and can be. In society, the distillation experience is expressed as science and objective experimentation.

Physiologically, distillation is raising the life force repeatedly from the lower regions in the cauldron of the body to the brain (what Asian alchemists called the Circulation of the Light), where it eventually becomes a wondrous solidifying light full of power. Distillation is said to culminate in the Third Eye area of the forehead, at the level of the pituitary and pineal glands, in the brow or silver chakra. On the planetary level, distillation is the realization of the power of higher love, as the life force on the entire planet gradually seeks to become one force in nature based on a shared vision of Truth.

Operation 7: Coagulation

The seventh ray of the Azoth points to the realm of the Queen and contains the symbol that stands for both the metal gold and the sun. It is at the feminine level of soul where masculine consciousness is transformed, and this ray is usually colored lavender or purple, indicating the true royalty of the King.

The final, seventh circle shows an androgynous youth emerging from an open grave, with the Latin word *Lapidem*, meaning "the Stone," on the outer ring next to it. This is the operation of coagulation, in which the fermented child of the conjunction is fused with the sublimated spiritual presence released during distillation. The resurrection of the soul is accomplished by bringing together only the purest essences of one's body and soul into the light of meditation. In other words, coagulation incarnates and releases the purified soul that the Emerald Tablet described as the "Glory of the Whole Universe." Coagulation is the second or higher application of the elements Air and Earth in the tablet, and it results in a union of spirit with matter. At this stage, the alchemists felt they were working with the "new" or resurrected Salt.

Coagulation images include a soaring eagle, brilliantly shining gold, scales of justice, an egg-shaped Stone, a heavenly scented balsam, the elixir or ambrosia (food of immortality), wingless creatures borne away by winged creatures, the serpent and lion united, and the phoenix (a mythical bird that repeatedly rose from the ashes). The event is also indicated by the King and Queen breaking free of their chains to matter and appearing as naked Sol and Luna (personages with heads of the Sun and Moon respectively). One drawing of this stage shows a purple moon fallen to the earth with a red bird ascending into the sky. In alchemical metallurgy, the baser metals are transformed into incorruptible gold during this stage. In many alchemical experiments, coagulation is the precipitation or sublimation of the purified ferment from distillation.

Psychologically, coagulation is first sensed as a new confidence that is beyond all things, though many experience it as a Second Body of golden coalesced light, a permanent vehicle of consciousness that embodies the highest aspirations and evolution of mind. Coagulation incarnates and releases the *Ultima Materia* of the soul, the Astral Body, which the alchemists also referred to as the Greater or Philosopher's Stone. Using this magical stone, the alchemists believed they could exist on all levels of reality. In society, it is the living wisdom in which everyone exists within the same light of evolved consciousness and knowledge of Truth.

On the bodily level, this stage is marked by the release of the elixir in the blood that rejuvenates the body into a perfect vessel of health. A brain ambrosia is said to be released through the interaction of light from the phallic-shaped pineal gland and matter from the vulva of the pituitary. This heavenly food or *viaticum* both nourishes and energizes the cells without any waste products being produced. These physiological and psychological processes create the Second Body, a body of solid light that emerges through the crown or gold chakra. On the planetary level, coagulation is a return to the Garden of Eden, this time on a higher level in tune with the divine mind.

The Three Magisteriums

While the operations of alchemy appear to be a linear sequence of processes to be applied in order to the substance at hand, this is really not the case in practical work. The overall pattern of the operations tends to be serpentine with the processes Above (fermentation, distillation, and coagulation) and the processes Below (calcination, dissolution, and separation) forming two circles in a figure-eight pattern with the conjunction in between (see figure 17 below).

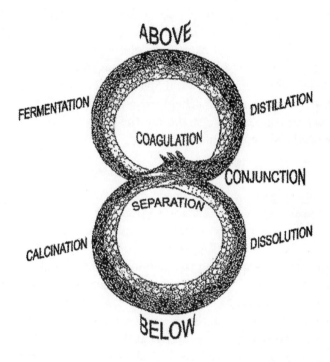

Figure 17. The seven operations form a spiraling pattern of gradual transformation that creates a new Conjunction or higher manifestation of the powers Above and Below. (D. W. Hauck)

Furthermore, the alchemists believed that ultimate success came in three passes through the seven operations. Thus our spiritual maturity is achieved in twenty-one steps, just as we are considered physically mature at the age of twenty-one. They referred to the successful completion of each of the cycles of seven operations as "magisteriums," to which they gave the names of different stones. During the First Magisterium (or first working through the operations), the Lunar Stone is created. It represents gaining control and perfecting the life force as it is expressed in the body, so that the alchemist might live long enough to complete the Great Work in one lifetime. The Second Magisterium, the Solar Stone, is achieved when the mind is perfectly controlled and directed through willpower, so that fear, ego, and other psychological baggage do not interfere in the full expression of the powers of mind. The Third Magisterium is the union of the Lunar and Solar Stones with the cosmic presence of Universal Spirit to create the Stellar Stone. In many writings of the alchemists, especially Paracelsus, this is seen as a true Golden or Astral body, the perfection of the physical body on the spiritual plane.

Experiment 6: The Hidden Keys to the Azoth

There are deeper secrets contained in the Azoth drawing that are only revealed through meditation. Although there are only seven operations shown, there is another implied or eighth step in the mandala. This secret is suggested by the fact that while there are eight circles corresponding to operations there are only seven rays labeled. Only deeper meditation on this drawing will reveal the unlabeled eighth ray.

Begin your meditation by entering a relaxed and open state of consciousness while staring directly at the face in the center of the mandala. Many alchemists have actually replaced the central image with a small round mirror to facilitate this introspective process. While staring at the center of the mandala, try to incorporate into your peripheral view all the alchemical images of King and Queen, Spirit and Soul that are present. Go slowly and intuitively, and try to feel a sense of increased meaning and inspiration as you begin your journey through the operations.

First look at each ray in order, beginning with the black ray of calcination. Observe the symbols on the ray and its position on the "Star in Man." Then move your attention clockwise to the circle explaining the operation of transformation to be performed here. Look at the scene depicted and try to get a feeling of actually being in the scene and witnessing what it depicts. Continue this way all around the mandala until you reach the final operation of coagulation that shows the androgynous youth emerging from the grave. This is a clue for you to do the same in your meditation with the mandala.

Sit back now and stare at the whole drawing. In other words, free yourself from the dead grave of the flat, square picture in which you have buried your consciousness in this meditation. Let your attention be free and see where it lands. In almost every case, you will be drawn to the black ray at position one, which points to the Cubic Stone. This is the Salt or unpurified matter at the beginning of the Work, as well as the new Salt or Stone at the end of the Work.

Further meditation on the meaning of this "eighth" ray leads us directly above this ray to the crowning sphere of conjunction. This is the operation that works with Earth to manifest the new Salt in material reality. It is also the turning point between the Below and the Above. In other words, the operation associated with the hidden eighth step is conjunction. It is the beginning and end of the Work. Some alchemists felt so strongly about this that they actually changed the entire process to show the final step of transformation depicted by gold and the Sun in ray number four instead of ray number seven. In any drawings based on Basil Valentine's version that appeared in his *Azoth des Philosophes* (1659), the Sun and its metal are shown in this ray of conjunction instead of in the final ray of coagulation.

This is an overwhelming confirmation of the importance of the ancient alchemical principle known as the Law of the Octaves. Just as the seven first notes in the musical scale lead to an eighth note that is a repetition of the first at a higher level of vibration, so do the seven operations of alchemy lead to a return to the realm of matter at a higher frequency of consciousness. In other words, the goal of alchemy is not to remain in the realm of spirit, as it is in all the Abrahamic religions. Like Buddhist and Taoist doctrine, the goal is to become purified in the realm of spirit and then return to the earth as seeds of spirit. The Great Work of alchemy is nothing less than the "consecration of the Whole Universe" as the Emerald Tablet tells us. It is the coagulation of spirit in matter, the full awakening of the hidden spark of light and consciousness that is trapped in matter. That can only be accomplished by a second conjunction, a Sacred Marriage between Soul and Spirit that takes place on both the Vertical Axis and the Horizontal Axis of reality. This is the true message of the Rosicrucians, cabalists, and mystical Christians. To bring spirit or the divine will into the world, we must sacrifice ourselves at the center of the cross of matter.

There is also one last message hidden in the Azoth drawing. All the Latin words contained in the outer ring that connects the rays of transformation spell out a summary of what has taken place: *Visita Interiora Terrae Rectificando Invenies Occultum Lapidem.* This condensation of the operations means "Visit the innermost parts of the earth; and by setting things right ('rectifying'), you will find the hidden Stone." Furthermore, the first letter of these seven Latin words spells out "VITRIOL." This biting and highly corrosive liquid fire is symbolic of the soulful energy that drives the whole wheel of transformation. It is both the fundamental acid that drives chemical change and the inner Secret Fire, sometimes likened to a spiritual hormone, which brings about the bodily and spiritual perfection of the alchemist.

14

Personal Purification

THE UNIVERSAL OPERATIONS OF ALCHEMY described in the previous chapter are intended to transform and perfect anything, whether it be the base metals, a person's temperament, or the human soul. Within the operations of alchemy are also all the traditional stages of initiation necessary to become an alchemist. From the first teachings and purification of the initiate in the Outer Court, through the introspective lessons of the Inner Court, to the crowning of spirit in the Holy of Holies, these are the same steps that have been used to become an adept since ancient times.

The process of initiation always begins in the Outer Court. This is where the principles are revealed for all who will hear them, and it usually took place in an open courtyard. Sometimes even the public was allowed in such meetings, where lectures and discussions took place. In your initiation into alchemy, the Outer Court is the book you now hold in your hands. This is where the principles of alchemy have been given to you. These are the seeds of gold that will take root in you if you let them.

To proceed to the Inner Court, all we have to do is allow these principles or seeds to come alive. This inner process always takes place in an enclosed and darkened space such as the great hypostyle halls of Egyptian temples. Here you must nurture the seeds of thought and feeling given you in the Outer Court and work with them to see how they fit inside you and where they can take root. This is an introspective and meditative process in which you overcome the false parts, the weeds that grew up in you with a life of their own passed down from society—from our parents, schools, and churches. When the inner garden is properly weeded, the true growth and flowering of these new seeds can begin.

The Inner Court is concerned with what mystics refer to as the Lesser Mysteries, which involve a lot of psychological purification and inner work on one's soul. The Greater Mysteries are revealed in the Holy of Holies on a one-on-one basis. Traditionally, the Holy of Holies is a very small room inhabited by just the initiate and the initiator, who was usually a priest or hierophant. In alchemy, the traditional initiator was Hermes, and his teachings were passed on individually within the Holy of Holies of the initiate's heart. In other words, Hermes (as Thoth) is the final initiator for all alchemists. Thoth represents the power of inspiration (literally "bringing in spirit"), which can be seen in the ancient Egyptian greeting that went: "May Thoth speak to you daily." The Egyptians believed that inspired thoughts and states of enthusiasm (literally, "infused with god") came from outside them. They could not imagine how their own minds, so trapped in everyday reality, could come up with such high and inspired thoughts, so they truly believed that such thoughts came from the gods. The strange thing is that they really do, and that is the method of revelation in the Holy of Holies.

In this chapter, we will focus on processes that take place primarily in the Inner Court. The Inner Court is where most of the work is done to become an alchemist, and once you successfully pass through this court, Hermes will always be waiting for you in the Holy of Holies that is within you. At that point, all you have to do is open up to him, and he will reveal the Greater Mysteries in a secret gnosis that is unique to you. This is a one-on-one experience between you and your god, and it cannot be taught in any book.

The crucial work in the Inner Court begins in your mind and heart, and the primary tool here is the art of inner reflection and concentration known as meditation. Alchemical meditation, however, is very different from other kinds of meditation with which you might be familiar. As you will see in the following exercises, alchemical meditation tends to be more active and directed than other forms. The basic method of meditation was well known to the ancient alchemists, as is shown in the following quotation, which is the earliest known description of the process of meditation ever found. Although the original text probably dates back to 2000 B.C., the oldest copy we have found was in the tomb of Tutankhamen and dates from 1323 B.C. It is from a book called *The Destruction of Humankind*, which is really about how to avert the destruction of both our species and individuals through a process of spiritualization. In this ancient manuscript, we can easily recognize crucial Hermetic ideas, such as the guiding force of higher inspiration and the relationship between the seven operations and the three magisteriums.

Whensoever Thoth speaks to you and you wish to recite a composition on behalf of the Sun, then you must perform a sevenfold purification for three sunrises. Whether a person or a group shall so proceed, you shall make your position in a circle, which is made beyond you, and your eyes shall be fixed within the circle. All your actions shall be composed and motionless, and your steps shall not carry you away from the circle. If you shall attentively dwell within the circle and observe with the eyes of your heart, you will find the path that leads Above. Even so shall the image become your guide, for the divine sight has this peculiar charm: It holds fast and draws unto it those who succeed in opening their eyes in this way. Now whosoever shall vocalize the sacred words shall visualize themselves as Thoth or as Ra in the redness of the dawn of his birth. Thus shall a thought exclusively occupying your mind be transformed into the actual state, and from this lesson, your house shall never fall into decay but will endure throughout eternity.

As beautiful and powerful as this process is, the first steps of personal transformation are not very comfortable. This Black Phase (*Nigredo*) is about the destruction of pre-existing structures and the freeing of trapped energy. To transform anything, it must first be reduced to its most fundamental ingredients—all the dross, falsity, and extraneous material must be removed. The job of the first two operations in alchemy is to ensure that this purification is done correctly and completely. After these revolutionary operations of Fire and Water, the essences of the matter at hand should be readily available to be recombined in a new and more perfect way. It is important to keep this overall process in mind during these first stages, which can seem very chaotic and confusing.

The alchemists summed up the larger process of destruction and rebirth as *Solve et Coagula* (Dissolve and Coagulate). It is short for the Latin phrase *Solvite Corpora et Coagulate Spiritus*, which means "Dissolve the body and coagulate the spirit." In other words, we are destroying or dissolving structures and pre-existing incarnations (what the alchemists would call Salt) to release the essences (what they called Spirit) and create a new body that is a more true or perfect expression of these essences.

Personal Calcination

We experience the fires of calcination on the personal level as the great forces of change over which we have no control like loss, failure, and humiliation. These hellfires usually erupt by the spontaneous combustion of all the extraneous garbage and falseness we carry around with us. Paramount among these artificialities are our own egos. While we were growing up, the center of focus in personalities shifted from our true essence to the artificial, social construct of ego. By the time we are adults, we spend most our life force enshrining or protecting our ego and supporting its little lies, tricks, and self-deceptions. This loss of innocence and energy has real consequences, and we pay for it in worldly terms. Our hopes and dreams turn to mockeries, our relationships sour, "dis-ease" erupts in our minds and bodies. Calcination can be viewed as a natural humbling process as we are gradually assaulted and overcome by the trials and tribulations of life.

Have you ever felt as if everything was going wrong in your life no matter what you did? Ever have days when whatever you attempted seemed to backfire on you? Then you have experienced

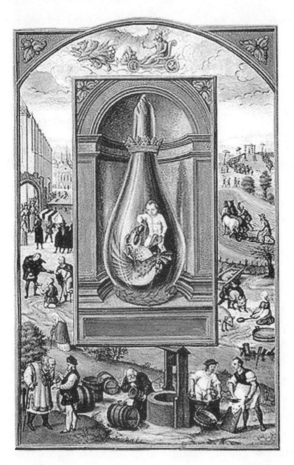

Figure 18. Dragons pull Saturn's chariot above, while images of worldly affairs dominate the scene below. In the retort of transformation, the spirit of Mercury gives the dragon of the First Matter a dose of poison and uses a bellows to fan the fires of Calcination. (Salomon Trismosin, *Splendor Solis*, 1535)

the fires of personal calcination. People caught up in calcination often feel as if they are trapped in the fires of hell, burning up and suffering through their lives yet unable to escape. As the Sufi alchemist Rumi described it: "I was raw, I cooked, I burnt to cinders!" Surprisingly, it is not until these fires are burning that your transformation begins. It seems the only way out of hell is to rise up with the flames, or as poet T. S. Eliot put it, "We are redeemed from fire by fire." The fire with which the alchemist works within during calcination is the flame of concentrated consciousness.

The only way out of this self-imposed hell is to sacrifice the former identity in a controlled burn, a deliberate calcination. You have to get rid of all traces of mistaken ideas. Calcination is like book burning in your own mind. Imagine a bitchy voice in your head exposing all the absurdity in your life. We have to sacrifice our own egos for that golden presence that is the essence in each of us. That is the meaning of the Green Serpent shown nailed to a cross in many alchemical drawings. Unless you completely destroy what was previously built, you are building the new on the foundation of the old. If you have creative thoughts of transforming yourself but build the new identity on the old belief system, you will fail at personal transformation. And the more you cling to the previous level, the hotter the fires of calcination become.

By applying the fire of introspective conciousness, you recognize falsity and burn away the leaden or crystallized thoughts that often take on a mind of their own and become unintended responses or robotic reactions to people and events. You have to burn through illusion, self-deception, defense mechanisms, bigotry, and all the other dogmas and dramas of your Tyrant Ego. The tyrant has usurped the throne of the deeper transpersonal Self, who is the rightful ruler of the personality. As in the Grail legend, the kingdom of your personality will wither and decay until the true King is restored.

As strange as it seems, the quality of your consciousness or inner attitude has a lot to do with how life treats you, with what kind of "justice" comes your way on a daily basis. The universe destroys falseness, and a false, leaden consciousness invites the fires of hell. A life-affirming golden consciousness attracts gold in your life, invites the light of heaven to shine down upon you, and produces an environment of wisdom and power. That, in a nutshell, is the alchemy of our lives.

Experiment 14: Crushing Ego

Pulverization is considered one of the sub-operations of calcination. It is a process in which the matter is crushed in a mortar and pestle or ground into small pieces. For instance, in the making of tinctures, the heated and dried herb is crushed before it is placed in alcohol to extract its essences.

Attacking one's own ego is a painful but necessary first step in personal transformation. Like the fire and acid used in the lab, we try to reveal the deepest essences of the subject at hand to "start over" in a conscious way and create a more perfect substance. Most of the work at this stage focuses on tearing down the ego, or the Salt of the personality. The operations are the same as in the laboratory and the subject of the work is something already existing that must be perfected by destroying it. During the initial stages of personal transformation, our ego becomes the enemy, the suspicious self that fosters illusions, generates false beliefs, judges and classifies things, imposes habits in thought and body, and literally incarnates an imperfect robotic self.

During this work, however, it must be constantly kept in mind that the ego is not the devil inside us but an essential part of us that allows us to function in society and the world. It is a focal point of self. Like the unperfected First Matter at the beginning of the work, it is the beginning and most important component of transformation. It is like lead and Saturn—both despised by the unenlightened, who fail to see their inner nature. The ego, like lead and the saturnic forces, carries the secret fire that fuels the whole transformation. The ego is our salted identity, fashioned by the forces of family, society, and religion imposed on innocent children.

The goal now is to dissolve the ego, to break down its structure in order to reveal the true original essences that will make up the new salt or new identity. These are essences of soul and spirit, Sulfur and Mercury. In fact, we must become Mercury to do this. Like the mirror-like surface of the metal, we are free to take on any image, any identity, once the slate is swept clean. So, just as in the dregs and ashes of laboratory work, the lowly despised ego eventually becomes the Stone. In other words, *identity* is the key to personal and spiritual transformation, as well as the grander Hermetic power of existing on all levels of reality. In the words of the master George Gurdjieff:

> If a man can develop within himself a permanent "I" that can survive a change in the external, it can survive the death of the physical body. The whole secret is that one cannot work for a future life without working for this one. He must become a master of his life to become a master of his death.

For most of us, there have been moments of utter humiliation in which ego has been at least momentarily pulverized. If we can relive those moments, the process can be used to crush the structure of the current imperfect ego. During this work, it is important not to attack one's self-esteem but to focus on the artificial everyday identity we have created in our lives. You have to know yourself objectively like you would another person and learn to see your ego as a foreign invader that has taken control of your life from your true self.

Simply think back and relive those moments of humiliation with as much detail and feelings as you can. Realize that the part of you that was humiliated is the part you need to work on. Think back to all those times when someone tried to deliberately embarrass you, or when you were caught performing some act you were not supposed to be doing. Have you ever lost your train of thought or did something clumsy in front of a lot of people? Were you ever blamed for something bad happening, when it was not your fault? Did you ever hurt a person or an animal, and then try to forget about it? Remember, your ego is constantly rewriting history to portray itself in the best light. Bring back those embarrassing events and hurt feelings as vividly and completely as you can, and you will feel your ego start to shrink and deflate.

If you cannot muster the objectivity to crush your own ego, you might want to ask for honest feedback from friends and loved ones, but be careful and only ask people you trust. Most of us have built up a support system of people around us who only respond to our ego and have little feeling for our true essence. Be careful of your own ego, too, which will do anything in its power to protect itself from attack.

Experiment 15: Mantra of the Self

The power of self-reflection is nowhere more apparent than in this meditation, which is based on just saying your name to yourself over and over. Sit alone in a quiet, dark room and repeat your name to yourself over and over, trying to determine what it really means. Choose any name with which you are identified or by which others know you, such as your first name or a nickname. You are calling yourself forth because you know the ego's name. Let feelings rise but not thoughts; replace extraneous thoughts with the mantra of your name. The ego cannot survive that kind of intense scrutiny. By observing yourself observing yourself, you enter an infinite progression or mental loop—until finally there is no difference between the observer and the observed, between you and your consciousness. Alternatively, you could concentrate on the breath, while periodically asking yourself the question "Who is aware?" or "What is the Source?" In the silence of the response, you will slowly start to sense the ground of your being. The poet Alfred Lord Tennyson was familiar with this process of burning out your name by repeating it over and over.

> A kind of trance I have frequently had, quite up from my boyhood, when I have been all alone. This has generally come upon me through repeating my own name to myself silently, until all at once, as it were out of the intensity of the consciousness of individuality, the individuality itself seemed to dissolve and fade away into boundless being; and this is not a confused state but the clearest of the clearest, the surest of the surest, the weirdest of the weirdest, utterly beyond words, where death was an almost laughable impossibility, the loss of personality seeming no extinction, but the only true life.

Experiment 16: Bodily Calcination

As with all the operations in alchemy, calcination takes place not only on the psychological and spiritual levels but also within the body itself. In alchemical terms, your body is the vehicle of your transformation, truly the temple of God. In this view, your organs and glands are like laboratory retorts in which alchemical processes are taking place to support the body. Oriental alchemists and Renaissance European alchemists firmly believed that the human body was the instrument of alchemical transformation. Unfortunately, like our minds and souls, the body becomes polluted over time and its life force diminished.

Bodily calcination uses aerobic exercises to fan the fires of metabolism and purify the body. Jogging, biking, and swimming can all be alchemical operations. One method of raising the metabolism is known as the "Bellows Breath." It is an ancient hatha yoga technique called *kapala bhati pranayam*. Sit cross-legged on the floor and start breathing very rapidly with a pause between inhaling and exhaling. The rate is about two exhalations per second. As you exhale, push out the air like a bellows by pulling the navel point in toward the spine. When you inhale, use a forward thrust of the navel to bring air into the lungs. Try to keep a smooth, balanced breath. After a few minutes of "fanning the fire," you will start to feel a warmth rise from the stomach and accumulate in the head, which causes a blunting of ego consciousness. If you stop suddenly at this point, there is a bouncing or spilling sensation, as the energy returns to the base of the spine. If you continue, a fluid warmth spreads slowly to other locations in the body, as the consciousness is diffused.

The result of bodily calcination is a biological purification and elimination of toxins, reduction of leaden adipose tissue, and a concentration of life force in the body. Mindful physical exercise is a powerful tool in personal transformation if performed with a positive attitude. This application of Fire in the body is eventually expressed in a kind of "second puberty," a rebirth into a more youthful and healthy state. The body is not only the temple of the soul, it can become a sacred talisman to remind us that alchemy is real and works on many levels.

Personal Dissolution

Just as calcination works on the mind and ego to destroy decep-
tions and impure thoughts, so does dissolution work on the heart
and the id to release buried emotions that conceal or distort our
true nature. Dissolution is working with the Water element by
opening our personal floodgates and generating fresh energy to
fuel our further transformation.

We have all seen how the powerful waters of emotions and feelings just wash away the petty concerns of ego, perhaps during an
illness or depression. We have all been overcome by our feelings at
one time or other, and the fact that water wells up in our eyes as
tears during such moments is just another signature of dissolution.
Medieval alchemists believed that tears actually result from the
decrystallization or breaking down of thoughts, that the salt in
tears is actually dissolved and discarded thoughts.

During dissolution, the lunar powers (as expressed in dreams,
visions, fleeting intimations and impressions, and bodily sensations)
take precedence over the linear approach of the rational mind. Successful dissolution requires letting go of control, allowing feelings
to flow and repressed thoughts and feelings to surface. You might
be overwhelmed by images, wordless impressions, and strange feelings, and feel like you are really floating around aimlessly in a giant
sea, but this is only a temporary process in the long road to renewal
and perfection. In fact, undergoing dissolution is a contradictory
phase that is hard to describe to others. Nothing is really "accomplished" in the worldly sense, but we are slowly becoming more
alive and more aware of a landscape we have been trying to ignore.

Dreams often carry important personal information during personal dissolution, and it is useful to keep a dream journal whenever
you feel like you are in this phase. Remember that your dreams are
intended for you alone and usually carry information about what is
happening in *your* life. Not all images have the same meaning for
everyone, and you have to interpret dreams in context with your current situation, feelings, and stage of transformation. In cases where
alchemical images start appearing in your dreams, the information

carries more universal or archetypal content that is shared by all human beings. It was Carl Jung's work with the dreams of his patients that proved to him that alchemy dealt with transpersonal energies being experienced by people undergoing transformation.

As the first psychologists, the alchemists knew that another way to defeat the ego is to try to drown it in deep feelings over which it has no control. The ego is terrified of the tremendous power of the subconscious and is constantly running from feelings and emotions—burying all those hurtful and humiliating experiences in the shadows, tying up emotional power in knots in our bodies, thinking faster and faster so feelings never catch up.

One of the hallmarks of dissolution is a temporary slowing down of mental processes and an increase in moodiness and depression. In today's upbeat, overstimulated world, it seems shocking to say that depression serves a good purpose, but that is exactly how the alchemists viewed it. To them depression was just another part of personal dissolution. The alchemists welcomed distress and depression because they incite the soul to move forward. That is what the Sufi alchemist Rumi meant when he said "Feel joy in the heart at the coming of sorrow." What is more, in depression there is no mental energy to spare to support the ego and its games, and it is a wonderful opportunity to allow deeper feelings, whose suppression is often the source of the depression, to surface and become acclimated into the personality.

Spiritual alchemists would never take Prozac because they know that only through the darkness can you reach the light. That is not to say that there are no chemical correspondences to depression; that would be expected by an alchemist. But the suggestion that the cure lies strictly on the physical level is anathema to alchemists, who insist on working on all levels of mind, body, and spirit at once. So the darkness of depression is just another temporary phase of total transformation. During dissolution, we realize that no wound is ever silent until it is healed; what is more important, we discover that it is in our wounds where the gold of our genuine Self has accumulated.

Figure 19. Two peacocks pull Jupiter's chariot above, while his signatures of justice and benign rule are shown below. In the retort, three birds (the Three Essentials) dissolve into each other as the operation of Dissolution begins. (Salomon Trismosin, *Splendor Solis*, 1535)

Undissolved people are judgmental and self-centered, and their relationships can only be described as selfish. In such people, the process of dissolution results in a withdrawal of projections and judgments and a breakdown of mental habits. Personal dissolution dissipates the egocentric nervous energy that blindly drives most of us. Being dissolved means being truly relaxed, stopping the endless stream of thoughts to try to feel our way and connect with deeper energies. Dissolution results in a wonderfully flowing presence that is free of inhibitions, prejudgments, and restrictive mental structures.

Experiment 17: The Bain Marie Meditation

As we have noted earlier, Jewish alchemist Maria Prophetissa invented a method of dissolution that became the standard process for washing the ashes from calcination. Called the "bain marie," it is basically a double-boiler in which the water in the bathing vessel is kept at a gentle and constant temperature by immersing it in a second container of water or sand being heated directly. Its mystical power is based on the correspondences between the two types of waters employed in the bain marie. The outer boiler represents earthly Water, and the inner boiler represents heavenly Water.

"The Water is an Angel and descends from the sky," said Prophetissa of her process, "and the earth accepts it on account of the earth's moistness. The Water of the sky is held by the Water of the earth, and the Water of the earth acts as its servant. Its sand serves the purpose of honoring it. Both the waters are gathered together, and the Water holds the Water. The vital principle holds the vital principle, and the vital principle is whitened by the vital principle."

The bain marie is also a powerful meditative tool for handling the destroyed psychic remains resulting from calcination. The meditation exudes a maternal warmth, and the fire of personal consciousness is turned down considerably to accept the spiritual energy from Above. The idea is to dissolve or melt away the burnt-out thoughts and emotions dredged up during the previous blaze of introspection during calcination. That means not thinking about the individual incidents behind emotions but rather trying to feel and work with only their pure energy or "vital principle." If you can successfully dissolve the connections between the emotions and their source, the energy will be set free to be used for your spiritual transformation.

Seated or lying down, start taking deep belly breaths with the abdomen, expanding on every inhalation. Try to feel the warmth in this area, which is very significant in bodily alchemy. In the Eastern traditions, it is known as the Hara or Lower Tan Tien vessel, a great cauldron of physical energy just behind the navel. Continue breathing this way until you feel a buildup of heat in your belly, which is the lower vessel of the bain marie that is heated directly.

Keep breathing by first expanding the belly and then filling the upper chest with air. This upper area is the second boiler or bathing vessel of the bain marie. Feel the difference between the energy in this upper bathing vessel, which is much cooler and calmer than the more intense energy in the belly. Next, wih each breath imagine you are adding ingredients to the gently dissolving waters of the second bathing vessel. These ingredients are fiery emotions, the still warm ashes of calcination. Hold the breath for a moment and let it work out painful memories or fiery emotions that overcome you. Then exhale slowly and deeply, as deep as you can, and imagine those hardened, hurtful "salts" melting away. Repeat this circulation of dissolving baths for as long as it takes you to feel genuine relief. If you can learn to circulate these calm waters through the body and direct them to painful or swollen muscles or joints, you will be amazed at the instant relief this simple visualization brings.

Experiment 18: Cibation

This meditation is based on a technique in alchemy called cibation, which is the addition of water or other fluids to the dried-out matter at precisely the right moment in the experiment to completely dissolve it. In this meditation, we will examine the areas of our emotional makeup that appear the driest and most crystallized, then we add or revitalize them with emotional energy to re-experience them again from a more objective viewpoint. This is a sensitizing process in which painful memories or hardened reactions are purposely dredged up and relived.

Put on your lab coat of relaxed awareness and enter the inner laboratory. Go back to your childhood, where some of our most painful experiences occurred, and retrieve the most painful memory you can think of. Perhaps it was the day a loved one died, the day you lost a pet or relative, or sometime when you were really deeply hurt by someone. Bring the energy into the throat area and feel it well up. Now try to cry from the memory—and cry until you can cry no more. For cibation to occur, you must make yourself cry at the same moment you are feeling the emotion. This crying technique is used by psychologists all over the world to treat eating disorders, sex problems, drug abuse, insomnia, and anger, and it is one of the fastest working methods in the arsenal of psychologists.

Experiment 19: Bodily Dissolution

An ancient and powerful method for bodily dissolution is fasting, which has long been part of many religious disciplines. Not only does fasting for two or more days purge the body of toxins and the effects of overindulgence, but it also activates a healing response from the body. Most animals respond to illness by seeking solitude and refusing to eat, as the body's energy resources are entirely directed toward healing. Fasting therapy has been employed to treat a wide variety of diseases, including cancer, diabetes, tuberculosis, high blood pressure, and even schizophrenia. Fasting clears the mind, refreshes the memory, and can even lead to mystical experiences. Fasting and its connection to the operation of dissolution was well known to Paracelsus and other alchemical healers, who associated it with the benefits of physical depression. One alchemical motto of this phase goes, "The Moon settled, does not eat." Like most methods of dissolution, fasting is a way of becoming stronger by letting go.

If you are not used to fasting, start with juice fasts for a single day or over the weekend. Eat no solid foods but as much fruit and vegetable juices as you want. Notice how not eating affects your mind and body. The more toxins in your body and mind, the more uncomfortable are the first fasts. It is necessary to drink a lot of water so toxins can be easily flushed from the body. True alchemical fasts continue for three to thirty days and should only be undertaken in a spiritually relaxing environment under the supervision of a doctor.

Personal Separation

The alchemists saw this operation as bringing the essences back to life by exposing them to Air, and there are a lot of alchemical images showing swords slicing through space and knives cutting things open at this stage. The archetype of Air is an invisible force with a will of its own and total freedom to exercise it. Down through the ages, archetypal Air has always been associated with life force, spirits, and spiritual energy. The physical signature of the essence of Air is life-giving oxygen, and its subtle component is the *prana* or *chi* that is the focus of Eastern alchemy. This *prana* (Indian alchemy) or *chi* (Taoist alchemy), is the vital breath responsible for a person's state of health, and can be harnessed for psychospiritual growth and rejuvenation.

During personal separation, we retrieve the purified essences of soul and spirit from the dregs of our body and mind. These two essences become very important to us and worth fighting for to keep pure. They are present at all levels of our being and are part of the basic trinity of Mercury (soul), Sulfur (spirit), and Salt (body). The two most immediate expressions of soul and spirit are our own feelings and thoughts (respectively), which we now realize offer us important tools of transformation. Soul expresses itself in feelings and is associated with the act of attention, and spirit expresses itself in thoughts and is associated with the act of intention. These two components of attention and intention make up a kind of binary software of transcendence.

Thus, Separation is coming into focus about our true nature and what has to be done to clean up our lives. This usually becomes a holy war in which we define ourselves by our level of determination. We realize the dross we carry is why we feel dirty and guilty instead of golden. All of a sudden we want to live spiritual principles, be true to our spiritual essences, and be around spiritual people. Because we still have to deal with the impurities of personal ego, organizational ego (bureaucracy), and social ego (what Jung called the superego), this can be a very challenging phase.

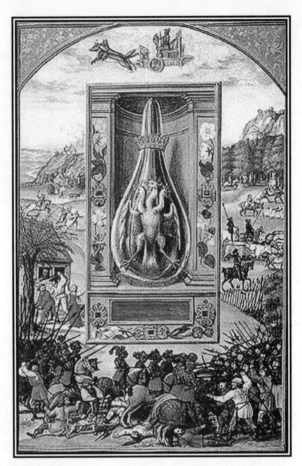

Figure 20. The dogs of war pull Mars's chariot above,
while scenes of war and pillage are shown below. In the
retort, the operation of Separation concludes, and the Three
Essentials emerge as individual identities in the same body.
(Salomon Trismosin, *Splendor Solis*, 1535)

Often during this phase, there is an abrupt separation from family
and friends, and everyone notices that you are willing to *fight* for
what you believe in all of a sudden. During separation, we learn
how to sharpen our will to conquer temptations, overcome abuse

and habitual patterns, live our own lives, and protect the essences we carry within. We now are willing to live our lives closer on the edge and be real no matter what.

The iron individual that emerges during separation is a willful, aggressive, and sometimes hot-tempered person, whose actions are dominated by a conquering energy that wants to change the world. Pollution from ego during separation is disastrous. Such people can be overly assertive and controlling, refusing to compromise in even the most mundane matters. In relationships, the ego-bound Mars is domineering and can even be abusive. At their worst, they are driven by frustration and anger and can become cruel or violent. On the other hand, people successfully handling separation are courageous and daring, often initiating major changes in the world and in the lives of the people around them. In relationships, they are fiercely loyal and can fight for the rights of others with unquenchable passion. The key to successful separation is letting go of the anger or anxiety that is the source of the separative impulse and letting the eternal essences of their personalities guide them.

Experiment 20: Cutting Through Reality

A method called Cutting Through Reality is a separation meditation in which you simply relax, concentrate on your breathing, and periodically ask yourself the question "What are the dregs of my life?" The object is to identify and cut away all but the purest essences of everything around you. It is what alchemists called dealing only with the true signatures of yourself, other people, things, events, and situations. The sword you use to cut through reality is your own consciousness honed to penetrate even the deepest illusion. You sharpen this sword of knowing by living on the *edge* between this world and the next, between matter and mind, between life and death. You no longer give yourself away to the everyday world but maintain a certain objectivity about what is true and what is false. By entering a state of "not doing"—not automatically going along with everything through some misguided sense of participation or politeness—we learn to halt the internal dialogue that supports the false or horizontal world and develop a second attention focused on the spiritual principles on the vertical axis of reality.

Experiment 21: Bodily Separation

There are many methods for bodily separation, in which the essences or energies of soul and spirit are isolated in the body. Some of these methods date back over thirty-five hundred years to Egyptian alchemists who taught spiritual energy techniques in Pharaoh Akhenaten's School of Breathings. Other techniques were developed by Eastern alchemists. All these methods center on working with the subtle life force that, according to the Emerald Tablet, the Wind "carries in its belly." In bodily separation, this energy is split into its masculine (yang) and feminine (yin) by directing the arms and legs in purposeful movements. Generally, movements up and to the right focus yang, and movements down and to the left focus yin.

Such separating, moving meditations, as practiced in Chi Kung and Tai Chi, are a kind of alchemistic aeration that separates and purifies the energetic essences of soul and spirit. By focusing attention on the breath and using intention to move the breath through the body, the essences of the life force (the yin component of soul and the yang component of spirit) are separated and recombined in a new constellation of energy during the final operation of alchemy (coagulation). While a full description of these movements are beyond the scope of this book, the reader is urged to follow through with local instructors in Tai Chi Chuan, Tai Chi Chih, Chi Kung, Aikido, and other disciplines that follow the path of martial arts in the sense of becoming a spiritual warrior.

At this point, we will make the transition from the purification and isolation of the individual essences of soul and spirit, to the conjunction, in which everything is brought back together again in a simpler and purer form. We will begin this work on the new identity or higher ego in the next chapter.

15

Becoming an Alchemist

CALCINATION, DISSOLUTION, AND SEPARATION, which work to expose and purify our thoughts and feelings, are the major operations of our lives. They seem to be a part of nature itself, and we can see them at work in the forces of Fire, Water, and Air that shape the whole planet. Overall, these three processes take place Below, in the realm of matter, the body, and the personality. The result is a purified and simpler substance that contains all the essences to continue the work but none of the complicating and illusory "dregs" that have polluted the original matter.

The next operation involves working with the element Earth, which the alchemists considered as anything that is manifested and solid. The goal at this stage is to *recombine* the essential ingredients into something entirely new on a more highly evolved level. You are fully committed to living in truth and doing whatever is necessary to maintain your integrity.

Personal Conjunction

The operation of conjunction, which means combining or conjoining things, is the turning point in personal alchemy. It is the marriage of the Sun and Moon within, the union of spirit with soul to produce a new identity. The alchemists saw this as a passionate coming together of the elements Fire and Water, an act of inner love. Conjunction is the creation of a whole new personality

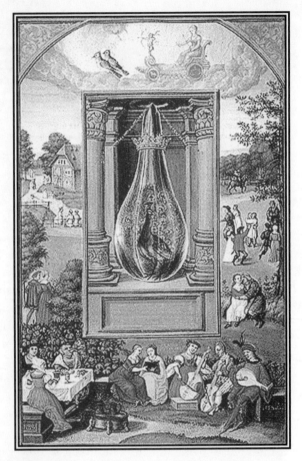

Figure 21. A pair of lovebirds pulls Venus's chariot above,
while images of love and championship are shown below.
In the retort, a peacock spreads its tail indicating that the
Conjunction has succeeded and the next operation is about
to begin. (Salomon Trismosin, *Splendor Solis*, 1535)

from the essences of soul and spirit we have discovered within us,
and it takes a lot of courage, passion, and devotion to succeed in
uniting them. Conjunction is what we experience when we fall in
love with another person, and it is also the communion we feel
with all of nature.

Personal conjunction is difficult for most modern people because it involves the merging of opposites, which is a mysterious and paradoxical operation. In order to achieve personal conjunction, we have to be able to redefine ourselves in paradoxical terms. The personal essences of spirit and soul come together in a new form of higher reasoning or intuition. There is really no single English word for this kind of alchemical way of thinking. The Chinese word for it means "heartmind," and the ancient Egyptian word means "intelligence of the heart." Yet this concept of the complete merging of thoughts and feelings is crucial in achieving personal conjunction.

In psychological terms, conjunction unites our thoughts with our feelings in moments of true wisdom. The alchemists referred to these two opposed ways of knowing as Solar and Lunar consciousness. Solar consciousness is the rational, deductive, argumentative, intellectual thinking that is the hallmark of science and our patriarchal Western culture. The alchemists assigned it many code words, such as the Sun, Sulfur, the King, the Father, and ultimately Spirit. Lunar consciousness is a nonlinear, image-driven, intuitive way of thinking that is an accepted tool of the arts and religion. Among its many symbols are the Moon, Mercury, the Queen, the Holy Ghost, and ultimately Soul. The union of Solar and Lunar consciousness produces a superior third way of knowing called Stellar consciousness. Stellar consciousness is a state of incorruptible wisdom symbolized by the heroic Child of the Philosophers, the metal gold, a diamond or pearl, the Philosopher's Stone, the astral body, and of course, the stars themselves. Remember, in the view of the alchemists, we have all embarked on a journey through the manifested planets—a journey home to the stars.

Experiment 22: Creating the Overself

The work in this experiment is done in the everyday world, and it is not necessary to enter a meditative state. The idea is to create a permanent vessel for the newly conjuncted consciousness within the existing personality. Nineteenth-century psychologists called this new identity the Overself. To create the Overself, you simply begin practicing to maintain your higher or stellar presence no matter what happens, no matter how confusing things get, no matter what emotions swell up within you, no matter how cruel or thoughtless others are toward you. Every problem, every personal challenge, every nuisance or annoying person, is another opportunity for you to develop presence and strengthen the Overself. In trying to maintain your presence and to keep centered in all situations, you soon learn that you can rely on neither intellect nor emotions. To be really connected to what is real, you have to make use of inner talents and resources you cannot explain.

It is important to remember that the two opposing ways of knowing only come together when they are *used* together. In order for the Overself to manifest you have to practice not relying on either alone on a daily basis in the real world. The Overself can overcome the onslaughts of ignorance, insensitivity, and illusion one encounters in the world because it is not of this world. This larger presence within you corresponds to the Lesser Stone of alchemists, which is gradually perfected to emerge during the last operation as a permanent state of higher consciousness that is the Greater Stone.

Experiment 23: Bodily Conjunction

That the human body must be perfected, as well as the mind and spirit, is a basic tenet of alchemy. Yet how do the King and Queen manifest in the body, and what exactly is the Child of the Philosophers in terms of human physiology? According to Tantric alchemists, the phallic-shaped pineal gland at the center of the brain and the bi-lobed pituitary body play the roles of King and Queen respectively. Their union, achieved through meditative exercises, produces a golden pill of immortality, which is released at the back of the throat and is activated when it reaches the stomach. This inner sex act, which the alchemists sometimes referred to as an act of incest because it takes place within, releases powerful energies that perfect and rejuvenate the body. This process is facilitated by using active imagination and meditations based on these ideas.

Personal Fermentation

The work of personal fermentation begins in the spiritual realm. But how do you work in unmanifested reality? How do you enter the Above; how do you get to the Other Side? The answer is plain. You have to die in this world and be reborn in the next. The alchemists called this universal process of death and rebirth fermentation, and just like natural fermentation, it starts with putrefaction, in which the matter is killed and allowed to decompose and rot in sealed containers or coffins. People, too, first must die to their own ego reality to grow and be reborn on a higher level. There is always a dark period of unconsciousness to pass through. "Clothe yourself in the garment of Nothingness and drink the cup of self-annihilation" said Attar, a twelfth-century Sufi alchemist.

Psychologically, putrefaction is the dark night of the soul in which our ego, everything we thought was our identity, suffers a final and complete death. Despite the optimism of the conjunction, we realize the impermanence of our personality. Putrefaction is a necessary, if painful, step to enlightenment in which we truly realize the futility of a merely physical existence.

The modern alchemist Fulcanelli, in *Les Demeures Philosophales* (Dwellings of the Philosophers), wrote:

> One can thus understand why the Philosophers place so much insistence upon the necessity of material death. It is through death that the spirit, imperishable and always active, stirs up, sifts, separates, cleans and purifies the body. It is from death that there proceeds the possibility of assembling the purified parts, to build with them a new lodging place, finally to transmit to the regenerated form an energy which it does not possess.

The sudden breakthrough of light and imagination that follows purtrefaction is the most inspired part of alchemy. During this phase of true fermentation, the alchemists felt they were working on a whole new level of reality. During fermentation, according to French alchemist Rene Schwaller de Lubicz, we "leave all dialectic behind and follow the path of the Powers." This is the inspiration of new life and energy from a higher level that changes the vibratory level of soul.

The peacock's tail that appears in the laboratory to mark this stage represents the activation of the dawn of the True Imagination, a world of light in the realm of pure mind. Alchemists called it the "true" imagination to differentiate it from mere fantasy or idle daydreaming; to them, the light of the True Imagination was the same divine light of mind that shown down from Above into the darkest recesses of matter. It is the nature of this mercurial light to encompass everything and to contain all possibilities.

Carl Jung commented on this process:

> The concept of *Imaginatio* is the most important key to understanding the alchemical Opus. We have to conceive of these imaginal processes not as the immaterial phantoms that we readily take fantasy pictures to be, but as something corporeal, a subtle body. The *Imaginatio*, or the act of imagining, was a physical activity that could be fitted into the cycle of material changes, that brought these about and was brought about by them in turn. The alchemist related himself not only to the unconscious but directly to the very substance that he hoped to transform through the power of imagination.

Experiment 24: Capturing the Fermental Light

The fermental light of the true imagination is always close at hand and only the veil of our assumptions of materiality needs to be lifted to see it. Sit back in a comfortable chair, fold your hands in your lap, and relax. When you are completely relaxed, close your eyes and concentrate on the first image that pops into your mind. Do not be concerned if it is something you had just seen or if there is no image at all. Simply allow the image, pattern, blankness, or whatever, to change and grow. Pay attention to the morphing image and try to remember as many details or impressions as you can. Now, ask yourself a question—something you really want to know—and see what

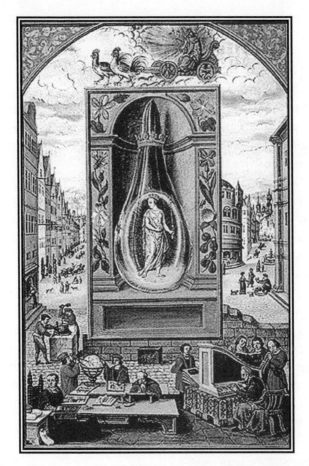

Figure 22. Two cocks pull Mercury's chariot above, while images
of learning, inspiration, and music are shown below. Inside the
retort, the white Virgin Queen is pregnant with the Child of
the Philosophers, indicating that Fermentation was successful.
(Salomon Trismosin, *Splendor Solis*, 1535)

happens. Observe how the image or feeling alters and what the final
version looks like. Finally, open your eyes again, and summarize
your experience in as much detail as you can.

If you visualized someone from the office lying naked on your
bed, you have probably missed the point. The idea is not to engage
our fantasies but to allow images to rise on their own from an

unconscious source. Try it again at a later time if your images are being driven by wish fulfillment or from instincts such as hunger, if you missed a meal. The curse of modern man is that he confuses fantasy for the amazing power of true imagination and thus relegates both to the psychic trash heap. However, if you experienced something that you had not previously noticed or something that an independent part of your mind was dwelling on, then you have had a breakthrough to the fermental light, and you should reflect on what higher meaning it carries.

Experiment 25: Bodily Fermentation

During the initial stages of personal fermentation, the level of inspiration can become so intense that it is experienced as a palpable warm light circulating in the body. As fermentation progresses, people report feelings of extraordinary grace and "flow" as the physical body raises toward perfection, toward an ideal or archetypal image that is slowly taking on reality within.

After the conjunction or marriage of the pineal gland and pituitary body, the pituitary (as the "master gland") floods the body with new types of hormones that cause fundamental changes in the organs, blood, and genetic material. The alchemists referred to this flood of psychospiritual chemicals as the vitriol humor, which initiates a kind of second puberty in the body.

Personal Distillation

Fermentation is like a mystical or religious experience for most people, and it can even take the form of psychedelic or paranormal experiences. It occurs whenever we confront the tremendous power of the transpersonal or spiritual realm. This can be an overwhelming experience in which we temporarily lose our balance and have to readjust to the real world. What we need is objectivity, a distilling of the experience. That is exactly what distillation means on the psychological level.

Personal distillation is gaining objectivity by taking a step back to get an overall view of the extremes of personal experience, the ups and downs in life. In that way, it is a purification of consciousness or the rising of consciousness to a higher level. For the modern adept, distillation consists of introspective techniques that attempt to raise the content of the psyche to the highest level possible, free from all sentimentality and personal attachments. Success at distillation is measured by how clear and focused your mind can become. We not only open up to our own pain and confusion but relate to the pain and suffering in a more compassionate way.

In spiritual distillation, we finally realize that we are all sparks of light trapped in matter and our only hope for survival is the union of our light with the divine light Above. This is actually an extremely refreshing experience of becoming clear and staying clear on all levels of our being. We now see that our thoughts and feelings are the thoughts and feelings of the whole universe; the center of our being and the center of the cosmos are one and the same during distillation. Distillation takes us into the rarefied realm of spirit where base emotions cannot follow. It is the purification of the unborn Self—all that we truly are and can be spiritually.

By bringing together the powers Above with the powers Below during distillation, we create what has been called a Hermes Field, in which we raise our consciousness to the highest level to bring back the miraculous possibilities of pure mind and directed consciousness into the manifested world. The Hermes Field forms at the juncture of Above and Below, in the twilight between unmanifested and manifested reality. Truly amazing things can happen there.

Experiment 26: Circulation of the Light

Chinese alchemists became proficient at personal Distillation thousands of years ago. In a meditation called "Circulation of the Light," the aspirant is taught to concentrate on the light of the innermost region while freeing oneself from all outer and inner entanglements. During the first stage of this distillation, a mercurial or watery consciousness is used, and the light is gathered by quieting the body and mind through breath awareness and meditation. Breathe slowly

Figure 23. Two midwives pull the Moon's chariot above, while scenes of humankind's dominion over nature are shown below. In the retort, the child has been born and appears as the magical Red King, indicating a successful Distillation. (Salomon Trismosin, *Splendor Solis*, 1535)

and deliberately and with each inhalation, feel the chi or spiritual energy in the air moving down into a reservoir of energy in the abdomen. Just relax and breathe long deep breaths originating in the belly. Feel the warm yellow energy enter with the breath and accumulate in the belly. The object is to store all this fresh energy in a vessel, such as a retort or cauldron, that is visualized in the abdominal cavity just below and about an inch behind the navel. In Taoist alchemy, this is called the Lower Tan Tien (Lower Elixir Field).

In the second phase of the Circulation of the Light, the alchemist's directed consciousness is used to initiate the movement of the accumulated light energy. With concentration fixed at the level of the abdominal vessel, the practitioner uses intention and attention to will and feel the light circulate up the Channel of Control up the back along the spinal column and into the vessel or "precious cauldron" of the brain, which is the Upper Tan Tien (or Upper Elixir Field). There, the light energy is condensed and accumulated, and any unconverted energy returns to the navel area via the Channel of Function, which runs along the front of the chest.

The adept repeats the Circulation of the Light daily for months or even years, until enough of the liquid light collects to crystallize in the brain cauldron. According to Chinese alchemists, the subtle matter distilled through this process congeals into a golden pill, which is the adept's passage to perfect health and even immortality.

The overall process is summed up admirably in a 2,500-year-old alchemy text from the Chou dynasty:

> In transporting the breath, the inhalation must be full and the breath should be held and gathered. If it is gathered, it becomes magic. If it becomes magic, it descends and quiets down. If it quiets down, it solidifies. If it is solidified, then it germinates. If it germinates, it grows. If it grows, it retreats upward. If it retreats upward, it reaches the top of the head. If it reaches the top of the head, it still presses up, for the secret power of Heaven moves Above, and the secret power of Earth moves Below. He who follows this will live; he who acts contrary to this will die.

Experiment 27: Bodily Distillation

There are many "moving meditations" designed to accomplish distillation of the life force in the body. The slow and graceful movements of the ancient art of Tai Chi Chuan and Tai Chi Chih are designed to make the practitioner aware of the subtle light energy (chi) as it circulates in the body. The sadhana postures of Kundalini Yoga actually attempt to bind one's awareness to this energy, so it can be followed upward as it is distilled from the body in a union of the individual's consciousness with the infinite consciousness of God. All these exercises work with the vertical axis in the human body, which is the Hermetic caduceus or ladder of transformation along which the seven operations in the Emerald Formula are used to release and purify knots of blocked or impure energy.

Personal Coagulation

Surprisingly, personal coagulation is one of the easier processes in our spiritual transformation. If everything proceeded well through the higher operations of fermentation and distillation, the goal of the Work almost automatically forms or congeals. The alchemists saw this final stage of personal transformation as working with a higher form of Salt, which is the uninflammable component found in the ashes from Fire or in the crystallized remains of Water. In other words, the final Salt is that which can be changed no more; it is the perfected essence of matter and the soul.

In the transformed person, this Salt is a new identity, a new ego or center of consciousness. We can only be resurrected from the cross of matter by sacrificing our individual identity, the Green Mercury Serpent of our ego. We can only join the One by becoming Nothing. We can only grow into the greater spirit by surrendering our separate individuality.

Personal coagulation produces a very genuine and alive person with a deep respect and connection to the processes of nature. It is sensed in the world as a higher love, a deeply felt compassion for the whole world and everyone in it, and also an appreciation for the processes of birth and death in the universe. This is a crowning individuation resulting in peace of mind, heightened energy, and a free-flowing adaptability to new situations. In the material realm, it entails the production of synchronistic events that enhance the life

Figure 24. Two horses pull the Sun's chariot above, while images of men working and playing harmoniously are shown below. In the retort, the dragon of the First Matter reappears, now refined and balanced, indicating a successful Coagulation of the powers. (Salomon Trismosin, *Splendor Solis*, 1535)

of the alchemist, as all parts of one's life become golden. That also means the healing of the body and simply living long enough (and comfortably enough) to apply the knowledge it has taken a lifetime to accumulate.

Personal coagulation incarnates and releases a higher state of consciousness, which the alchemists also referred to as the Greater Stone. Using this magical touchstone, the alchemists believed they could create an elixir that would cure all diseases and heal all wounds on all levels. They also believed that the perfected human would be able to solve a multitude of problems that seem insurmountable in our human civilization. As Albert Einstein once noted: "You cannot solve a problem with the same mind that created it." The mind of the coagulated person has been fundamentally and permanently transmuted and is open to vistas of time and space to which most of us are unaware.

Experiment 28: Coagulation of the Second Body

This unique quality of emotion and holistic thought acts like a forgotten switch, turning on our genetic codes and creating a hormonal "elixir"—to use the alchemists' term—that inaugurates a spiritual revolution in our bodies, a coming of age in spirit that rejuvenates and revitalizes us. On the spiritual level, coagulation is the creation of a perfected Second Body, a golden body of coagulated light that the great alchemist Paracelsus named the Astral Body. Alchemists believed that if you could not create this perfected body during your lifetime, you were destined to be reabsorbed into the cosmos and recycled until you got it right.

In Christianity, the culmination of the Great Work is expressed as the "seamless garment" or in the words of Jesus: "I and my Father are one." In occult terminology, spirit and soul are permanently united in a body of light that acts as a mobile center of consciousness spanning all dimensions of existence and described in out-of-body and near-death experiences. In terms of spiritual chemistry, the immortal soul (the volatile "saved" feminine variable) has united inseparably with the human spirit (the fixed masculine invariable principle) to form the Living Stone. Soul and Spirit are one in a new body. The difference between the lowest state of consciousness in alchemy and the highest is like the difference between soft, black coal and a hard, clear diamond. Yet they are both made out of the same material. As one Renaissance alchemist put it: "You break through space, fly to heaven in broad daylight, and shed the flesh-and-bone bag, which is now as useless as the alchemical workshop and vessels once the elixir has been perfected."

To practice the coagulation of the light, the first step is to spiritize the body and mind. This can be done in meditation by going through the previous operations in order to reach a purified state of consciousness. You could also begin with the rising and falling waves of the Circulation of Light meditation. While doing the circulation, observe how the energy moves in your body and then try to increase the vibrations of the light itself by visualizing it changing from a yellow or white color to a deep violet color. In increasing the frequency of the light, you increase its energy and it becomes a soft violet flame circulating in your body. This is the divine energy within you. Visualize softly undulating violet flames sweeping over your entire body until they engulf you. You are now within the flame. As you surrender to the flame and let go of any of your control over it, try to sense how the flame imparts a feeling of vibrancy and vitality. Its action has been described as a welcomed feeling of being boiled and cleansed, like being immersed in a warm bubbling hot tub. Feel the bubbling flames caressing your body, internally and externally.

Now retake partial control of the increased vibrational state and start to crystallize the subtle flame into an etheric double or replica of your physical body. Begin the formation of this body gradually, by trying to extend a hand or foot just beyond your physical frame. Increase the limb's vibrational rate if necessary and project more of the violet flame into it. Then try to touch some object near you, such as a chair arm, carpet, or mattress. Now return your limb to coincide with your physical body and relax the vibrational rate to change the violet color back into the yellow hue the energy had at the beginning. Let the two bodies merge again. This is enough for the first time. Continue this exercise until you truly feel as though you are separating from your physical body by directing the intensity of the violet flame. With continued practice and by expanding the process to other parts of your body, you begin to build a new Salt or new body of light.

Experiment 29: Making Visions Real

One of the characteristics of the coagulated spirit is the ability of the individual to make his or her personal reality part of the real world. This is nothing supernatural or even mystical, but a practical expression of the higher reality that is part of the natural "Operation of the Sun" described in the Emerald Tablet. In this exercise, we will begin to train our minds to take advantage of our divine image-making ability to project our visions into reality.

Taoist alchemists are very proficient at this activity. At the advanced levels of Tai Chi and Chi Kung, the practitioner does not actually perform the movements at all but visualizes performing them in the mind. In many well-documented cases, the mental performance of the movements produces the same changes in body and brain chemistry as actually doing the movements.

A story about Native American athlete Jim Thorpe also illustrates this idea. When he was on the ship crossing the Atlantic to Sweden on his way to the 1912 Olympics in Stockholm, Thorpe was told that he had to be entered in at least two events to participate in the games. His assigned events were long-distance running and the broad jump, which was a completely new sport to him. Thorpe's tribal name was Wa-Tho-Huk, which means "Bright Path." There is no doubt that he took the path of light in his physical training. He had learned the power of visualization as a child and applied it in his amazing feats of running. And now he would apply it to this entirely new sport.

Thorpe put a wide strip of white tape on the deck of the ship and then lined up a deckchair twenty-three feet, three inches away from the line. This was one inch more than the current world record. But he never attempted to actually jump the distance. He simply sat in the chair visualizing the playing field and the distance he had to clear. His preparation for the event was in the inner laboratory he created on the ship's deck. For most of the day during the eight-day journey, he sat stubbornly in the chair creating a focused and purified space, until it resonated perfectly between how he would perform on the playing field and what he knew he could do in his own mind. In his own words: "I just sat in that chair until I truly believed I could jump the distance."

The first time Jim Thorpe ever broad jumped, he set a world record. He went on to win both the pentathlon and decathlon events. The same year he led his Carlisle football team to the collegiate championship by scoring nearly two hundred points. After that, he went on to play six years of major league baseball. Perhaps the most fitting description of Jim Thorpe's abilities came at the 1912 Olympics, when King Gustav V of Sweden presented Thorpe with his trophies. "Sir," the King told the Indian, "you are the greatest athlete in the world."

All you have to do to apply this alchemical principle in your own life is to start "rehearsing" things in your mind before actually doing them. One of the first things you learn is that we are our own worst enemies in most of what we do. We tend to focus on the negative aspects of things and of everything that can go wrong. By clustering our doubts and fears in our minds and imagination, we project the means of our own defeat. Try alchemical visualization a few times and you will be convinced of its power. Remember, if you do it with a blasé or skeptical attitude that will be projected. Be open and relaxed yet determined to not leave your visualization until you really believe that is the way it will turn out. Or, as the alchemists would say, make your images come alive in you or they will have no life at all.

THE OPERATIONS OF ALCHEMY offer us real and time-tested methods for personal transformation. They are a path to the divine powers that dwell within us. It is never an easy path, and it involves as much destruction and negation of existing structures in the personality as it does encouraging and building up new structures. You have to learn to work both left-hand and right-hand paths and move freely between the Above and the Below. The important thing to remember is that it is the work itself as much as accomplishing your goals that brings real power into your life. As the great yogic alchemist Pantanjali wrote over twenty-one hundred years ago:

When you are inspired by some great purpose, some extraordinary project, all your thoughts break their bonds; your mind transcends limitations, your consciousness expands in every direction, and you find yourself in a new, great, and wonderful world. Dormant forces, faculties, and talents become alive, and you discover yourself to be a greater person by far than you ever dreamed yourself to be!

APPENDIX 1:

Glossary of Alchemy

Air: one of the Four Elements of alchemy. Air in the alchemical sense carries the archetypal properties of spirit into the manifested world. It is associated with the operation of separation and represented by the metal iron.

Albification: making the matter in the alchemical work become white. Refers to both physical and spiritual processes.

Alchemy: the word is derived from the Arabian phrase "al-khemia," which refers to the preparation of the Stone or Elixir by the Egyptians. The Arabic root "khemia" comes from the Coptic "khem" that alluded to the fertile black soil of the Nile delta. Esoterically and hieroglyphically, the word refers to the dark mystery of the primordial or First Matter (the Khem), the One Thing through which all creation manifests. Alchemy, then, is the Great Work of nature that perfects this chaotic matter, whether it is expressed as the metals, the cosmos, or the substance of our souls.

Alembic: the upper part of a still; a stillhead, a type of retort. The term is often used to refer to a complete still. (see cucurbit; distillation)

Alkahest: the power from Above that makes possible alchemical transformation. The word is usually translated as "universal solvent," which alludes to the ability of the alkahest to dissolve or reduce all physical matter to its basic essence. With metals, this meant transmuting them to their purest form, which was gold. In the human body, this meant the creation or revealing of a golden body of consciousness, the Astral Body.

Aludel: a pear-shaped earthenware bottle, open at both ends. It was used as a condenser in the sublimation process and thus came to signify the end stages of transformation. Also called the Hermetic Vase, the Philosopher's Egg, and the Vase of the Philosophy.

Amalgamation: the formation of an amalgam, or alloy, of a metal with mercury. This term is sometimes extended to mean any union of metals.

Animals: often used to symbolize the basic components and processes of alchemy. They may be used to symbolize the Four Elements such as the lion or ox (Earth), fish or whales (Water), eagles (Air), or salamanders or dragons (Fire). Aerial animals generally indicate volatile principles, while terrestrial animals indicate fixed principles. Whenever two animals are found, they signify Sulfur and Mercury or some relationship between the fixed and the volatile.

Antimony: from the Latin word "antimonium," which was probably used by Constantinius Africanus (1050 A.D.) to refer to stibnite ore. According to one legend, alchemist Basil Valentine named the metal, after feeding it to some monks in a Benedictine monastery. The monks got violently ill and some even died, hence the Latin name that means "anti-monk." Spiritually too, monks feel most threatened by their own animal nature. Oddly enough, the Tincture of Antimony cures venereal diseases. Associated with the attributes of Lead.

Aqua fortis: Latin for "strong water" and refers to nitric acid. Various grades of *aqua fortis* were prepared depending on the length of its Distillation, which concentrated the acid. A mixture of *aqua fortis* and *spiritus salis* ("spirit of salt," i.e., hydrochloric acid) produces *aqua regia* ("royal water," so named because it can dissolve gold). It was first prepared by distilling common salt with *aqua fortis*.

Aqua vitae: "living water" or water "with spirit." An aqueous alcohol concentrated by one or more distillations.

Arcana ("magical secrets"): archetypal influences that transcend space and time. According to the ancient text *Archidoxies*, the arcana are pre-existing powers that "have the power of transmuting, altering, and restoring us." In this view, the arcana are the secret workings of the mind of God, the *logos* of the Greeks or what the alchemists referred to as the thoughts of the One Mind. In the Tarot, the arcana are represented by symbolic drawings that the reader tries to work with through meditation. In the cabala, the arcana are represented by the esoteric properties of the letters of the Hebrew alphabet, energies that the cabalist tries to work with in the Tree of Life. In the ancient Chinese system of divination, the *I Ching*, the arcana are represented by the sixty-four trigrams, each with its own properties and influ-

ences. The alchemists believed the arcana were expressed on all
levels of reality, from chemical compounds to our innermost moods
and desires.

Arcanum Experiment: early alchemists divided their chemicals into
major and minor arcana. The major arcana consisted of the four
compounds: Vitriol, Natron, Liquor Hepatis, and Pulvis Solaris.
Three out of the four consisted of dual ingredients that were easily
separable. Vitriol could be broken down into sulfuric acid and iron.
Natron appeared as sodium carbonate and sodium nitrate. Pulvis
Solaris was made up of the red and black varieties. Thus, the seven
chemicals comprising the minor arcana were: Sulfuric Acid, Iron,
Sodium Carbonate, Sodium Nitrate, Liquor Hepatis, Red Pulvis
Solaris, and Black Pulvis Solaris. The alchemists believed that these
secret chemicals could be combined in the Arcanum Experiment,
the single laboratory experiment that would demonstrate the archetypal forces and evolution of the universe. Ideally, such an experiment should succeed on many levels, not only corroborating the
deepest philosophical and psychological principles, but also providing concrete evidence of their veracity. The Arcanum Experiment
exposed the hidden principles connecting heaven and earth, offering a framework in which to explain both microcosmic and macrocosmic events.

Archaeus: the "Thing Itself" of a substance. According to Paracelsus,
it is the "secret inner matter of a substance," its oldest part that goes
back to when it was just an ideal image, thought, or vibration of
spirit in the Above.

Archetype: an elementary idea rooted in the mind. It is the ideal or
essence from which an existing thing has been copied and is part
of creation itself. Archetypes are primordial patterns that show up
on all levels of reality.

Athanor: from the Arabic word *al-tannur* (oven), the athanor is the
furnace used by the alchemists to perfect matter. Built of brick or
clay, the athanor usually was shaped like a tower with a domed roof
and was designed to keep an even heat over long periods of time.
The alchemists considered it an incubator and sometimes referred to
it as the "House of the Chick." Symbolically, the athanor is also the
human body and the fire of bodily metabolism that fuels our transformation and the ultimate creation of a Second Body of light. The
mountain is a symbol for the athanor, since the perfection of

the metals takes place under the guise of Nature within mountains. Sometimes a hollow oak tree is used to symbolize the athanor.

Azoth: the term "Azoth" is formed from the first and last letters of the English alphabet ("a" and "z"), which stand for the beginning and end of all creation—the alpha and omega of the Greek philosophers, the aleph and tau of the Hebrew cabalists. Therefore the Azoth is the ultimate arcanum, the universal spirit of God in all created things. The alchemists believed that the liquid metal mercury carried the signature of this omnipotent archetypal spirit.

Bain Marie (Balneum Marie): a warm alchemical bath. Chemically, it is a double boiler in which a container of water is suspended in a simmering cauldron. Psychologically, it is the gentle warmth of emotionally centered meditation used in the dissolution process. The bain marie was named after Maria Prophetissa, a Jewish alchemist who wrote much about the methods and equipment of the Water operations of dissolution and distillation.

Balsam: a resinous or waxy semi-solid compound that captures the essence of a liquid medicine or perfume. To Paracelsus, the balsam was the "interior salt" that protected the body from decomposition, and earlier alchemists considered the Balsam of the Elements to be the Quintessence, the result of the conjunction of alchemical principles. Because of its amalgamating ability, mercury was considered the balsam agent of the metals. In the chemical arcana, Liquor Hepatis mixed with fat or wax was known as the Balsam of the Soul.

Basilisk: a symbolic alchemical creature said to have the head of a bird and the body of a dragon. The wingless serpentine animal was hatched from a hermaphroditic cock's egg and nursed by a serpent. Psychologically, the basilisk represents the melding of our higher and lower natures in conjunction, a process that must be continued in the next three operations of alchemy for this "Child of the Philosophers" to become the Living Stone of the fully integrated self. Biologically, the basilisk represents the mammalian embryology, the genetic replaying of the stages of evolution within the egg or womb. The basilisk also has chemical connotations, which probably have to do with a metallurgical process involving cinnabar.

Baths: symbolize the dissolution process in alchemy in which the metals are cleansed and purified.

Birds: ascending birds indicate the volatilization of compounds or their sublimation. Descending birds indicate the fixation of compounds or their condensation and precipitation. Birds shown both ascending and descending indicate the process of distillation.

Black Lion: the darkest part of a substance, its *caput mortum* or black salt that cannot be purified any more. Carbon.

Black Phase (or Nigredo): the first stage in alchemy. This phase begins with the operation of calcination and lasts through the putrefaction stage of fermentation.

Blue Vitriol (or Bluestone): cupric sulfate.

Brimstone (from German *Brennstein* or "burning stone"): sulfur.

Caduceus: the magical staff of Hermes, the Messenger of the Gods and revealer of alchemy. The staff is entwined by two serpents representing the solar and lunar forces. Their union is the conjunction of alchemical principles; their offspring, if it lives, is the Stone. This stone is represented as a golden ball with wings at the top of the caduceus.

Calcination: the first operation in alchemical transformation. It is denoted by the symbol for the first sign of the zodiac, Aries. Breaking down of a substance by fierce heating and burning usually in an open crucible.

Child: a naked child symbolizes the innocent soul. In alchemy, the child is the offspring of the King and Queen, the result of their marriage or union. A child crowned or clothed in purple robes signifies Salt or the Philosopher's Stone.

Cibation: the addition of new material to the contents of the crucible. During dissolution, it requires adding liquid to the desiccated matter at precisely the right moment.

Cinnabar (Vermillion): the bright red ore of mercury sulfide. Known as "Dragon's Blood," the roasted rocks emit a thick reddish smoke, as pure glistening mercury oozes from cracks. Psychologically, cinnabar represents the hardened habits and terrestrial marriages of soul and spirit that must be broken asunder in calcination to free the essences with which the alchemist intends to work.

Circulation: the purification of a substance by a circular distillation in a pelican or closed distillation apparatus. Through heating, the liquid component separates, is condensed and descends again to the substance in the flask. Sometimes it refers to a rotation, in which a liquid is circulated over a solid in a sealed vessel.

Coagulation: the thickening of a thin liquid into a more solid mixture through some inner change, as with the curdling of milk. This can

be accomplished by a variety of means—by the addition of a substance or by heating or cooling. Coagulation is the seventh and last
operation in alchemical transformation.

Coction: the cooking or heating of a substance at a moderate heat for
an extended period.

Cohobation: a kind of distillation in which the distillate is poured
back into its residue; a method of redistillation. Cohobation involves
the frequent removal of the moist component of a substance by
heating. Often the moist component (or some other liquid) is
added and the process continued.

Congelation: a loose or temporary conjunction of opposites; a mixture
in which a liquid is gelled or made semi-solid; intercourse. The
process is represented by the sign for the constellation of Taurus.
The conversion of a thin, easily flowing liquid into a congealed
thick substance, often by heating.

Conjunction: the fourth operation in alchemical transformation. It is
the coming together of the opposing archetypal forces of the Sun
and Moon or the King and Queen. Conjunction is the joining of
two opposite components, often seen as the union of the male and
female, the subtle and gross, or even the elements. Copulation is a
conjunction, or joining of two opposite components, seen through
the metaphor of the union of the male and female, or the union of
the fixed and the volatile.

Copper: one of the seven metals of alchemy. Copper (and sometimes
bronze and brass) is associated with the operation of conjunction
and the element Earth.

Crown: symbolizes the successful completion of an alchemical operation or the achievement of a magisterium. It also signifies chemical
royalty or the perfection of a metal.

Crows: symbols of the black phases of calcination and putrefaction.

Crucible: the melting vessel of the alchemists. It is made of inert
material such as porcelain and can withstand great heat. Used to liq-
uefy the metals.

Cucurbit: the lower part of a still, containing the original liquid. It is
made of glass or earthenware and was also known as a "gourd" on
account of its shape; a receiver. (see alembic; distillation)

Dew: symbolic of divine incarnation or manifestation from Above.
Alchemists believed natural dew contained the divine Salt (thoughts
of the One Mind) that could transform the Sulfur and Mercury of

the First Matter. In many ways, dew represented the Elixir or contents of the cup of God, the Holy Grail.

Diana: appearances of the Greek goddess Diana in alchemical drawings and treatises signify the Moon and Lunar consciousness.

Digestion: is a kind of putrefaction in which the nutrients or essences are reabsorbed; the slow modification of a substance by means of a gentle heat.

Dissolution: the second operation in alchemical transformation. The process of dissolving a solid in a liquid; the reduction of a dry thing in water. Represented by the sign for the constellation of Cancer. The dissolving or transforming of a substance into a liquid.

Distillation: the sixth operation in alchemical transformation. Denoted by the symbol for the constellation Virgo. It is essentially a process of concentration, no matter on what level (physical, mental, or spiritual) it occurs. The separation of a volatile component from a substance by heating so as to drive off the component as a vapor that is condensed and collected in a cooler part of the apparatus. The entire setup consisting of the boiling flask, condensing tube, and receiving flask is called a distillation train.

Dogs: signify primitive matter, natural sulfur, or material gold. Dogs represent a domesticated life force in the service of man. A dog fighting with a wolf symbolizes the process of purifying gold using antimony.

Dove: a symbol of renewed spirit or infusion of energy from Above. Chemically, it signifies the change from the Black Phase to the White Phase of transformation.

Dragons: represent the spirits or life force of the metals. A dragon in flames is a symbol of a metal undergoing calcination. Several dragons fighting is symbolic of metals undergoing putrefaction. Dragons with wings represent the volatile (spiritual or pure) principle; dragons without wings represent the fixed (crude or material) principle. A dragon biting its own tale is the Uroboros and signifies the fundamental unity of all things. In formulae, the term "the Dragon" usually refers to the mercury-acid obtained from metals.

Eagle: a symbol of volatilization. For instance, an eagle devouring a lion indicates the volatilization of a fixed component by a volatile component. Denotes sublimation or distillation.

Earth: one of the Four Elements of alchemy. Earth in the alchemical sense carries the archetypal properties of manifestation, birth, and material creation. It is associated with the operation of conjunction and represented by the green ore of copper.

Egg: symbolic of the hermetically sealed vessel of creation. Stoppered retorts, coffins, and sepulchers represent eggs in many alchemical drawings.

Elixir: essentially a liquid version of the Philosopher's Stone and has the same ability to perfect any substance. When applied to the human body, the Elixir cures diseases and restores youth.

Exaltation: an operation by which a substance is raised into a purer and more perfect nature. Exaltation usually involves the release of a gas or air from a substance.

Fermentation: the fifth operation in alchemical transformation. It is represented by the sign for the constellation of Capricorn. After the rotting of a substance, usually of an organic nature, digesting bacteria appear and are often accompanied by the release of gas bubbles.

Filtration: a kind of separation, in which material is passed through a sieve or screen designed to allow only pieces of a certain size to pass through. The operation is represented by the sign for the constellation of Sagittarius, the Archer. The process of removing the grosser parts of a substance by passing through a strainer, filter, or cloth.

Fire: one of the Four Elements of alchemy. Fire in the alchemical sense carries the archetypal properties of activity and transformation. It is associated with the operation of calcination and represented by the metal lead.

Fixation: making a volatile subject fixed, stable, or solid, so that it remains permanently unaffected by fire. The process of stabilizing and incarnating a substance; depriving a substance of its volatility or mobility to congeal or combine it. The process is represented by the sign for the constellation of Gemini.

Flores: the oxide of a metal.

Fountain: the alchemical Fountain of Fountains is a symbol of the Uroboros. Three fountains represent the three principles of Sulfur, Mercury, and Salt. The King and Queen sitting in a fountain signifies a bath or the Water operations of dissolution and distillation.

Geber (or Jabir): the Latin name of Jabir ibn Hayyan (721–815 A.D.). He is the father of both Islamic and European alchemy. He knew of the existence of the Emerald Tablet and spread the doctrines of the Four Elements and the Mercury-Sulfur theory of the generation of the metals.

Gold: the most perfect of the metals. For the alchemist, it represented the perfection of all matter on any level, including that of the mind, spirit, and soul. It is associated with the final operation of coagulation.

Green Dragon: probably an acetate of lead, which originates from a green oil, but in general, it refers to the underlying essence and source of all the metals. Philosophically, the Green Dragon is a "tamed" dragon sharing the crystallized energy that it had formerly so ferociously protected. Psychologically, it represents elements of the unconscious that have been assimilated into consciousness.

Green Lion: the green acetate of lead in its liquid or crystallized form. Philosophically, it is the same as the Green Dragon.

Griffin's Egg: the griffin is a half-lion and half-eagle creature that symbolizes the conjunction of the fixed and volatile principles. The Griffin Egg is an allusion to the Vessel of Hermes.

Head: the top of a retort flask used in distillation. Sometimes it also refers to the spout/condenser of the classical retort.

Hermaphrodite (or *Rebis*): represents Sulfur and Mercury after their conjunction. *Rebis* (something double in characteristics) is another designation for this point in the alchemy of transformation.

Hermetically sealed: sealed airtight so no outside influence can corrupt the contents.

Impregnation: the alchemical process is sometimes paralleled with the gestation of a child. Thus impregnation follows from the union or copulation of the male and female, and leads to the generation of a new substance.

Inhumation: to bury under the earth; sometimes used to mean any process that buries the active substance in a dark earthy material. Also applied to placing a flask in the warm heat of a dung bath.

Iron: one of the seven metals of alchemy. It is associated with the operation of separation.

Jungian alchemy: Psychiatrist Carl Gustav Jung rediscovered the images and principles of alchemy surfacing in the dreams and compulsions of his patients and began a lifelong study of the subject. He concluded that alchemical images explain the archetypal roots of the modern mind and underscores a process of transformation leading to the integration of the personality.

King: in alchemy represents man, solar consciousness, or Sulfur. The King is naked in the early operations of alchemy and regains his royal robes at the end of his transformation. The King united with the Queen symbolizes conjunction.

Lead: the first and oldest of the seven metals of alchemy. It is associated with the operation of calcination.

Lion: any salt or fixed substance obtained from metals. It is red, green, or black according to its state of perfection.

Litharge (or letharge): the leftover scum, spume, or ashes of a metallic operation; reddish-yellow crystalline form of lead monoxide, formed by fusing and powdering massicot.

Magnesia: a mystical term to the alchemists that denoted the primordial transforming substance in the universe. It was one of many symbols used to describe the central mystery of alchemy that was never to be spoken of in common wording.

Matrass: a round-bottomed flask with a very long neck. Also called a "bolt-head."

Menstruum: an alchemical term meaning a solvent or alkahest having both the power to dissolve and coagulate at the same time. Based on the belief that the ovum takes its life and form from the menses, the menstruum was also referred to as the Mercury of the Philosophers.

Mercury (called quicksilver by the ancients): a liquid metal that could be found weeping through cracks in certain rocks or accumulating in small puddles in mountain grottoes. It was also obtained by roasting cinnabar (mercury sulfide). The shiny metal would seep from the rocks and drip down into the ashes, from which it was later collected. The early alchemists made red mercuric oxide by heating quicksilver in a solution of nitric acid. The acid, which later alchemists called "aqua fortis," was made by pouring sulfuric acid over saltpeter. The reaction of quicksilver in nitric acid is impressive. A thick red vapor hovers over the surface and bright red crystals precipitate to the bottom. This striking chemical reaction demonstrated the simultaneous separation of mercury into the Above and the Below. Mercury's all-encompassing properties were exhibited in other compounds too. If mercury was heated in a long-necked flask, it oxidized into a highly poisonous white powder (white mercuric oxide) and therapeutic red crystals (red mercuric oxide). Calomel (mercury chloride) was a powerful medicine, unless it was directly exposed to light; in that case it became a deadly poison. When mixed with other metals, liquid mercury tended to unite with them and form hardened amalgams. These and other properties convinced alchemists that mercury transcended both the solid and liquid states, both earth and heaven, both life and death. It symbolized Hermes himself, the guide to the Above and Below.

Mortification: a process during which the substance undergoes a kind of death, usually through a putrefaction, and seems to have been destroyed and its active power lost, but eventually is revived.

Multiplication: a process of distillation and coagulation in which the power of transmutation is concentrated; an increase in the amount of the Stone as obtained from its pristine form. It is represented by the sign for the constellation of Aquarius. Multiplication is the operation by which the powder of projection has its power multiplied.

Natron: it means salt, though this word usually refers to native sodium carbonate. To the early alchemists, however, the word natron stood for the basic principle in all salt formation and the creation of bodies in general. The Egyptians accumulated the white salts formed from the evaporation of lakes and used them to preserve mummies. Known as soda ash (sodium carbonate), the oldest deposits are in the Sinai desert. Another naturally occurring sodium compound mined by the Egyptians was cubic-saltpeter (sodium nitrate). The alchemists referred to both these salts as natron (from the Arabic word for soda ash), because they suspected that both had a common signature or archetypal basis. Common salt is sodium chloride (NaCl).

Oil of Vitriol: sulfuric acid made by distilling Green Vitriol.

Orpiment (auri-pigmentum): yellow ore of arsenic; arsenic trisulfide.

Pelican: is a circulatory vessel with two side arms feeding condensed vapors back into the body. It has a fancied resemblance in shape to a pelican pecking at its breast. Pelicanization is the circulation or rotation of a liquid over a solid performed in the pelican retort.

Philosopher's Stone: the ultimate Stone is the goal of the Great Work of the whole universe. It was viewed as a magical touchstone that could immediately perfect any substance or situation. The Philosopher's Stone has been associated with the Salt of the World, the Astral Body, the Elixir, and even Jesus Christ.

Precipitation: a process of coagulation in which solid matter is created during a chemical reaction and falls out of solution. The descent of a substance out of a solution; the precipitate descends to the bottom of the flask.

Projection: the final stage of coagulation in which the power of transformation is directed toward a body; the final process in making gold, in which the Stone or powder Stone (the powder of projection) is tossed upon the molten base metal to transmute it. It is represented by the sign for the constellation of Pisces. The throwing of a ferment or tincture onto a substance in order to effect a transformation of the substance.

Pulverization: the breaking down of a substance to smaller fragments through being repeatedly struck with a blunt instrument, such as a hammer or mallet.

Purgation: the purifying of a substance by casting out a gross part of it.

Purple Phase (or *Iosis*): the Great Work is the third and final stage of transformation. It is marked by the purpling or reddening of the material and occurs during the coagulation operation.

Putrefaction: the first stage of the fermentation operation; a digestion in which decomposing essences are reabsorbed. The process was represented by the symbol for the constellation of Leo. The rotting of a substance, often under a prolonged, gentle, moist heat. Usually the matter becomes black.

Queen: symbolizes woman, lunar consciousness, and Mercury. The Queen is naked during the early stages but regains her royal robes at the end of her transformation. The Queen united with the King is the operation of conjunction.

Quintessence (Quinta Essentia): the fifth element with which the alchemists could work. It was the essential presence of something or someone, the living thing itself that animated or gave something its deepest characteristics. The Quintessence partakes of both the Above and the Below, the mental as well as the material. It can be thought of as the ethereal embodiment of the life force that we encounter in dreams and altered states of consciousness. It is the purest individual essence of something that we must unveil and understand in order to transform it.

Receiver: the flask attached to the outlet of the condenser tube during distillation, which contains the distillate or distilled product.

Rectification: the purification of the matter by means of repeated distillations, the distillate being again distilled.

Red Dragon: the pure red oil of lead; the untamed dragon or First Matter. It is also associated with the Red Dragon of Projection at the end of the Great Work.

Red Lion: the red acetate of lead in its crystalline form. It carries similar signatures as the Red Dragon.

Retort: a spherical container (usually glass) with a long neck or spout. It is used to distill or decompose solutions by the action of heat or acids.

Salt: the third heavenly substance in alchemy, which represents the final manifestation of the perfected Stone. The Emerald Tablet calls it "the Glory of the Whole Universe." For Paracelsus, Salt was like a balsam the body produced to shield itself from decay. It has also been associated with the Uroboros, the Stone, and the Astral Body. In general, Salt represents the action of thought on matter, be it the One Mind acting on the One Thing of the universe or the alchemist meditating in his inner laboratory. Common salt is sodium chloride.

Separation: the third operation in the alchemy of transformation. Symbols of separation include swords, scythes, arrows, knives, and hatchets. The operation is symbolized by the sign for the constellation of Scorpio. The making of two opposite components separate from each other; often alternated with the conjunction process.

Serpents: two serpents represent the opposing masculine and feminine energies of the Work. Three serpents stand for the three higher principles of Sulfur, Mercury, and Salt. Winged serpents represent volatile substances; wingless serpents represent fixed substances. A crucified serpent represents the fixation of the volatile.

Silver: one of the seven metals of alchemy. It is associated with the operation of distillation.

Skeletons: signify the processes of calcination and putrefaction, on all the levels in which they occur.

Soul: in alchemy is the passive presence in all of us that survives through all eternity and is therefore part of the original substance (First Matter) of the universe. Ultimately, it is the One Thing of the universe. Soul was considered beyond the four material elements and thus conceptualized as a fifth element (or Quintessence).

Spirit: in alchemy is the active presence in all of us that strives toward perfection. Spirit seeks material manifestation for expression. Ultimately, it is the One Mind of the universe.

Square or cube: symbolic of matter and the four elements of creation.

Stone: the end result or product of a working. See Philosopher's Stone.

Sublimation: the first stage of coagulation or last stage of distillation, in which the vapors solidify; represented by the sign for the constellation of Libra. The vaporization of a solid without fusion or melting, followed by the condensation of its vapor in the resolidified form on a cool surface. The elevation of a dry thing by fire, with adherency to its vessel. This occurs when a solid is heated and gives off a vapor that condenses on the cool upper parts of the vessel as a solid, not going through a liquid phase. An example is sal ammoniac.

Sulfur (Sulphur): one of the three heavenly substances. It represents passion and will and is associated with the operation of fermentation. Flowers of Sulfur is light yellow crystalline powder, made by distilling sulfur.

Three Levels: the key to understanding alchemy is to realize that alchemical thought is extremely dynamic and takes place on three levels at once: the physical, the psychological, and the spiritual. Thus turning lead into gold meant not only physically changing the base metal into the noble metal, but also transforming base habits and emotions into golden thoughts and feelings, as well as transmuting our dark and ignoble souls into the golden light of spirit. By developing this ability to think and work on all three levels of reality at once (becoming "thrice-greatest"), the alchemists created a spiritual technology that applied not only to their laboratories but also to their own personalities and to their relationships with other people—and with God.

Tin: one of the seven metals of the alchemists. It is associated with the operation of dissolution and the element Water. Pewter (a mixture of lead and tin) represents a metallic state between the operations of calcination and dissolution.

Transudation: occurs if the essence appears to sweat out in drops during a descending distillation.

Trees: symbolize the processes of transformation. A tree of moons signifies the Lesser or Lunar Work; a tree of suns signifies the Greater or Solar Work.

Triangle: represents the three heavenly principles or substances of Sulfur, Mercury, and Salt.

Trituration: the reduction of a substance to a powder, not necessarily by the use of grinding but by the application of heat. To grind a solid into a powder; to pulverize with a mortar and pestle. Crush. A process just after calcination, when the ashes are ground into a fine powder for dissolution.

Uroboros (or Ouroboros): the symbolic rendition of the eternal principles presented in the Emerald Tablet. The great serpent devouring itself represents the idea that "All Is One," even though the universe undergoes periodic cycles of destruction and creation (or resurrection). In Orphic and Mithraic symbology, the Uroboros was called the *Agathos Daimon* or "Good Spirit" and was a symbol for the "Operation of the Sun." In Greek terminology, the Uroboros was the *Aion*, which Herakleitos likened to a child at play. To the Greeks, the *Aion* (from which our word "eon" is derived) defined the cosmic period between the creation and destruction of the universe.

Vitriol: was the most important liquid in alchemy. It was the one in which all other reactions took place. Vitriol was distilled from an oily green substance that formed naturally from the weathering of sulfur-bearing gravel. This Green Vitriol is symbolized by the Green Lion in drawings. After the Green Vitriol (ferrous sulfate) was collected, it was heated and broken down into iron compounds and sulfuric acid. The acid was separated out by distillation. The first distillation produced a brown liquid that stunk like rotten eggs, but further distillation yielded a nearly odorless yellow oil, Vitriol. The acid readily dissolves human tissue and is severely corrosive to most metals, although it has no effect on gold. White Vitriol is zinc sulfate; Blue Vitriol is copper sulfate.

Water: one of the Four Elements of alchemy. Water in the alchemical sense carries the archetypal properties of cleansing and purification. It is associated with the operation of dissolution and represented by the metal tin.

White Phase (or *Leukosis*): the second stage of the Great Work and takes place during distillation.

Wine: symbolic of the process of fermentation and the spiritization of matter.

Winged Lion: the sublimated salt used to make the Philosopher's Stone. It is the volatile or spiritual aspect of an ingredient.

Wolf: symbolizes the animal nature or wild spirit of man and nature; often associated with the metal antimony.

Yellow Phase (or *Xanthosis*): an intermediate stage that takes place between the Black and White phases of the Great Work. The term was used by Chinese and Alexandrian alchemists to describe changes that took place during the fermentation operation.

Zodiac: According to the Doctrine of Correspondences in the Emerald Tablet ("As Above, so Below"), the stars must find expression on earth and in mankind. In alchemy, it was essential to consult the zodiac before commencing any of the major operations.

APPENDIX 2:

✦ Resources ✦

Recommended Alchemy Books

Alchemical Psychology is a look at ancient alchemical recipes for living in the modern world. Thom Cavalli. Jeremy Tarcher, 2002.

Alchemical Reader is a collection of original writings by alchemists from Hermes Trismegistus to Isaac Newton. Stanton Linden. Cambridge University Press, 2003.

Alchemist's Handbook: Manual for Practical Laboratory Alchemy is an excellent guide to labwork. Frater Albertus. Samuel Weiser, 1974.

Alchemy & Mysticism is a stunning pictorial presentation of the spiritual practice of alchemy in the Middle Ages. Alexander Roob. Taschen, 1997.

Alchemy: The Great Secret is an illustrated history exploring aspects of alchemy's mix of science, philosophy, art, religion, and magic. Andrea Aromatico. Harry N. Abrams, 2000.

Anatomy of the Psyche: Alchemical Symbolism in Psychotherapy is an in-depth description of the Seven Operations of alchemy in psychological terms. Edward Edinger. Open Court, 1991.

Book of Alchemy presents the Seven Operations of the Emerald Formula, as well as an overview of alchemy. Francis Melville. Barron's Quarto, 2002.

A Dictionary of Alchemical Imagery documents alchemical symbolism from Hellenistic Egypt to the late-twentieth century. Lyndy Abraham. Cambridge University Press, 2001.

Emerald Tablet: Alchemy for Personal Transformation is the definitive history of the Emerald Tablet and the application of its principles to alchemy and personal transformation. Dennis William Hauck. Penguin Arkana, 1999.

Four Temperaments describes the alchemy of the Four Elements in human beings. Randy Rolfe. Marlowe & Co., 2002.

Jung on Alchemy is a collection of psychiatrist Carl Jung's writings on alchemy. Selected by Nathan Schwartz-Salant. Princeton University Press, 1995.

Modern Alchemist is a guide to personal transformation using the principles of alchemy. Richard and Iona Miller. Phanes Press, 1994.

Practical Handbook of Plant Alchemy: An Herbalist's Guide to Preparing Medicinal Essences, Tinctures, and Elixirs, Manfred Junius. Healing Arts Press, 1993.

Secret of the Golden Flower is a Taoist alchemy treatise with insightful commentary by C. G. Jung. Wilhelm Reich. Harcourt Brace, 1988.

Tao and the Tree of Life: Alchemical and Sexual Mysteries of the East and West decodes the mysteries of both the Tao and Cabala to show their underlying basis in alchemy. Eric Yudelove. Llewellyn, 1996.

Taoist Yoga and Sexual Energy; Internal Alchemy and Chi Kung is an alchemical view of Chinese alchemy. Eric Steven Yudelove and Mantak Chia. Llewellyn, 2000.

Transformation of the Psyche is a look at the symbolic alchemy of the beautiful paintings from *Splendor Solis*. Joseph Henderson and Dyane Sherwood. Brunner-Routledge, 2003.

Tower of Alchemy is a look at the occult principles of alchemy. David Goddard. Samuel Weiser, 1999.

Internet Resources

Alchemy Guild: The official Web site of the International Alchemy Guild.
www.AlchemyGuild.org

Alchemy Lab: Dedicated to personal transformation and has been

described as "one of the most stunning web archives ever" by the London Times.
www.AlchemyLab.com

Alchemy Website: A large resource of original texts, drawings, and articles on the ancient art with an even blend of spiritual and practical material.
www.levity.com/alchemy

Crucible Catalog: Carries lab supplies, chemicals, herbs, jewelry, and many esoteric and Hermetic items of interest to alchemists.
www.Crucible.org

Flamel College: An Internet portal for all kinds of esoteric and Hermetic instruction that has a large online library of original texts.
www.FlamelCollege.org

Hermetic Order of the Golden Dawn: Presents alchemy from the viewpoint of the Golden Dawn organization.
www.golden-dawn.com/temple/index.jsp?l=eng.

Paracelsus College: An Australian site that offers information on the practical and psychological aspects of alchemy.
homepages.ihug.com.au/~panopus.

Rubellus Petrinus Web site: The Portuguese alchemist's personal Web site devoted to practical and laboratory alchemy.
pwp.netcabo.pt/r.petrinus

Spagyria Web site: Practical plant alchemy and the art of spagyrics from John Reid.
www.spagyria.com

ᴝ Index ᴄ

❧ About the Author ❧

DENNIS WILLIAM HAUCK is an author, consultant, and lecturer working to facilitate personal and institutional transformation through the application of the ancient principles of alchemy. As one of the world's few practicing alchemists, he writes and lectures on the universal principles of physical, psychological, and spiritual perfection to a wide variety of audiences that range from scientists and business leaders to religious and New Age groups.

Hauck's interest in alchemy began while he was still in graduate school at the University of Vienna, and he has since translated a number of important alchemy manuscripts dating back to the thirteenth century. His book, *The Emerald Tablet: Alchemy for Personal Transformation* (Penguin Arkana, 1999), presents startling new revelations about the mysterious "time capsule of wisdom" that inspired over thirty-five hundred years of alchemy. A dedicated explorer of consciousness, Hauck has done considerable research into "exceptional human experiences"—a term used to describe a wide variety of mystical phenomena. Convinced that a serious study of such events will lead to a better understanding of the true nature of human consciousness, he has written several ground-breaking books along these lines. His guidebooks to thousands of sacred energy sites and locations of paranormal activity, *The International Directory of Haunted Places* (Penguin, 2000) and *Haunted Places: The National Directory* (Athanor, 1994; Penguin, 1996; Penguin Putnam, 2002), have led hundreds of people to places where they have experienced such altered states of consciousness.

Hauck has been interviewed on nearly four hundred radio and TV programs, including such popular national shows as NPR's

"Morning Edition," "Sally Jessy Raphael," "Geraldo," "A&E Unexplained," "Sightings," "Extra," and "CNN Reports." He also serves as a special consultant to several leading film production companies and a number of popular television programs.

Hauck has an award-winning Web site: www.alchemylab.com. He is the editor of the *Alchemy Journal* and a regular columnist for several publications and a pioneer in introducing transpersonal concepts to businesses and government agencies. He is a regular contributor to dozens of magazines, including *Perceptions*, *Fate*, *Intuition*, *PSI Review*, *New Age Retailer*, and *Whole Life Times*. He has been featured in *USA Today*, *Wall Street Journal*, *New York Times*, *Chicago Tribune*, *New York Post*, *Boston Globe*, *Seattle Times*, *Harper's*, *Magical Blend*, *Lingua Franca*, and over a hundred other periodicals.

Hauck is an instructor in the Alchemy Home Study Program and conducts alchemy tours to Egypt, India, and Europe. He is also an instructor at Flamel College and serves on the Board of Governors of the International Alchemy Guild. He is a professional member of the Association for Transpersonal Psychology (ATP), the Institute of Noetic Sciences (IONS), the Association for Comprehensive Energy Psychology (ACEP), and the Center for Research into Science (CRIS). He is presently working on two new non-fiction alchemy books, *Egyptian Alchemy* and *Principia Alchemia: A Revelation and Compendium of the Ancient Spiritual Technology Known as Alchemy*.

Dennis William Hauck holds lectures and workshops throughout the world on the various aspects of practical, mental, and spiritual alchemy (for more information, go to www.AlchemyLab.com/lectures.htm). He lives in Scaramento, California.